EUROPEAN DISCOURSES ON ENVIRONMENTAL POLICY

European Discourses on Environmental Policy

Edited by
MARCEL WISSENBURG
University of Nijmegen, The Netherlands
GÖKHAN ORHAN
Balikesir University, Turkey
UTE COLLIER
WWF UK

Ashgate

Aldershot • Brookfield USA • Singapore • Sydney

Published by
Ashgate Publishing Ltd
Gower House
Croft Road
Aldershot
Hants GU11 3HR
England

Ashgate Publishing Company
Old Post Road
Brookfield
Vermont 05036
USA

British Library Cataloguing in Publication Data
European discourses on environmental policy
   1.Interdisciplinary Research Network on Environment and
   Society - Congresses 2.Environmental policy - Europe -
   Congresses
   I.Wissenburg, M. L. J. II.Orhan, Gokhan III.Collier, Ute,
   1964-
   333.7'094

Library of Congress Catalog Card Number: 99-72595

ISBN 1 84014 777 6

Printed and bound by Athenaeum Press, Ltd.,
Gateshead, Tyne & Wear.

Contents

PART I: THEORETICAL PERSPECTIVES

PART II: STRUCTURE AND BACKGROUND

Figures

Tables

Contributors

Dr. *Susan Carr* is Lecturer in the Systems Discipline and Researcher in the Centre for Technology Strategy at the Open University, Milton Keynes, UK. Correspondence: Centre for Technology Strategy, Open University, Milton Keynes MK7 6AA, UK.
E-mail: S.Carr@open.ac.uk

Dr. *Ute Collier* is Climate Change Policy Officer with the World Wide Fund for Nature (WWF UK) in Godalming, Surrey, UK.
Correspondence: WWF UK, Weyside Park, Catteshall Lane, Godalming, Surrey GU 7 1XR, UK.
E-mail: UCollier@wwfnet.org

Dr *Jan Eberg* is a Research Fellow in the Department of Political Science at the University of Amsterdam, the Netherlands.
Correspondence: Department of Political Science, University of Amsterdam, O.Z. Achterburgwal 237, 1012 DL Amsterdam, The Netherlands.
E-mail: eberg@pscw.uva.nl

Brendan Flynn is a Lecturer in Comparative Politics with the Department of Political Science and Sociology, National University of Ireland at Galway. Correspondence: Department of Political Science and Sociology, National University of Ireland, Galway. Ireland.
E-mail: flynbm@hotmail.com

Prof. *Detlef Jahn* is Research Professor in the Department of Economics and Politics, The Nottingham Trent University, Nottingham, UK. (England). Correspondence: Department of Economics and Politics, The Nottingham Trent University, Burton Street, Nottingham NG1 4BU, UK.
E-mail: Detlef.Jahn@ntu.ac.uk

Dr. *Andrew Jordan* is Senior Research Associate in the School of Environmental Sciences at the University of East Anglia, Norwich, UK. Correspondence: CSERGE, School of Environmental Sciences, University of East Anglia, Norwich NR4 7TJ, UK.
E-mail: a.jordan@uea.ac.uk

Dr. Les Levidow is a Research Fellow in the Centre for Technology Strategy at the Open University, Milton Keynes, UK.
Correspondence: Centre for Technology Strategy, Open University, Milton Keynes MK7 6AA, UK.
E-mail: Levidow@open.ac.uk

Gökhan Orhan completed his PhD at the Department of Government, University of Essex. He is a Lecturer at the Department of Public Administration at Balikesir University, Turkey.
Correspondence: Balikesir Üniversitesi, Bandirma Iktisadi ve Idari Bilimler Fakültesi, Kamu Yönetimi Bölümü, Bandirma, Balikesir, Turkey.
E-mail: Gorhan@balikesir.edu.tr

Dr. Paul Pestman is Research Associate in the Department of Environmental Policy Sciences at the University of Nijmegen, the Netherlands.
Correspondence: Department of Environmental Policy Sciences, University of Nijmegen, P.O. Box 9108, 6500 HK Nijmegen, the Netherlands.
E-mail: P.Pestman@BW.KUN.NL

Dr. Jan van Tatenhove is Lecturer in Environmental Policy Sciences at the University of Nijmegen, the Netherlands.
Correspondence: Department of Environmental Policy Sciences, University of Nijmegen, P.O. Box 9108, 6500 HK Nijmegen, the Netherlands.
E-mail: J.vanTatenhove@BW.KUN.NL

Prof. Albert Weale is a Fellow of the British Academy and Professor of Government at the University of Essex, Colchester, UK.
Correspondence: Department of Government, University of Essex, Wivenhoe Park, Colchester CO4 3SQ, UK.
E-mail: Weala@essex.ac.uk

Dr. Marcel Wissenburg is Lecturer in Political Theory and the Philosophy of the Policy Sciences at the University of Nijmegen, the Netherlands.
Correspondence: Department of Political Science, University of Nijmegen, P.O. Box 9108, 6500 HK Nijmegen, the Netherlands.
E-mail: M.Wissenburg@BW.KUN.NL

Foreword

ALBERT WEALE

According to one dominant paradigm in social science theory, the Interdisciplinary Network on Environment and Society (IRNES) ought not to exist. It is the product of voluntary action among a large number of busy, young scholars, all with pressing career priorities of their own. It organises scholarly meetings open to a wide range of new researchers, many of whom have to scour their own institutions for some support in order that they can attend. The constituencies that it serves are heterogeneous, coming from many disciplines and from diverse national backgrounds. The barriers to successful organisation are thus formidable. Of course, this is not the whole story. The UK's Economic and Social Research Council has been far-sighted enough to provide some resources (congratulations to that all too often maligned institution), and the publications that IRNES has sponsored provide a wider readership for their work than research students often secure. Even so, rational choice theory tells us that voluntary action to provide public goods is rare. We should wonder, then, not only that IRNES exists but that it also flourishes.

The present volume is devoted to the topic of discourse in European environmental policy. The term 'discourse' denotes one of those marvellously flexible concepts that has managed to appeal to a wide range of theoretical traditions in the social sciences, including recent work in the policy sciences, studies of ideology, post-structuralism and Anglo-Saxon political theory drawing on linguistic philosophy. Its occurrence at the conjunction of such diverse theoretical traditions might suggest that its significance is difficult to pin down. Yet, it is the merit of the essays collected in this book that the reader comes to understand the different ways in which the understanding of discourse helps makes sense of European environmental policy.

In the first place, an emphasis upon discourse highlights the technical complexity of environmental policy, and therefore draws attention to the way in which a framework of concepts and understandings is necessary in order that policy learning can take place, either within different political groups in the same country or across national boundaries. In the absence of a discursive framework that at least partially fixes the understanding of what policy is feasible and effective, whether in the form, say, of the waste-management hierarchy or in the implications of the precautionary principle, policy makers and members of the attentive public are unable to evaluate prevailing practices and policies.

The importance of public understanding becomes more important in environmental policy once we acknowledge that many environmental problems have their origins in the dispersed consumption activities of citizens who drive their cars more and more, buy an increasing volume of material goods and dream in larger and larger numbers of holidays in hitherto scarcely visited sites of natural beauty. Governments cannot simply regulate this activity, but must instead appeal to the understanding and revaluation of social norms that make citizen self-regulation possible. In other words, environmental governance becomes a matter of sharing understanding, not the promulgation of authoritative commands.

A special place for understanding policy through its discourse is also prompted by the politics of European integration. Multi-level governance in Europe is not simply the centralising trend of the creation of nation states writ large. It is a process with its own dynamic and form of growth. Central to this process is the need to secure sufficient common understandings of environmental problems and policies to ensure that collaborative European action is productive rather than counter-productive. From the Babel of national environmental policy paradigms in Europe we are unlikely to see a common language emerge that all are equally happy speaking. But we might hope to see emerging areas of understanding among state and non-governmental actors on specific topic that at least provide the framework within which transnational approaches can be developed.

Behind these specific occasions for a discursive understanding of European environmental policy we can also see more general features of politics and human action that make discourse important, including the politics of reflexive modernisation making citizen understandings a feature of all policy development and the fact that humans are irreducibly symbol-using creatures whose way in the world is marked by the need to define their environment and the meaning that it has.

Discourse is therefore an irreducible feature of environmental politics and policy, but does this mean that it is fundamental? Does it provide a rock-bottom account of how policies are formed and implemented? Here the careful reader will note that throughout this volume the contributors are aware of the limits as well as the strengths of a discursive analysis. Discourse may be no more than rhetoric, adopted to disguise the balance of economic and political forces that are in play in the making of policy. Perhaps environmental discourse in Europe has developed as far and as fast as it has because its practical effects were limited. Understanding the interaction of (dare I use the term?) 'material' interests with discursive formations still remains a challenging task. The reader who has benefited from this volume will hope that it will not be the last on the topic that IRNES will produce.

Acknowledgements

The editors would like to thank the UK Economic and Social Research Council for its trust in and financial support for IRNES, the volunteers running IRNES for their immense efforts and unwavering enthousiasm, all contributors to the IRNES European seminars for their interest and active participation, all host institutions for the warm welcome they offered, and the Netherlands Organisation for Scientific Research NWO/REOB for its grant 415-31-001. Most of all, we wish to acknowledge our debt to Penny Law of the London School of Economics. As the tireless IRNES European officer, she initiated and organised the European seminars, traveled through Europe to find people and connect them, and with her unlimited energy and zeal persuaded many that network and seminars were worthy of their active support. In the final analysis, those seminars, this book and the European network would never have existed without her.

Ute Collier
Gökhan Orhan
Marcel Wissenburg

Introduction

MARCEL WISSENBURG

The book which you are about to read serves two purposes. It is, of course, intended to enlarge the existing body of scientific knowledge, and to contribute to its further development, in the fields of environmental policy and policy studies in general and environmental policy in Europe in particular. In addition to this relatively innocent academic vindication, there is a more profane reason the existence of this book. It is a means of introducing the work of promising young scholars, and it was expressly intended as such.

The chapters collected in this book are all based on papers presented at a series of European seminars organised by or on behalf of the Interdisciplinary Research Network on Environment and Society (IRNES). During 1996, IRNES received a grant from the UK Economic and Social Research Council (ESRC) for European networking, to establish contact with researchers elsewhere in Europe working on environmental topics from an interdisciplinary perspective. One immediate result was that enthusiasts from all over Europe gathered on five occasions: in London at the headquarters of the ESRC, in Florence at the European University Institute, in the Netherlands at the University of Nijmegen, in Colchester at Essex University and during several workshops at the annual IRNES conference at the University of Lancaster. During the seminars, over fifty papers were presented and discussed, papers originating in all the disciplines of the social sciences from social psychology to political philosophy, all dealing with aspects of European environmental policy. In the months and years following, the network expanded to include dozens of scholarly groups and individuals all over Europe. The aims of the grant were met.

Yet IRNES has more aims than networking alone. IRNES is itself an independent academic network, set up in 1990 with funding from the UK Economic and Social Research Council. It holds research seminars every two months at UK universities and organises an annual environmental research conference. Its newsletter *Interdisciplinary Strands* is published three times per year. The network was founded expressly to facilitate liaison between active researchers from all disciplines who are working in various environmental fields, and to facilitate research collaboration between more

1

established and less established academics. Among other things then, IRNES hopes to create a forum for the broadest possible dissemination of new and innovative research by new and innovative researchers, for whom it is often notoriously difficult and time-consuming to gain entrance to the community of established scholars.

One of the most effective ways of reaching this aim is by enabling people to publish their work. Volumes based on papers from the annual IRNES conferences have, for instance, been published in 1993 (Holder et. al.) and 1995 (Elworthy et. al.). The book you are now holding tries to set forth this tradition. The editors of *European Discourses on Environmental Policy* have tried to bring together some of the best contributions to the IRNES European seminars. Unfortunately, this volume is not representative of the diversity in terms of disciplines and nationality of the network. The duty to produce a book with a unifying topic rather than a series of separate texts stapled together forced us to exclude, with deep regrets, a number of excellent texts that simply did not fit in. We thus ended up with a group of authors whose research focuses on environmental policy and whose roots lie in Germany, Italy, Ireland, the Netherlands, Sweden, Turkey and the UK 'only'. Yet we hope that it is still representative in one respect: that of the quality and promise of Europe's present and future academics.

Aside from all this, the primary aim of this book remains to contribute to an existing body of knowledge, in this case environmental policy in Europe. Environmental policy as such has received increasing attention from all corners of the social sciences, even among academics who until recently showed little interest in environmental affairs (cf. e.g. several contributions to Young 1997). An important reason for this quantitative and qualitative expansion lies in the (apparently) new and creative ways in which environmental policies at the national, transnational and global levels are designed, institutionalised and implemented. The European Union in its current and past stages of development deserves a special place within this rapidly expanding field due to its unique structure: it is not quite a state, yet sometimes acts as one independent and sovereign body, not quite a shared administration of sovereign nations yet is often used as such, not quite an international political or economic organisation and not quite the opposite, whatever that may be. As a result, widely differing European environmental policies and policy styles exist at sub-national and national, cross-border, regional and European levels, sometimes to the advantage of the environment, sometimes to its disadvantage. European environmental policy is about as complicated as policy can get. No surprise then that authors often focus on one very specific policy area (e.g. climate change policy or industrial competitiveness). It is extremely difficult to provide a broad and detailed assessment of the complete environmental policy area (e.g. Liefferink, Lowe and Mol, 1993; Judge 1995) and keep it up to date.

Our purpose in compiling this book has been to offer the reader a representative selection of the work currently being done on environmental policy in Europe, with respect to the scope and policy instruments used, the level of application from global to local, and the relation between the European Union and its constituent parts, as well as with respect to the role of policy studies within the social sciences. Three unifying topics seem to return in every possible context: the role of discourses, the benefits and burdens of policy diversity, and the heavily politicised character of environmental policy processes in Europe.

As it turns out, the formulation, design and implementation of environmental policy are not 'post-political': after a political decision has been taken to instigate some sort of policy aimed at some particular environmental goal, the political battle simply goes on. The same political actors plus several new ones (scientists, public servants, economic and civic agents) now gather to form a new political arena where new decisions have to be taken. In explaining the behaviour of these policy actors, institutional and structural factors are often insufficient, just as their behaviour and relative power alone are insufficient to explain the design and implementation of the resulting policies. It appears that discourses play an independent role in policy-making. The conceptions and interpretations not just of the given aim of an environmental policy but also of 'environment' (or 'sustainability') itself, hence of criteria for success, differ widely at any given moment in time. More important: they change and develop, as do the opinions and positions of policy actors themselves. Discourse, both in the sense of a unified set of conceptions and rules allowing an interpretation of the world, and in the sense of plain, ordinary exchange of views, actually contributes to the shaping of environmental policies. The result, given different sets of actors operating in different environments at different political levels, is policy diversity: the co-existence within Europe of several types of policy aimed at solving the same problem. Whether this is a beneficial development, in terms of the problem-solving capacity of European environmental policy as a whole, depends on a series of factors that will be identified in the next nine chapters.

The chapters have been organised in three parts: one part on theoretical issues, one on the background conditions for environmental policy and one on policy formulation and implementation itself.

That an analysis of environmental policies in Europe is relevant for the quality of the environment as well as for adapting existing policies and designing new ones goes without saying. That it can and should also be relevant to scholars of European politics is far less obvious. In the opening chapter of Part One, Andrew Jordan argues for exactly this thesis. According to him, policy analysis could bridge the gap between the existing International Relations and Comparative (national) Politics approaches in European studies, each of which fails to be able to account for the exact role of the European Union as something in between an independent actor on the stage of an international anarchy of states, and as a stage itself, an organisation of states. The case of pan-European environmental policy illustrates Jordan's argument that an analysis of 'post-politics' (read: the policy process) might help to enlighten us as to where the power in the EU really lies, and why it lies there: in Brussels, or in some or all member states.

Gökhan Orhan, in the second chapter, maps the history of environmental policy in Europe from its invention in the form of national, end-of-pipeline stategies to its present state of diversification. He points to the crucial role played by environmental ideas and discourses, next to structures and institutions, in this evolution. For him, ideas are more than necessary elements in explaining the arrival of environmental issues on the political agenda and in understanding the existence of 'the environment' as a topic in its own right. They are also partly responsible for the design of policies, later judgements on their effects, changes in strategies and, most importantly, for the increasing divergence in European environmental policies. Orhan argues that policy diversity is, at least in principle, a virtue next to a necessity: it is a necessary condition for learning (processes), allowing us to experiment on a wide scale.

Jan van Tatenhove takes up the same topic, the role of ideas and discourses, in the third chapter, but his conclusion is almost opposite: he predicts the end of the era of policy diversification. He also relates environmental policies in Europe to environmental discourses, yet argues that these are in turn products of the more general process of modernisation. In our present time, we find on the one hand a development in politics away from classic modernisation and the classic state towards a 'diffuse negotiating state' more and more immersed in and communicating with civil society, which at least in part explains policy diversity. Yet in the economic sphere, where the role of the state is (also) diminishing rapidly due to internationalisation, particularly in Europe, ecological modernisation of production and consumption will, he suspects, actually force political actors to develop more homogeneous policies.

Part Two opens with a look at the everyday world of policy: an overview of environmental policies in Europe by Ute Collier. She focusses on the integration of the sustainable development concept into EU policy-making, which has coincided with an increasing emphasis on the application of subsidiarity and deregulation as guiding principles in the EU policy process. While in principle, ideas such as 'action as close to the citizen as possible' and the application of a market-based approach appear compatible with sustainability objectives, especially considering the shortcoming of EU environmental policy to date, political and economic realities mean that subsidiarity and deregulation are two-edged swords. Collier demonstrates this through the example of the EU's response to the climate change issue. In this case, the subsidiarity principle has been exploited in the interest of national sovereignty, while the search for a more market-based approach for environmental instruments has mainly focused on self-regulatory tools with dubious effectiveness. Overall, despite much rhetoric, EU environmental policy has lost momentum in recent years and, beyond marginal adjustments, there has been little progress with the integration of environmental concerns into other EU policy areas.

Brendan Flynn, in the fifth chapter, investigates the relative weight of national and European environmental policies in the light of today's official Prime Directive in European Union politics: subsidiarity. In order to solve the decennia-old debate on national sovereignty and European co-operation versus loss of sovereignty and European federalism, or at least to dodge it, member states of the European Union have on several occasions embraced the idea that 'in principle' only those policies that require support from more than one state can become the object of EU policy. Flynn discusses the effects that adoption of this subsidiarity ideology has had on the position of six actors in European environmental policy: DG XI, the European Environmental Agency (EEA), the European Court of Justice, the European Parliament's environment committee, the (Environment) Council of Ministers, and the European Council. On the one hand, he argues, subsidiarity is a blessing: it supports the current trend of creating 'soft law', regulation after broad processes of negotiation between politics and civil society (cf. Van Tatenhove's negotiating state), thus increasing the chance that environmental policies can be implemented with success because they are widely perceived as legitimate. On the other hand, subsidiarity allows environmental policies to become increasingly less general, less radical and less opportune. Flynn therefore fears that the popular vindication of subsidiarity in environmental policy as 'doing less yet better' may end up meaning little more than 'doing less'.

The issues of the legitimacy of environmenal policies and the role of ideas and discourse are investigated once more in the sixth chapter, where Detlef Jahn discusses the mobilisation of ecological world views in Sweden and Germany between 1970 and 1995. In his comparative case study, Jahn tries to combine discourse analysis with an institutional approach to the political process in modern society. Discourse analysis, he argues, has become unavoidable in the social sciences, due to processes of fragmentation and disorganisation in public communication and political life, a transformation known as reflexive modernisation. On the other hand, institutions and collective actors themselves are more stable factors, allowing one to trace changes in their voiced opinions and hence to map the (alleged) greening of society over the past decades. Jahn first describes the incorporation of ecologial protest into established politics in Sweden and the absence of integration in Germany since the 1970s, supporting the popular conviction that Sweden had and Germany had not left the 'productionist path' of economic growth and materialism. However, more recent figures indicate that Sweden is now in fact the more productionist country. Jahn concludes that 'the character and changes of the national ecological discourse of relevant collective actors provide a better understanding of social developments in both countries than the analysis of the political opportunity structure'.

In the final part of the book, three examples of real existing environmental policy fields are discussed: biotechnology, waste policies and large infrastructure projects. Susan Carr and Les Levidow (Chapter 7) inquire into the role of science and expertise in the formulation and implementation of biotechnology policies in Europe. Like others in previous chapters, they highlight the increased role of debate and the influence of non-state actors other than scientists in the policy process. Drawing attention to the uncertainty of scientific data and the normative aspects of scientists' environmental policy recommendations, non-state actors have turned hard science into negotiated science. The authors stress the positive side of this development in terms of an increased attention to precaution and a possible improvement in the legitimacy of policies. Yet they point to a (for policy scientists often unexpected, but among social psychologists familiar) risk of negotiated science and negotiated policy in general: the danger of group-think and group fallibility. A widely supported policy is not necessarily an effective policy; it may be based on wishful thinking. Since there is no way back to the time of rigorously closed politics, Carr and Levidow conclude that an actual expansion of open debate and negotiating processes to the policy implementation phase is necessary in order to diminish the dangers of group-think.

Learning from the experience of implementation is precisely what interests Jan Eberg in Chapter 8. Eberg argues that policy diversity can only serve a purpose if we do not learn from our own experiences with our own policies only, but also compare policies between polities, across borders. This may help us not only to understand why different background factors lead to the development of different policies, but also to see whether and in which ways it makes sense to 'import' successful policies. As illustrations of both theses, he discussed Dutch and Bavarian waste policies. In closing, Eberg picks up a theme introduced earlier by Van Tatenhove: the internationalisation, or more precisely Europeanisation, of the economy. Eberg is more pessimistic in that he does not expect economic Europeanisation to involve ecological modernisation. More or less in line with Van Tatenhove, he argues that the development of more homogeneous, pan-European policies will be unavoidable, but as his case-study of Bavarian waste policy shows, such policies may not be equally effective in and sensitive to local circumstances.

Finally, Paul Pestman picks up the subject of mobilisation again, now in the post-politics phase of the (highly controversial) formulation of two large infrastructure projects in the Netherlands: a railway for high-speed passenger trains connecting Amsterdam to Brussels, Paris and beyond, and a freight train connection between the port of Rotterdam and Germany. Pestman is interested in the effects of mobilisation processes on policy practises, policy organisation and the 'paradigm' of the policy field. He argues that decision-making can be seen as a battle between groups of actors about the definition and interpretation of certain aspects of a policy issue. Since the interests of the parties may themself be at stake, these groups are not necessarily stable coalitions; the two cases Pestman studies supports this conclusion. The outcome of the battle depends on the political room available (in terms of rules and resources) and the discursive space in which these are positioned. The extent of this room for manoeuvre can be influenced by processes of mobilisation: classical mobilisation where actors, rules and resources are mobilised, and performative mobilisation when, as a result of the introduction of new conceptualisations, the meaning of existing actor-relations, rules and resources change. The battle ends with a temporary cease-fire: a provisional definition of the most important aspects of the policy problem and a temporary stabilisation of the configuration of actors, rules and resources. The approach Pestman introduces will, he argues, offer new perspectives on the analysis of the strategic, institutional and discursive aspects of power and its long term consequences.

The picture of European environmental policies that emerges out of these nine chapters is not one of utter confusion. These policies did not develop in a totally random way out of political battles between changing coalitions under contingent and diverging circumstances. Structural and institutional factors can be identified, the crucial role of discourses traced. What remains is a far from perfect system of environmental rules, regimes and policies, a system that has in many ways been designed rather than evolved. Its diversity, dividing risks and multiplying experience, can be one of its strongest points, provided learning processes inside and across borders really take place. Yet diversity can also become the Achilles heel of the system: it allows issues that are important on a European scale to be neglected in local arenas where they might require unpopular measures. Despite its promises, the present shape of European environmental policy seems about to change, for better or for worse, under the influence of Europe's economic unification.

PART I
THEORETICAL PERSPECTIVES

1 'Post-Decisional' Politics in the European Union – A Threefold Agenda for Future Research

ANDREW JORDAN[1]

The evolution of the European Union

Until relatively recently, the manner in which the European Union (EU) was researched and taught was dominated by the theoretical models and organising principles of International Relations (IR). For over forty years analysts struggled to comprehend the behaviour of European states as they manoeuvred to exert control over the macro-level process of integration. Early theorists such as Stanley Hoffman (1966), pondered the 'fate' of the nation-state in such an arrangement (was it 'obstinate' or 'obsolete'?), centring on questions of sovereignty and state power, rather than what actually happened *within* particular policy sectors – such as the environment, transport or energy – at the meso and micro-levels. It was, as Stephen George (1996: 11) explains, entirely logical for the discipline to have developed in this way. After all, 'what was taking place... was an experiment in putting *inter-state* relations on a new footing' (emphasis added).

It was only in the mid- to late-1980s, when the tremendous surge of regulatory activity unleashed by the Internal Market Programme had spilled into cognate sectors and permeated down to the national level, that European policy processes began to mature, with their own legal bases and bureaucratic characteristics. In a comparatively short space of time, the Union began take on the attributes of a neo-state with structures similar to those normally found *within* states. Lobbying in Brussels proliferated, supranational institutions such as the European Parliament began to make their presence more directly felt at *all* stages of the policy process, and the output of legislation burgeoned (Armstrong and Bulmer, 1998). These were

11

the 'golden years' of EU environmental policy when the environmental *acquis* expanded exponentially; before the post-Maastricht backlash against deeper integration and the arrival of the more 'messy' politics of sustainability, subsidiarity and environmental policy integration (Jordan, 1999).

There was, of course, a short time lag as academics struggled to respond to this integrative thrust, but by the early 1990s the blurred outlines of a new sub-discipline, European public policy, had begun to emerge out of what was left of the largely moribund field of regional integration theory, its practitioners keen to apply theories of domestic public policy to understand the *internal* politics of the EU. There is a rapidly emerging consensus among scholars of the EU that theories of IR help to explain the creation of the Union and the periodic alterations to its basic institutional structures, but they are too blunt to cut into the day-to-day process of policy-making which unfold prior to and after states, meeting in the European Council, have decided to integrate more intensively (Rhodes and Mazey, 1995; Caporaso and Keeler, 1995; Sandholtz and Stone-Sweet, 1998).[2] In a provocative article, Simon Hix (1994) suggests that the metamorphosis of the EU into a something far more complicated and internally differentiated than a conventional international organisation, renders theories of IR of limited value if the aim is to understand what he termed its internal 'politics' or policy-making processes. To understand these, he argues, scholars must reach into the tool box of Comparative (or national) Politics (CP). Peterson (1995) similarly argues that no single theory can explain EU governance at all levels. Theories of IR explicate the 'history making' decisions at the macro level (Jordan, 1998b), and the crises which periodically threaten to bring the whole edifice crashing down. But when it comes to the day-to-day decisions at the meso- and micro-levels which 'set', 'shape' and implement individual policies, 'macro theories tend to lose their explanatory power.'

Hix has been rightly criticised for positing too hard a distinction between internal politics and integration (Hurrell and Menon, 1996; Hix, 1996; Risse-Kappen, 1996; Hix, 1998). We know, for example, that the steady output of 'history making' rulings by the European Court of Justice (ECJ) facilitates deeper integration (Burley and Mattli, 1993), while the 'high politics' of Treaty adjustment do fundamentally re-balance the power relations between different actors. CP alone cannot *explain* the EU because it was developed to explain what happens within and between states. Indeed well known comparativists such as Richardson (1996: 27) openly admit to being unable to describe let alone theorise the EU policy process using the standard tools of policy analysis, hence recent interest in fostering theoretical and methodological cross-fertilisation (Rhodes and Mazey, 1995; George, 1996: 23; Caporaso, 1997; Hix, 1998). This willingness to cross disciplinary boundaries notwithstanding, there is still a strong sense in which macro and meso-level studies of the EU remain on adjacent but not necessarily convergent paths. It is notable that in their critique of Hix, Hurrell and Menon (1996: 397 *et seq*) leave tantalisingly open the question of exactly *how* to overcome the 'divide' between CP and IR, although they do explicate some of interconnections between 'politics' and 'integration' (*ibid*: 390-3).

The main purpose of this chapter is to place policy implementation firmly on the research agenda. Why does implementation deserve greater attention? Is it simply to discover whether individual policies are put into effect, the implicit aim being to close 'gaps' and 'deficits' in performance? (see: Jordan, 1999b). This is certainly one of the traditional concerns of implementation analysis (see: Hill (1997) for an honest assessment of the field by a former protagonist), but there are at least three other good reasons for paying closer attention to the 'downstream' aspects of the EU policy process: (1) broadening the scope of analysis to include long-term policy outcomes as well as short-term outputs offers a fuller understanding of the '*internal*' politics of the European Union through which the 'grand bargains' are given concrete effect; (2) tracking statutes as they travel down the policy cycle reveals a lot about the continuing *Europeanisation* of national political spheres; and (3) studying implementation will expand our understanding of the broader process of European *integration*, thereby bridging the divide between CP and IR approaches to the EU. The crucial distinction is between what Easton (1965) famously termed policy *outputs* (the laws, regulations and institutions employed to deal with policy problems) and policy *outcomes* (the effect of those measures upon the state of the world and actors' perceptions of it). The existing literature has a lot to say about the former, but neglects the latter (see Armstrong and Bulmer, 1998: 38). Before elaborating these three in greater detail, I will unpack the term 'post-decisional' politics then explain why implementation has received such scant attention in the extant literature. I do this from the standpoint of British politics, although many of my arguments are probably generalisable to other Member States.

'Post-decisional' politics in the EU

The current popularity of EU public policy is reflected in a growing number of new books, articles and even the appearance of a specialist journal, the *Journal of European Public Policy* (Sbragia, 1992; Mazey and Richardson, 1993; Wallace and Wallace, 1996; Hayes-Renshaw and Wallace, 1997). The primary concern of this stream of work is to look below and beyond the Treaty level, paying closer attention to the EU's 'internal' policy processes using the tools of CP and public policy. In contrast to IR theorists, practitioners take as given the existence of integrated institutional structures and seek to understand what takes place within them rather than how they were formed or how they evolve over time. Their primary concern is understanding EU public policy, not European integration. Typically, they treat the EU not as an international organisation but a multi-tiered system of governance – a neo-state or confederal structure – with policy processes similar to those found within nation-states.

The blossoming literature on EU public policy continues, however, to elide a full consideration of what happens *after* common policies are formally adopted. The literature tends to concentrate on the more visible 'decisional' politics centring on the Commission and the concrete adoption of laws and policies in the Council of Ministers (CoM), rather than the less visible 'front' (agenda setting) and 'back end' (implementation) of the policy process (c.f. Peters, 1994). Token references are made to the implementation 'gap' in the EU and the power enjoyed by states in the implementation phase, but rarely does implementation constitute the main focus of analysis. There is an emerging literature on the comitology procedures through which the Commission and Member States administer EU legislation in collaboration with committees of national experts (Docksey and Williams, 1994; Dogan, 1997), but these do not really explore the detailed aspects of implementation at the national and sub-national level.

Over two decades ago, Donald Puchala (1975: 497) observed that 'most work on the politics of the [EU] to date has focused upon decision-making in Brussels.' 'Yet... in order to understand European integration, we must devote at least as much analytical attention to postdecisional politics as we have been devoting to decision-making' (*ibid*: 518). 'Very simply put, the politics of compliance and non-compliance slow down the rate at which transnational harmonisation and standardisation can be accomplished.' 'The transmission downward and outward of regional directives from Brussels to the national peripheries, and the problems, pitfalls, and impacts involved, constitute postdecisional politics in the [EU]' he explained (*ibid*: 497-8). Of course Puchala was by no means alone in identifying this lacuna. Around the same time, Helen Wallace (1977: 33-4) was also arriving at very similar conclusions:

> the Community process is not confined to what takes place within the formal framework of the Community institutions. Rather it embraces a network of relationships and contacts among national policy-makers in the different Member States...[It]... can be analysed only as the tip of a much larger iceberg formed by the domestic contexts that set constraints on each member government... These arenas of discussion sometimes complement or reinforce the Community process but on occasion may complicate or undermine it.

Crucially, it is precisely the submerged portion of this policy 'iceberg', the continuing relations between international and domestic politics, which intrigues implementation analysts.

Why have 'post-decisional' politics been neglected?

There are several reasons why implementation has been neglected by EU scholars. Some of them have to do with the way in which the discipline of politics is organised. Social scientists like to divide the world into discrete parts to simplify the task of understanding its operation (Becher, 1989). If political science comprises a collection of tables each, to paraphrase Almond (1990: 19), conducting its own separate conversation, then scholars of IR have occupied one while comparativists have occupied another in a different part of the room. With few exceptions, scholars have tended to work within one tradition or the other, departing only insofar as it useful to their broader purpose (Gourevitch, 1978). Standing, as it does, mid-way between these two stools, it is not entirely surprising that until relatively recently the implementation of international environmental agreements received little sustained attention. These divisions have left their imprint on European studies: one of the main paradigms of integration – inter-governmentalism – is ontologically committed to studying the interaction between states. According to Moravcsik (1993: 473):

from the signing of the Treaty of Rome to the making of [the] Maastricht [Treaty]... the [EU] has developed through a series of celebrated intergovernmental bargains, each of which set the agenda for an *intervening period of consolidation*. The most fundamental task facing a theoretical account of European integration is to explain these bargains (emphasis added).

Inter-governmentalism evinces little interest in internal politics: it is assumed to unfold along the lines specified by the grand bargains which determine the 'rules of the game' in individual policy sectors. Meanwhile, the main alternative, (neo)functionalism, predicts a largely self-sustaining process of integration that gradually binds states and non-state actors together, preventing them from descending once again into war. For (neo)functionalism, the 'intervening periods' are precisely when integration takes place; the grand bargains only consolidate and/or institutionalise what precedes them. Writing from a broadly neofunctionalist perspective, Marks (1993, 392, 395) suggests that:

a convincing analysis of institution building in the [EU] should go beyond the areas that are transparently dominated by Member States... Beyond an beneath the highly visible politics of member states bargaining lies a dimly lit process of institutional formation... there is the less transparent but very consequential, process of post-Treaty interpretation and institution building. The causal logic of this process varies across policy areas.

(Neo)functionalist theorising has, however, always contained a strong normative attachment to the integrationist project. William Wallace (1982: 65), who did much to raise the profile of EU public policy in the late-1970s, recalls that it was 'considered indecent, even anti-European, to draw attention to the problems raised by national governments for the further development of the Community.' Residues of this idealistic support for faster and deeper integration are still discernible today; there is undoubtedly *still* a sense in which the pressure groups which orbit the Commission and the 'high summitry' of the CoM are more excitingly *communautaire* than day-to-day events at the 'coal face' of the EU policy process. Witness, for example, the current popularity of interest group lobbying and inter-institutional relations as research topics in EU public policy.

If analysts working at the European level have been guilty of not looking down to lower levels, those working in national contexts have been just as slow to recognise the steadily growing role of the EU. There has definitely been a marked tendency in British political science to treat Britain 'as though it were a self-contained political system untouched by the implications of... being part of an international political and economic order' (Dearlove and Saunders, 1991: 508). Peter Hennessy (1990: 253), for example, devotes only a few pages of his monumental study of British Government to the EU, noting almost in passing that the 'European dimension in Whitehall is as important as it is unexciting.' In spite of claims made about how far the locus of policy-making has shifted upwards to the EU, 'the precise impact of EU action on the Member States has been curiously under-researched' (Kassim and Menon, 1996: 1).

Implementation has also been a poor relation of policy analysis at the national level too (Parsons, 1995: 462). It is often viewed as a straightforward, almost 'boring', bureaucratic process of putting into effect pre-determined policies. For many, the more visible politics of decision-making within and around Parliament and Whitehall hold a more obvious appeal. Indeed, surprising as it may sound, it was not until the mid-1970s that implementation was identified as a 'missing link' in the analysis of the policy process. For various reasons, the practical problem of implementing EU policies has also been overlooked by policy-makers in Brussels and by national governments (see Jordan (1997) for a fuller analysis). For their part, European bureaucrats and politicians have tended to devote their energies to extending the Community's competence into new issue areas and building up as wide a corpus of policy as possible, without inquiring too closely into whether it is being properly implemented and enforced. The first ever book written on EU environmental policy by a well known insider devoted just two pages to formal compliance and said nothing about practical compliance (Johnson, 1979).[3] It was not really until the mid-1980s, a full decade after the EU first turned its attention to environmental matters, that implementation rudely emerged as an issue of debate and policy discussion, and a focus of study in its own right (Haigh, 1984; Jordan, 1999b).

In many ways this was understandable: one cannot study the implementation of policies that do not exist or that have not had sufficient time to generate political outcomes. Many of the water policies adopted by the EU in the 1970s, for example, set compliance deadlines of five and ten years. However, increasing interest in issues of enforcement and compliance, which reflected growing public concerns for environmental issues and the political determination to develop a Single Market, soon revealed a serious implementation deficit or 'gap', with many policies selectively or only tardily enacted. This gap is now viewed widely as a fundamental problem which challenges the legal integrity of the Union and undermines its efforts to promote more environmentally sustainable forms of economic development. Given that the underlying purpose of the EU environmental policy is to improve environmental quality, it is hardly surprising that many analysts now study implementation in order to understand how such 'gaps' can be closed.

Implementation and the 'internal' policy process

If implementation is under-researched, what needs to be done to address the imbalance? What, in other words, should studies of 'post-decisional' politics actually address? There is much debate within the public policy literature on this question. Most of the relevant material dates from the 1970s and 1980s and is ably summarised by Paul Sabatier (1986). Traditionally, implementation theorists have been almost obsessed with the question of goal attainment or policy effectiveness, specifically the delivery or non-delivery of political outcomes, rather than the processes that lay behind them. The implicit aim of more 'top down' accounts is to improve policy, to learn from mistakes and to solve problems. Normally the criterion of success is whether the goals embodied in the policy in question are achieved, although there are several other alternative perspectives. Conditions for prompt and full implementation are often specified and include the setting of clear, the provision of adequate resources and the availability of compliant implementing officials etc. These help to identify why gaps occur and how they might be corrected. Here, one is talking about a fairly narrow legal-bureaucratic review of the organisations and institutions of control – an approach taken by many of the early implementation studies (Van Horn, 1979: 9-10).[4] Many 'black letter' accounts of the transposition of EU law into national law fall into this category (Daintith, 1995; Somsen, 1997). A great number simply describe the Commission's enforcement powers (Barav, 1975; Evans, 1979; Dashwood and White, 1989).

However, it is questionable whether such accounts actually address the 'real' implementation problem, that of delivering political outcomes. Policy analysts are more likely to want to know whether, for example, polluting emissions are reduced by the stated amount and what effect this has on environmental quality. Intuitively speaking, this may appear to be a more pertinent question given that the ultimate purpose of EU policy is to protect or improve the environment. Sabatier for instance, believes that focusing on outcomes reveals whether the causal theory embodied in a policy is sound (i.e. whether or not it is properly conceived). After all, some policies are ineffective not because they are poorly implemented but because they target the wrong actors or require the wrong actions. Again, the implicit aim is to *improve* life and make things 'better'.

The mid-1980s witnessed the appearance of a number of general surveys of implementation in the EU which focused on outputs or, more rarely, outcomes (Azzi, 1985; Siedentopf and Ziller, 1988; Haigh *et al*). Siedentopf and Ziller (1988: x), for example, consider 19 statutes in 10 countries using a methodology which 'satisf[ied] the practical needs of the Commission.' Indeed, many were not only targeted at the needs of policy-makers in the Commission and Whitehall, but financed by them. It is not surprising, then, that many were eager to prescribe solutions to implementation problems.[5] In general, the implicit aim was to find out whether legally prescribed goals are achieved and if not why not.

Other theorists take a different view, arguing that policy statements, laws and policies made by those at the top are poorly related to political outcomes. It would be more realistic, suggest 'bottom uppers', to focus on what actually influences action on the ground, especially the interaction between groups of street level bureaucrats and their clients, 'rather than faulting it for not living up to the assumptions of the traditional top-down perspective' (Hanf, 1982: 160). Analysts therefore start with a policy sector or problem rather than a single piece of legislation and work backwards to provide a map of the full range of actors involved, showing their needs and aspirations. In caricature, discretion is seen as beneficial rather than the source of 'steering' problems; it allows implementors to cope with, better still improve, 'bad' policies. Insofar as they study them, bottom uppers take a more relaxed view of implementation 'deficits': street level bureaucrats are seen to be closer to policy problems and hence better placed to develop solutions which may deviate from those sought by the top.

In an EU context, bottom uppers would be keen to elucidate the 'shaping' role of front-line (i.e. sub-national) bureaucrats upon whom policy delivery often depends. It is often the case that the Commission and the ECJ only really become involved when a Member State's behaviour is plainly egregious. Normally, day-to-day enforcement activities such as permitting, site designation and monitoring are conducted without any input from or scrutiny by supranational authorities. Perhaps the greatest strength of 'bottom up' models is their ability to generate descriptively accurate accounts of who actually interacts in a particular policy area. As such, they offer an excellent method of uncovering more of the submerged 'iceberg' of the EU policy process, revealing the extent and nature of policy delivery systems. The challenge posed by bottom uppers to our understanding of policy processes is still properly to be addressed in mainstream accounts of EU public policy.

Assessing how 'effectively' – however defined – individual policies are put into effect is undoubtedly an important component of an implementation analysis, although it raises a raft of issues including which criteria to use. But an examination of what happens after EU policies are adopted may still yield important insights into the operation of European and British political systems. Certainly from a political science perspective, it is perhaps more interesting to put aside notions of policy 'success' and 'failure', and analyse the *process* as opposed to the outcome of implementation. What types and forms of political conflict are triggered at the national and local level for instance? What implications do European policies have for the procedures and structures of national, regional and local government? Do they lead to the centralisation of powers in national capitals (as seems to be the case with more regulatory policies areas such as the environment (Haigh, 1986)), or the creation of a 'multi-level governance' structure (Marks, 1992: 1993), where powers are shared by actors at different levels, including the regional and local, rather than monopolised by state executives? The latter has been identified in distributional policy areas such as social and regional policy. And how does EU policy interact and ultimately become entwined with domestic policies, or undermine existing practices? In what ways does it constrain or enable the actions of actors at the sub-national level? And in what ways does it conflict with established policy paradigms and bureaucratic procedures? All these questions demand sustained empirical research.

This lacuna was identified by Nigel Haigh as long ago as 1984. His handbook (Haigh, 1984) (now Manual) of EU environmental policy and Britain remains the only, sustained attempt to document every single item of EU legislation in a single policy area and assess its impact on the national sphere. Although he reached this conclusion intuitively rather than through a process of theoretical reasoning, he has consistently and very correctly argued that properly to understand EU 'policy', attention must be paid to the manner in which it is implemented:

> A consideration of... items of [EU] legislation cannot... give a complete picture of Community policy since all they can do is to set out the *intentions* of policy. To discover whether these policy goals are being achieved it is necessary to examine how they are being implemented within the Member States. Community policy cannot therefore be regarded as some abstract concept existing on its own and separate from national policy. Community policy only comes to life when it is implemented in the Member States and has thereby become inseparably intertwined with national policies and practices (Haigh, 1992: section 1.1).

The key point being made is that EU environmental policy does not exist in Brussels or in Strasbourg – although important decisions are made there -. Nor is the same set of policies replicated across the 15 Member States. Rather, policy developed at the European level permeates down through the administrative tiers of the Union, altering as it comes into contact with national traditions and practices. By the same token, the same national traditions and policy styles influence the positions adopted by states during discussions over new initiatives. When examined over time, the flow of influence can be seen to be two way: states seek to affect the process of integration to suit their particular circumstances but in so doing are affected by it.

Arguably, the fact that EU policy is 'European' – born of a fusion of ideas and practices from many states – rather than purely 'national', renders it more vulnerable to refraction and mutation during the implementation process at the national level. Indeed the main legislative instrument of EU environmental policy - the Directive – deliberately allows states to determine the precise means of implementation, although the objectives to be met are clearly defined. Whether and how that discretion is applied by states fundamentally shapes political outcomes. Throughout the 1970s and 1980s, for example, Britain deliberately adopted a narrow, *de minimis* view of EU water Directives in order to reduce public spending on water improvement schemes (Jordan and Greenaway, 1999c; Ward, 1998). Large gaps remain in our understanding of the bargaining games played out between the Commission and Member States over the precise scope and speed of implementation (Jordan, 1995; Mendrinou, 1996). What is or is not adjudged to be 'full compliance' often arises from a 'political' understanding between Commission officials, who are keen to push a maximal interpretation of the law, and national bureaucrats, who procrastinate in order to attend to domestic 'difficulties'. Puchala (1975: 517) referred to the wily devices deployed by national bureaucrats as 'smoke-screening'.

But as impressive and illuminating as it is, Haigh's is not a theoretically informed account. There is still a marked absence of theory-led research in the area and studies that extend below the executive level to focus on sub-national and non-institutionalised forms of political activity generated by EU policies (Tarrow, 1995: 223). For example, what forms of political conflict are generated as EU policies are put into effect within national spheres? What types of protest are mobilised and new political opportunity structures created as fresh coalitions of interest come together? There are certainly high profile disputes between Member States and the Commission which the ECJ is sometimes called upon to resolve, but there are also myriad forms of non-institutionalised conflict and bargaining which develop around EU policies *within* Member States as they are implemented.

Implementation studies may thus usefully reveal who, to borrow Lasswell's memorable phrase, 'actually gets what, when and how' from an EU policy; who, in other words, ultimately enjoys power in the EU. After all 'winning' at the policy formulation stage does not necessarily ensure a beneficial outcome at the policy output stage. For the powerful, poor implementation is a useful way of thwarting demands for change to the *status quo* via a process of non-decision-making. The spectacle of 'doing something' is used to accommodate opponents or appease critics (Edelman, 1971). By concentrating on events in Brussels, existing studies of the EU policy process run the risk of concentrating on the 'winners' – the well mobilised interest groups who see the growing importance of Brussels and are capable of lobbying there and other elites identified by neo-functionalists, or get what they want without trying. In contrast, implementation studies are more likely to encounter the 'losers' – the ignorant and poorly mobilised actors whose activities remain nationally or locally focused – who played no part in the development of the policy or who simply capitalise on new agendas as policies are enacted.

Implementation and Europeanisation

It is now a commonplace that the domestic politics of the countries of Western Europe cannot properly be understood without taking EU legislation into consideration; that national politics and political systems have in effect been steadily and irrevocably 'Europeanised'. Richardson (1996: 27), for example, claims that the national and the European 'co-exist' in the same policy space, Rhodes (1994: 142) refers to the 'Europeanisation of everything', and Rometsch and Wessels (1996: xiii) identify a 'fusion' of national and European political arenas. Yet in spite of ritual claims made about the extent to which policy-making powers have shifted upwards to the EU in recent years, 'the precise impact of EU action on the Member States has been curiously under-researched' (Kassim and Menon, 1996: 1). Arguably implementation studies are uniquely placed to uncover the longer term and more deep rooted effects of EU membership on national spheres (Knill (1997) confirms this). This is a less applied and more detached view of 'post-decisional' politics than that described above; it is analysis *of* the policy process rather than analysis *for* improving the quality of public policy (Gordon, Lewis and Young, 1977).

The environment provides an interesting area in which to study the inter-penetration of national and European political systems. In many areas of British political life, the EU effectively functions as a third level of government intervening directly in areas of policy-making that were once exclusively domestic. In the environmental sphere, almost all British legislation is driven by or developed in close association with EU or international legislation. In 1990, Derek Osborn (1992: 199), then a Deputy Under-Secretary at the DoE, remarked that:

> In a relatively brief period of time the nature of the Community has evolved and expanded, so that its many strands are now woven in to most areas of [British] public policy. This is certainly true of environmental policy, where in the last 20 years the [EU] has rapidly become a major force, or even the dominant one.

But where do we begin to cut into such a complicated skein of cause and effect? Hall (1993) usefully divides policy into three different levels or parts. The first of his levels relates to the precise setting of policy instruments. The second is the instruments or techniques themselves, while the third comprises the overall goals that guide policy. These goals operate within a policy paradigm: 'a framework of ideas and standards that specifies not only the goals of policy and the kind of instruments that can be used to attain them, but also the very nature of the problems they are meant to be addressing.' This framework is largely taken for granted and is embedded in the terminology of a policy area. According to Hall, incrementalism and satisficing characterise policy-making at levels 1 and 2, whereas changes at the third level typically involve more obviously political or strategic factors. He (*ibid*: 270, 280) defines third order change as a 'disjunctive process associated with periodic discontinuities in policy' and a 'wider contest between competing paradigms.' He offers as an example the transition from Keynesian to Monetarist economic policy-making.

British environmental policy has traditionally been a flexible, pragmatic and piecemeal affair. In terms of underlying paradigms, Britain has commonly followed a 'science based policy approach' (Hajer, 1995: 141), which insists that interventions are justified on scientific grounds, and problems are dealt with when they arise and only to the extent necessary to maintain environmental quality at an acceptable level. This stands in contrast to continental – and especially German – notions of precautionary environmental protection, which insist upon protection in situations where scientific understanding is poor and the economic benefits of proposed measures cannot be directly related to the costs. In caricature, the traditional aim of environmental policy in Britain has been to *optimise* pollution rather than minimise it; to achieve a specified level of environmental quality. Whereas continentals, have sought to achieve the highest possible environmental quality regardless of the dilution capacity of the receiving air or water. Emphasis is therefore placed upon notions of practicability and balance; of making optimum use of the assimilative capacity of the environment using environmental quality standards set according to dosage levels which would guard against unacceptable environmental damage. Uniform standards and solutions, and other attempts to remove potential pollutants regardless of their likely impact are all completely alien to this tradition. Generally speaking, safeguarding human health rather than the intrinsic welfare of environmental systems has remained the main priority of policy.

These third level goals suggested certain tools of policy intervention. In caricature, the British have tended to rely upon informal quality objectives set according to a properly conducted scientific examination of the waste absorptive capacity of the environment, while continentals have used uniform emission limits and the best available abatement techniques. Staying at the second level, British governments have tended to prefer on loose administrative controls, informal guidelines and voluntary agreements with polluters rather than precise standards to achieve objectives (Jordan, 1998d). These are, of course, recognised hallmarks of the British policy 'style'. As in many other areas of British administration, processes of environmental protection have tended to be imbued with secrecy, have been consultative rather than openly adversarial, and reactive as opposed to anticipatory. Environmental policy tends to have a large technical core and there has been a long-standing willingness on behalf of both politicians and the public to leave matters to front-line officials at the local or regional level, who have tried to seek a balance between the costs and benefits of protection. In contrast, the EU develops policies with uniform standards, clear targets and timetables for compliance, in order to reduce cross-national variations which might otherwise constitute barriers to free trade.

Implementation studies which address the longer term and cumulative effects of EU policies as they are implemented at the national level offer a means of investigating the effects of Europeanisation along these three dimensions. Starting at the third level, it is commonly asserted that the EU has helped undermine the assimilative paradigm in several areas, by adopting policies based upon continental (but especially German) notions of precautionary environmental protection. These insist upon protection in situations where scientific understanding is poor and the economic benefits of proposed measures cannot be directly related to the costs. A good example is British coastal water policy. In the past, most sewage was disposed of untreated along pipes into the sea, but now it receives some form of treatment and in some areas is even disinfected. As for the other two levels, Osborn (1992: 206) suggests that EU legislation has altered profoundly the predominantly 'case-by-case approach' to environmental problem solving favoured in Britain. It has, he claims, brought greater codification and made policy more explicit, reduced the discretion normally enjoyed by local administrators, increased monitoring and boosted public awareness, injected a greater sense of urgency into domestic environmental policy-making and brought about higher standards than would otherwise have been the case. Haigh and Lanigan (1995: 29-30) claim that the EU has also: brought issues on to the domestic agenda that were once neglected or actively suppressed; empowered actors normally excluded from the policy process such as pressure groups; forced senior civil servants to deal with technical matters normally left to local officials; and, because EU legislation is addressed first and foremost to national governments, helped to centralise powers that were once exercised locally.

The task now is to generate clear hypotheses about where and when we would expect Europeanisation to occur. Has the incremental effect of successive Directives increased over time as EU institutions have grown in competence? Or has it decreased as British officials have learned how to function better in European networks and build alliances with other states? Have the changes been incremental or are other, more paradigmatic, influences apparent? Can we make general conclusions or is Europeanisation a sector specific process? How do states exercise discretion during the implementation process? Is it primarily determined by state executives at the national level, or do street-level bureaucrats retain an important role? Have the enforcement practices of local pollution control officers changed as a result of European policies or have they been left largely untouched? (Richardson *et al*. 1983; Hawkins, 1984; Jordan, 1993).

Implementation and European integration

Neither (neo)functionalism nor inter-governmentalism seriously considers the question of policy implementation. However, as long ago as 1971, Helen Wallace (1971: 538) underlined the fact that what actually gets put into practice at the national level is as important a measure of the extent and depth of integration as what new institutions are created and policies adopted in Brussels:

> For political integration of the character envisaged by the founders of the Communities to be achieved, changes at the national level are as important as the development of the Community institutions themselves.

Functionalism predicts a rational and incremental process of learning by association. Integration is viewed as a process of technical problem solving, dominated by elites operating in a largely apolitical atmosphere. As problems are solved, elites shift their loyalties from the nation-state to the supranational level, followed by interest groups who perceive their interests to be better served there. The outcome is a cumulative and expansive process, with a more or less automatic transfer of sovereignty from Member States to the EU institutions, who are assumed to have some autonomy from states. States are simply dragged along by a self-reinforcing dynamic, finding themselves bound to a much greater degree of integration than they had originally foreseen because of the prevalence of unintended consequences, or simply fail to notice the gradual draining away of power to Brussels.

Neo-functionalists such as Haas claim that integration is driven by an 'expansive logic of integration', normally termed 'spillover',[6] which brings actors together from different sectors and states. The sheer complexity of policy processes, the density of issues under consideration, the tendency for state bureaucrats to focus on near term (predominantly electoral) effects, and the inevitability that policies will generate consequences in policy realms beyond those originally considered (spillover), 'over the longer term... trap[s] governments in a web of unintended consequences spun by their own previous commitments' (Moravcsik, 1993: 475). Although there is conflict between participants, neo-functionalists assume an underlying consensus on the problems to be tackled and the solutions to be adopted, brought about by the frequency and intensity of interaction between officials from different states.

Neither approach, however, originally considered – and certainly did not predict – the emergence of a systemic implementation problem in the EU. Once 'European' solutions to national problems had been identified and adopted, the implicit assumption was that they would then be fully implemented by the states that had made them. In the language of CP, policy outcomes were automatically assumed to follow policy outputs. Consensus at the adoption stage was considered sufficient to drive integration forwards. But clearly without prompt and full implementation of these solutions, integration is just a meaningless abstraction. Haas (1964: 231) himself emphasized the importance of elites reaching consensus and of a process of 'upgrading the common interest', whereby states agree to stress what they have in common and to postpone the settlement of disagreements in the hope that agreement in the short term will increase the possibility of agreement in the longer term. The emphasis was upon searching for and adopting solutions. However, differences of interpretation or quarrels about these solutions or the ultimate objective to be achieved may only emerge in the 'post-decisional' phase, having been subsumed or deliberately withheld during the process of negotiation, as new problems arise and external circumstances change. In reality, Member States choose whether or not to fulfil their commitments; they retain a tight hold over the implementation of policy and have many opportunities to dilute or impede policies they find unpalatable. Problem 'solving' may be a pretence; a deliberate tactic used by states to buy time, pacify their neighbours and accommodate domestic critics.

Later formulations tried to adopt a less deterministic view, introducing the concept of 'spillback' (a 'situation in which there is a withdrawal from a set of specific obligations' (Lindberg and Scheingold, 1970: 137) or 'a return to a purely national framework of action' (Haas, 1968: xxix)) as one of a number of possible outcomes[7] of integration. The presumption was that when pressure groups realised the threat of non-compliance, they would normally lobby states to prevent them reneging on their commitments. But the qualification to the teleogical predictions of neofunctionalism was never clearly specified: while spillback 'does entail risks for the system as a whole, it is likely to be limited to the specific rules in question.' Spillback, in other words, is a temporary glitch, an 'integrative plateau' (Haas, 1968: xxix), on the road to deeper integration.[8] Haas continued: states may on occasions attempt to 'sidestep, ignore, or sabotage' EU policies, but 'they recognise a point beyond which such evasions are unprofitable, and in the long run they tend to defer to federal decisions' lest they set a precedent for other governments (*ibid*: xxxiv).

When integration failed to advance steadily across all policy areas, typified by the 1966 'empty chair' crisis, Haas began to question the automaticity of spillover and eventually proclaimed that the whole theory was obsolescent (Taylor, 1983). In a recent attempt to revive interest in neo-functionalism, Burley and Mattli (1993) argue that the cases brought by EU institutions before the ECJ and instances of non-compliance provide concrete evidence that supranational bodies do enjoy a degree of autonomy from Member States and the EU legal system has moved beyond the initial preferences of Member States and *gradually* imposed constraints on their ability to fight back – what they term 'transnational incrementalism.' This brings us back to Marks invocation to study more closely what occurs *between* the major Treaties.

Inter-governmentalists, who take an essentially realist view of international politics, on the other hand, see the sovereignty of Member States as essentially undiminished. States are seen to be in control of the EU and external from it. EU institutions are creatures of state executives, having little or no independent role. Integration proceeds only as fast and as far as states decree. States are powerful, hierarchic structures. They perform a 'gate-keeping' role at the nexus between domestic politics and IR. Bargains between them are a necessary condition for European integration. Supranational structures suit the preferences of Member States. When those preferences change, the structures and institutions are altered accordingly, having little or no autonomy of their own. Policy outcomes broadly correspond to those foreseen by states at the point of formal policy adoption.

Inter-governmentalists have devoted little attention to implementation however. While integration may proceed on matters of 'low politics' such as technical standards, inter-governmentalists such as Hoffman (1966) suggest it is blocked if it ever encroaches on issues such as defence and foreign policy (matters of 'high politics'). Even then, states still exercise strong influence over issues of 'low' politics such as environmental protection (Weale, 1996: 602-4). In general, sovereignty is *only* sacrificed to achieve carefully specified national political goals which can better be met by international collaboration (i.e. sovereignty is 'pooled' rather than lost). States possess the power to block policies and ignore rulings by the ECJ that cause domestic problems, and co-operate only when it suits them (Garrett, 1995). Like most other international organisations, they have traditionally held a 'double veto' in the EU: one during the process of policy adoption and the other during the process of implementation (Puchala, 1975: 510). In other words, states are free to pick and choose between those obligations they wish to obey and those they do not. Outputs having been adopted, they exercise a strong grip over the generation of outcomes.

However, if the EU were completely dominated by states, why would implementation problems arise at all? Poor implementation is potentially very politically embarrassing, may undermine trust in the EU and work against the creation of the Single Market to which all states are in principle committed. Surely, states would use various devices to 'erode' or block unpalatable policies at the point of adoption? There are several possible explanations. First, states *deliberately* sign up to policies they cannot implement: given the high cost of withdrawing completely from the EU, '*selective membership*' is one way to keep the rise of the European 'regulatory state' in check (Majone, 1992) while reaping the positive benefits of integration. Second, some policies might be accepted reluctantly during the process of horse-trading in the CoM. 'Cohesion' states, for example, might well agree to higher standards of sewage treatment in exchange for financial assistance. Third, because of the integration brought about by ECJ rulings or Commission entrepreneurship, states may sign find themselves bound to do more than they had originally envisaged: the obligation, in effect, may *tighten* in a manner unforeseen when the policy was first adopted. Fourth, states may lack the *internal* capacity to make good on their externally made promises: they may want to implement but find they cannot. Finally, state preferences, which tend to be treated as essentially fixed by inter-governmentalists, may shift throughout the period of implementation. Governments come and go and domestic political changes, such as the 'greening' of public opinion, may lead political leaders to question earlier policy stances. The first two are broadly consistent with classical realist thinking, the rest, to varying degrees, are not.

Thus in different ways, the question of implementation presents both traditions with a series of interesting puzzles. Golub (1996) suggests that the 'true test' of whether power remains with states or has been diffused among other actors, is whether policies are adopted in the face of state opposition or blocked by EU institutions in spite of state support. But this relies upon a truncated view of the policy process. It neglects the fact that sub-central actors are not pusillanimous; their support is needed by national governments for policies to be implemented fully. It also takes a snap-shot of what is often an evolving process. In contrast, an implementation perspective argues that a consideration of political *outcomes* offers a much better test of where power lies. Does integration really lead to the loss of state power or is it clawed back during the implementation stage? Or do states find themselves forced to implement rather more than they had originally intended. IR theories generate quite different answers to these questions. Neo-functionalism predicts that states will find themselves boxed into corners, obliged to accept policies they do not favour because of the emergence of unforeseen consequences and the gradual tightening of the legal context of implementation. Conversely, inter-governmentalism argues that states remain fundamentally in control of the EU policy process, and secure the objectives they set out to achieve. If unintended outcomes emerge, states exploit various mechanisms (e.g. Treaty revision, non-compliance etc.) to regain control (Garrett, 1995).[9]

Conclusion

This chapter argues that studying the implementation of EU policies sheds much new light on the both the 'external' process of integration and the 'internal' politics of particular policy sectors. It claims that a closer examination of policy outcomes over extended periods of time improves understanding of the pathways through which integration occurs by arbitrating between rival theories of integration. Existing accounts typically adopt a very short time frame and remain narrowly focused on policy outputs. Very often, the manner in which outcomes are perceived at the national level determines future negotiating positions via a series of complicated feedback loops. It is doubtful, for example, that Britain would have pushed the subsidiarity principle so hard in recent years had supranational EU institutions not significantly tightened the legal and political interpretation of Directives, which were once widely regarded as fairly loose statements of intent than binding articles of law, and insisted upon implementation to the letter.

In many ways the troublesome implementation of EU environmental policies represents a microcosm of the wider story of integration and the conflicting forces and contradictions which have characterised the EU since its inception. But these are, if anything, more starkly revealed in the implementation phase when the Community's policies *have* to be made to work, than at earlier stages in the policy process, where symbolic gestures and rhetorical commitments are more likely to secure consensus. Implementation is where a burgeoning supranational legal order meets a decentralised policy delivery system in which the Member States play the dominant role. It is in every sense the sharp end of the EU policy process.

Viewed in this way, implementation deficits are built into the very structure of the EU; they help to maintain the delicate 'balance' between governmental and supranational elements (Sbragia, 1993). It is significant that 'maximalist' agencies such as the Commission have been at the forefront of attempts to publicise and resolve failures of non-compliance, while Member States have sought to maintain a tight grip over policy delivery and ensure that it remains '[t]he last strong-hold of national control' (From and Stava, 1993). Setting the question of implementation in this wider context helps to counter the common perception of EU policies as being necessarily 'good' and poor implementation as pernicious. Rather, 'post-decisional' politics of implementation in the EU are but one part of a wider struggle between actors at different levels for autonomy and power.

Notes

1   The funding for this chapter was provided by the UK ESRC which core funds the Centre for Social and Economic Research on the Global Environment (CSERGE), which is jointly located at the University of East Anglia in Norwich and University College London. The text incorporates a number of very useful comments made by Tim O'Riordan and the participants at the IRNES conference held in Nijmegen in December 1996. All remaining errors and omissions are the sole responsibility of the author.

2   The debate is mainly about the most appropriate 'level' of analysis. IR theorists are mainly concerned with the macro (i.e. inter-state) level, public policy theorists the meso- and micro-level aspects of integration (i.e. intra-state). But it is also about where 'history' is made. Is it, as intergovernmentalists claim, made at the big 'history-making' meetings of the European Council or during the daily process of policy-making in particular policy sectors? The *sui generis* character of the EU has encouraged greater reflexivity within both camps and made EU politics one of the most active and intellectually vibrant sub-disciplines of political science.

3   At the time, Johnson was Vice-Chairman of the European Parliament's Environment Committee and later became a special adviser to the Director-General of DG XI.

4   Van Horn feels that implementation studies should be concerned *only* with measuring the extent to which policy outputs conform to the objectives set out in legislation.

5   'Our hope', wrote Siedentopf and Ziller (1988: xii) 'is that this publication... can contribute to solving the difficulties encountered in implementing... policies in the Member States.'

6   There are three main types of spillover: functional (the tendency for interventions in some areas to create the need for interventions in others), political (or *engrenage*) (the tendency for state elites to re-focus their activities on the supranational level in the belief that their interests will be better served there) and cultivated (the Commission's attempts to 'upgrade the common interest' by building alliances, constructing package deals etc.). Critics argue that neo-functionalism is much too deterministic.

7   The others were equilibrium, output failure (the inability of the political system to produce an acceptable set of policies despite political commitment) and spillover (forward linkage).

8   Haas (1968: xxx) suggests that the inter-linking of administrative practices among national and supranational agencies 'that cannot perceive themselves functioning except in terms of ongoing co-operative patterns', serves to limit the extent and rate of spillback.

9   But are intergovernmentalist accounts falsifiable? Garrett (1995) steers precariously close to tautology when he argues that states only accept the independent actions of supranational actors such as the ECJ (specifically 'constitutionalization of the Treaties') precisely because they further their interests, or because short term costs of tolerating an unfavourable policy are outweighed by the benefits of being in a Single Market. Moravcsik (1993: 514), on the other hand, retreats into a corner when he suggests that 'only when the actions of supranational leaders systematically bias outcomes away from the long term self-interest of Member States can we speak of a serious challenge to an inter-governmentalist view.'

2 European Environmental Policy at the Intersection of Institutions and Ideas

GÖKHAN ORHAN[1]

Introduction

Environmental policy is a relatively new but rapidly changing area of public policy. During the second half of the 20th century, environmental problems gained an increasing importance to became one of the most important political problems of contemporary societies. Parallel to the increasing salience of environmental problems, institutions designed to solve environmental problems were established both at the domestic and international level. During the last three decades, environmental policy has become institutionalised all around the world, although it is still subject to some changes in the face of new environmental problems and obstacles in solving existing environmental problems.

The institutionalisation of environmental policy has taken place through several steps. Although environmental policy is a new area of public policy, there is constant change in this field. Initially, the solution of the environmental problems was assigned to the existing branches of government. Later on, governments tried to solve existing environmental problems by establishing environment ministries. This piecemeal approach was unable to deal with existing environmental problems. Subsequently, a more comprehensive strategy was developed, namely sustainable development, for solving both environmental and development problems. Unlike previous approaches, the sustainable development paradigm required an integrated, co-ordinated and participatory environmental policy process, which required major institutional changes.

Explaining institutional change has been one of the main problems of social scientists. If we depart from an institutionalist assumption on the continuity of institutions and of already existing practices, it is difficult to explain policy changes and the establishment of new institutions. However, institutional changes did take place, both at the domestic and international level, in response to environmental problems. These changes in environmental policy can even be considered indications of a paradigm change. During these major changes new policy ideas coming from scientific community and environmental movements played a major role. Yet the role of some other factors in shaping new policies, like that of institutions, is undeniable as well.

In this chapter, the role of new policy ideas in the environmental policy process and the interaction of these new ideas with existing institutions will be discussed. New environmental policy ideas, like ecological modernisation and sustainable development, offer policy proposals towards solving environmental problems and towards providing effective protection of the environment. These new policy ideas and associated environmental discourses influenced environmental policies all around the world. The Brundtland Report itself is an exercise in such new ideas. Similarly, ideas like sustainable development and accompanying principles of ecological modernisation have mushroomed all around the world as viable solutions to environmental problems. In that sense, these ideas influence the efforts of the international community and national governments in solving environmental problems. However, the policy proposals are general and often do not take domestic institutional contexts of countries into consideration. Countries have different types of environmental problems and different environmental priorities. Similarly, countries define and solve their environmental problems in different ways. Furthermore, the institutional context of individual countries influences environmental policy outcomes, all of which results in policy divergence.

At this stage, there is a tension between the already existing institutions and the ideas surrounding them, and new institutions and ideas introduced to solve environmental problems. This tension or even clash of ideas and institutions is more evident in the EU context. There is a strong influence of new policy ideas on EU environmental policy and there is an ever increasing amount of European legislation on environmental policy. European environmental policy is supposed to be applied in the same manner all around the EU. However, EU environmental policy regulates a diverse Europe with different types of environmental problems, different environmental priorities and different understandings of environmental problems. Furthermore, its implementation is influenced by the institutional contexts of the individual countries and their national environmental regulations.

In the end, the question surfaces how we can deal with problems concerning institutional change in relation to EU environmental policy, and accommodate the impact of different national policy styles on the European environment. Is it possible to develop a European environmental policy, to be implemented all around the Union, or will the strong national traditions of regulation and national priorities on environmental issues override any attempt at developing a European environmental policy?

These issues will be discussed in this chapter in the light of recent developments in the field of environmental policy and some other theoretical discussions on the role of the institutions and ideas in the environmental policy process. The EU environmental policy process will be discussed at the intersection of new policy ideas and existing institutions. It will be argued that in the end, European environmental policy may benefit from the richness of the practices in EU member countries. Instead of presenting EU environmental policy as an affair of incommensurable processes, it should be considered a process of experimentation and learning from partners that can draw from various diverse national sources. In order to understand these sources, we should learn about the institutional parameters of the member countries and their understanding of environmental problems. This process requires us to analyse the general role of institutions and ideas in the environmental policy process first.

Institutional changes in the field of environmental policy

The first phase of environmental policy change, i.e., from non-environmental policy to the development of environmental policy as a new field of public policy, is a recent phenomenon. By the 1960s, environmental problems started to draw attention of governments. In the beginning, responses of the governments to the environmental problems focused on the establishment of specialist branches within the existing state bureaucracy. There was no talk yet a holistic and comprehensive approach to environmental problems at the institutional-organisational level. Different departments dealt with environmental problems within their own jurisdiction, without co-operation with other departments, despite the fact that environmental problems are interdependent and the solutions require comprehensive efforts. It was thought that environmental problems were well understood and that cause-effect relations between the sources and results of environmental problems were clear. Environmental policies and approaches to environmental management in the 1970s largely focused on after-the-fact repair of damage, which aimed at correcting past mistakes and eliminating previous harms to the environment. Policies were based on an unshakeable faith in the capacity of science and technology to solve environmental problems. End of pipe technologies were seen as typically adequate and instead of the sources, the effects of environmental problems were the object of the authorities' concerns.

One of the distinctive features of 1970s environmental policy was a belief in the inherent incompatibility of economic growth and environmental protection. The main focus was on the destructive effects on the environment of economic growth and industrialisation. Strict environmental policies were seen as a burden on the economy and believed to have a negative effect on economic growth.

These first responses to environmental problems had some success in solving some environmental problems, yet particularly pollution problems continued in a large scale. Furthermore, the international community came to understand the cross-boundary and global nature of the environmental problems and the necessity of co-operation to solve them. These international efforts played a major part in environmental problem solving. Among these efforts, the achievements of the World Commission of the Environment and Development (WCED) are especially worth mentioning. Sustainable development became a catch-word in the field of the environmental policy all around the world after the publishing of the WCED's *Our Common Future* and even more so after the Rio Conference on the Environment and Development. As a result, the 1980s and so far 1990s witnessed another paradigm change in this field. The new environmental policy approach, namely sustainable development, requires a co-ordinated and integrated environmental policy with the participation in environmental decision-making of all interested parties.

As a result, sustainable development became a major policy principle for both international organisations and individual countries. Achieving sustainable development requires substantial changes and restructuring in environmental policies which has important institutional implications: institutional change is one of the major pre-requisites of sustainable development.

Institutional change for sustainable development

Achieving sustainable development requires substantial institutional changes. According to the Brundtland Report, the most important and fundamental challenge to sustainable development comes from the systemic nature of environmental problems and the need for an integrated policy approach towards solving them. The source of this challenge is the interdependence between environmental problems and other sectors of the economy. The policy changes suggested by the Brundtland Report have deep institutional implications. The objective of sustainable development and the integrated nature of the global environment and economic development poses immense problems for institutions, national and international, that were once established on the basis of narrow preoccupations and compartmentalised concerns (WCED, 1987: 9, 310). These institutions tend to be independent, fragmented and working on relatively narrow mandates with closed decision processes. Those responsible for managing natural resources and protecting the environment are institutionally separated from those responsible for managing the economy (WCED, 1987: 9, 310). Separate policies and institutions, the WCED argues, can no longer cope effectively with these interlocked issues and with the need for the integration of environmental concerns into economic decision-making (WCED, 1987: 310).

According to the Brundtland Report, environmental protection and sustainable development must be an integral part of the mandates of all agencies of governments, of international organisations, and of major private sector institutions. They must be made responsible and accountable for ensuring that their policies, programmes, and budgets encourage and support activities that are economically and ecologically sustainable, both in the short and longer terms. They must be given a mandate to pursue their traditional goals in such a way that those goals are reinforced by a steady enhancement of the environmental resource base of their own national community and that of the world (WCED, 1987: 312). The integrated and interdependent nature of the new challenges and issues contrasts sharply with the nature of the institutions that exists today. This new awareness requires major shifts in the way governments and individuals approach issues of environment, development, and international co-operation. The challenges are both interdependent and integrated, requiring comprehensive approaches and popular participation (WCED, 1987: 9, 310).

Broad public participation in decision-making is seen as one of the fundamental prerequisites for achieving sustainable development. This issue was especially emphasized in Agenda 21 (UN, 1992: 217-245). As stated in Agenda 21, there is a need for new forms of participation, like participation of individuals, groups and organisations in environmental impact assessment procedures, as well as a need to know about and participate in decisions which potentially affect the communities in which they live and work. Individuals, groups and organisations should have access to information relevant to environment and development held by national authorities, including information on products and activities that have or are likely to have a significant impact on the environment, as well as information on environmental protection measures (UN, 1992: 219).

If we summarise the policy proposals of the Brundtland Report, they concentrate on a comprehensive, integrated and co-ordinated approach towards policy-making that incorporates environmental concerns into the decision-making process at all levels, and that requires the participation of all affected parties. These changes call for a fundamental re-structuring of current institutions, of the legal frameworks that regulate those institutions, and of their responsibilities according to their traditional mandates. In short, the definition of environmental problems in terms of sustainable development is very much related to the critique of current institutions. Institutional restructuring constitutes one of the major preconditions for the achievement of sustainable development. Thus, institutions are at the very centre of the problem of implementing sustainable development, both as something to be transformed and as something that will contribute to this transformation process. In the end, countries are required to restructure their domestic institutions. However, the implementation of these policy changes will not be as straightforward as the Brundtland Report suggested. Among other factors, national institutional traditions and already existing ideas are expected to form a major source of problems in the implementation of sustainable development policies.

Institutions and ideas in policy analysis

Policy proposals for achieving sustainable development require both institutional change and a substantial policy change with major institutional implications. Even apart from this, understanding the implementation of a new policy itself requires the study of institutions. Institutions work like a filter. They both constrain and enable actors, they provide a path dependence and persistence (concepts which will be explained below), but at the same time they are open to change. In order to understand policy change we should furthermore focus on some other factors like the role of policy ideas. The Brundtland Report itself is an exercise in new ideas. Various new policy ideas stemming from environmental movements and the scientific community have also played a major role in all these policy changes. Although these new ideas were filtered through already existing institutions, new ideas had a certain impact on the shaping of new environmental policies and institutions established to implement the new policies. In that respect, there is a two-way relationship between ideas and institutions.

Peter Hall's widely accepted definition of institutions, for instance, includes 'the formal rules, compliance procedures, and standard operating practises that structure the relations between individuals in various units of the polity and economy'. John Ikenbery breaks down his definition into three distinct levels that 'range from specific characteristics of government institutions, to the more overarching structures of state, to the nation's normative social order' (Cited in Thelen and Steinmo, 1992: 2). By and large, historical institutionalists define institutions as the formal or informal procedures, routines, norms and conventions embedded in the organisational structure of the polity or political economy. They can range from the rules of a constitutional order or the standard operating procedures of a bureaucracy to the conventions governing trade union behaviour or bank-firm relations. In general, historical institutionalists associate institutions with organisations and rules or conventions promulgated by formal organisations (Hall and Taylor, 1996. 938).

According to Hall and Taylor, historical institutionalists tend to conceptualise the relationship between institutions and individual behaviour in relatively broad terms. They emphasize the asymmetries of power associated with the operation and development of institutions, tend to have a view of institutional development that emphasizes path dependence and unintended consequences, and they are especially concerned to integrate institutional analysis with the contribution that other kinds of factors, such as ideas, can make to political outcomes (Hall and Taylor, 1996: 938).

According to new institutionalists there is an impact of these broader institutional characteristics of countries on the implementation of the public policies. Some research, especially on economic policies, and more recently in other areas of public policy, showed that there is a substantial impact of the institutional framework of a political system of a country on its public policy performance. Broadly speaking, the state tradition of the countries, its historical antecedents and institutional constraints play an important role in understanding the policy processes and policy capacities of countries. The institutional framework of the political system of a country thus has a substantial impact on public policy, as summarised in the following quotation:

> Public policies need to be understood in the light of the specific configuration of institutions and organisations that exist within the political system. Some configurations will create the conditions within which certain public policies may be pursued, whereas other configurations will prevent certain strategies of policy (Weale, 1992: 52).

What Weale suggests is that to understand the specific policies in a country we should have a look at the broader configuration of institutional factors. Similarly, Skocpol points to a tendency for studies on the capacities of states in specific policy areas to move towards macroscopic explorations of the broad institutional patterns of divergent national histories to explain why countries now have, or do not have, policy instruments for dealing with particular problems or crises (Skocpol, 1985: 18).

According to Weaver and Rockman, political institutions shape the process through which decisions are made and implemented; these in turn influence government capabilities. Features such as the extent to which decision-making is centralised, the degree to which decisions are subject to multiple vetoes, and the extent to which elites are stable and share common values and objectives may affect specific capacities (Weaver and Rockman, 1993: 7).

Weaver and Rockman depict the role of institutional constraints on the policy capacities of countries as in Figure 2.1 below.

If we literally present the chart, it says that *institutional constraints* encourage or discourage certain types of *attributes of the decision-making process* that enable or deter the emergence of *policy-making capacities* that influence governments' ability to make strategic *policy choices* that influence but do not necessarily determine the quality of social and economic *policy outcomes*.

Weaver and Rockman's arguments focus on to the role of institutional constraints on policy outcomes. Institutions constrain their behaviour and indicate a path dependence, but at the same time we observed changes in public policies and in institutions dealing with them. One of the potentially limiting or facilitating factors in the public policy performance of a country is the set of dominant ideas about these policies. As Hall and Taylor pointed out, historical institutionalists are especially attentive to relationships between institutions and ideas or beliefs (Hall and Taylor, 1996: 942).

Figure 2.1   The Role of Institutional Constraints

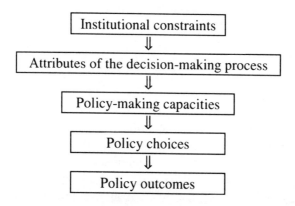

Source: Adapted from Weaver and Rockman, 1993: 9

The role of ideas in the policy process was mainly taken up by a number of researchers and scholars from the ranks of new institutionalism, who tried to make ideas a part of their explanations of the role of institutions. For instance Peter Hall states that

> the deliberation of public policy takes place within a realm of discourse... policies are made within some system of ideas and standards which is comprehensive and plausible to the actors involved... that is, policy-makers work within a framework of ideas...which specifies not only goals and instruments, ...but also the very nature of the problems they are meant to be addressing (Hall, 1993: 277).

Institutional analysis informs us about the constraints imposed by institutional arrangements – however, ideas provide the stimulus for change. As Peter Hall pointed out,

> [i]t is the ideas, in the form of economic theories and policies developed from them, that enable national leaders to chart a course through turbulent economic times, and ideas about what is efficient, expedient, and just that motivate the movement from one line of policy to another. Structural accounts tell us a great deal about the constraints facing policy-makers, but policy-making is based on creation as well as constraint. If we want to explain innovation as well as the underlying continuities in policy, we must recognise that 'knowledge basis of state action, as well as the processes by which the state itself influences the development and application of social knowledge, are indeed research issues of central importance (Hall, 1989: 361-2).

Hall, in his *Political Power of Economic Ideas*, focuses on the impact of Keynesian ideas across a number of countries. According to Hall, the Keynesian case confirms that ideas have an existence and force of their own that cannot be reduced to complete dependence on some set of material circumstances. Keynesian ideas, he argues, did not simply reflect group interests or material conditions. They had the power to change the perceptions that a group had of its own interests, and they made new courses of action possible that changed the material world itself. In these respects, Keynesian ideas had a good deal of independent force over circumstances (Hall, 1989: 369).

According to Hall, the Keynesian case also suggests that the influence of a new set of ideas does not depend entirely on the innate qualities of those ideas alone. First, the persuasiveness of economic ideas depends, in part at least, on the way those ideas relate to the economic and political problems of the day. In other words, persuasiveness is an inherently relational concept, determined as much by the shape of current economic and political circumstances as it is by the shape of the ideas themselves. It is congruence between the ideas and the circumstances that matters here, and changes in material circumstances can affect the pertinence and appeal of certain ideas. Secondly, many complex sets of ideas are ambiguous and far from immediately comprehensible. In these cases, interpretation is a necessary prerequisite to understanding; and to make such interpretations, individuals tend to refer to an existing stock of knowledge that is generally conditioned by prior historical experience. Hence, the same set of ideas can be interpreted quite differently in settings where the relevant historical experiences diverge. Finally, if it is to influence policy, an idea must come to the attention of those who make policy, generally with a favourable endorsement from the relevant authorities. However, the organisation of decision-making in each state can affect the flow of information within it, including the access that policy-makers have to particular ideas and the kind of authorities they consult them about (Hall, 1989: 369-70).

The apparent economic viability of Keynesian ideas had an important effect on how they were received. However, receptiveness to new ideas also depended on the *administrative viability* of those ideas, namely on the degree to which the new ideas fit the long-standing administrative biases of the relevant decision-makers and the existing capacities of the state to implement them, and on their *political viability*, judged in this case by the fit between the new ideas and the existing goals and interests of the dominant political parties and by the sort of associations that Keynesian ideas acquired in the political arena (Hall, 1989: 370-1).

According to Hall, a new set of economic ideas must be seen to have a minimum level of viability on all three of these dimensions – economic, administrative and political – in order to be incorporated into policy. Administrative considerations will carry greater weight in nations where a permanent civil service exercises considerable control over policy. Political considerations may become more important in periods of crisis and realignment when the initiative passes to the political arena (Hall, 1989: 375).

Policy-making takes place within an institutional framework, the configuration of which varies from nation to nation, but it also occurs within the context of a prevailing set of political ideas. These include shared conceptions about the nature of society and the economy, various ideas about the appropriate role of government, a number of common political ideals, and collective memories of past policy experiences. Together, such ideas constitute the political discourse of a nation. They provide a language in which policy can be described within the political arena and the terms in which policies are judged there (Hall, 1989: 383). Hall concludes in his study that the influence of Keynesian ideas within a nation depended heavily on the range of material circumstances, institutional structures, and the ideas that were already there. Similarly, Smith argues that a sharp dichotomy between institutions and ideas is unhelpful. The ideas that are forces in political affairs should always be thought of in terms of their institutional locations, just as institutions always have to be thought of in terms of the ideas embedded in and constitutive of them (Smith, 1995: 139).

Blyth takes this argument further and argues that, although there seems to be an elective affinity between ideas and institutions, the rediscovery of ideas is simply a reaction to the limitations of the 'new institutionalism' which emerged in the late 1980s (Blyth, 1997: 229). Blyth argues that ideas can be seen as both facilitators of radical policy change and as prerequisites of change. While it is true that policy changes in advanced capitalist states tend to be incremental, the espousal of critical economic ideas is nonetheless clearly related to periods of deep-seated institutional reform. Incrementalism is not the norm when economic ideas, as a prerequisite of policy change, advocate the dismantling or reform of existing institutions. Therefore, in this second instance economic ideas facilitate the institutional reformation of the state and are the prerequisites of radical policy changes. Thus we can conceive of ideas as having institutional effects without necessarily reducing them to institutions (Blyth, 1997: 246). As Blyth pointed out, ideas are not only the fillers of institutions but they also shape the institutions. We should therefore not only focus on the role of ideas as (part of) institutions, but on role of ideas in creating them as well.

In the next section, I shall try to explore the role of institutions and ideas in environmental policy change. Sustainable development and ecological modernisation can be considered new policy ideas which signify a paradigm change in the field of environmental policy. In that sense, we can apply the approaches discussed above to environmental policies, where new policy ideas have changed institutions, introduced new institutions, and this all around the world simultaneously.

Institutions and ideas in environmental policy

As mentioned before, environmental policy is a new area of public policy. Environmental problems only recently began to be considered as *environmental* problems. However, state bureaucracies have their already established methods to tackle new problems. Every country has its own way of tackling emerging problems, and its own distinctive style of politics and policy-making. Institutional traditions of a country and its specific configuration of state-society relations will play a major role in the development of its environmental policies and the implementation of sustainable development.

Hall's research on the role of Keynesian ideas in economic policy highlights the role of ideas as well as institutions. Similarly, new environmental policy ideas played a major role in recent environmental policy changes. In this process, findings of the scientific community played a major role.

For a long time scientific inquiry and research were assumed to be neutral and value-free processes. In the same manner, the making of public policies was supposed to be a value-neutral and technical process, independent of the values and interests of policy-makers. Post-positivist public policy[2] (Fischer, 1993a and 1993b) constitutes a challenge to these assumptions. Post-positivist approaches to public policy have a sceptical attitude towards the role of experts in scientific inquiry and in the making of public policy. Post-positivists, according to Fischer, shed doubt on the traditional conception of science as an objective mode of inquiry governed by universal criteria. The scientific community is itself revealed as a community of inquirers with their own interests and objectives. The world, it is argued, is not defined by its own inherent empirical properties; rather, its objects and relationships are named and described by the scientists themselves. The activity of science is thus seen to be a product of the very social world it seeks to explain. Revealing scientific research to involve more than a passive reception and organisation of sense data, post-positivist theory emphasizes science's dependence on the particular constellation of presuppositions, both empirical and practical, that prestructure empirical observations. Thus science, like all human knowledge, is grounded in and shaped by the normative suppositions and social meaning of the world it explores (Fischer, 1993b: 167).

In the field of environmental policy we come across a wide use of scientific inquiry and information. The role of professional expertise is indispensable and necessarily involved in making environmental policy: scientists alerted the world to the hole in the ozone layer, for example, and scientists uncovered the relations between carbon emissions in the UK and acid rain in Scandinavia. In these cases, the findings of scientists initiated a new phase in environmental policy. The way such problems are perceived and presented has an impact on the way policies are made: the construction and interpretation of a problem will be influenced by the belief system and conceptual frameworks that professional communities use in the conduct of their work (Weale, 1992: 60).

In that sense, the role of the ideas in the environmental policy is more evident than in any other field of public policy. For one, as we just saw, new discoveries made by the scientific community and the associated policy ideas are directly channelled into the environmental policy process. In addition, environmental movements have a distinct influence on the policy-making process. As mentioned above, and as Hajer points out for the case of ecological modernisation, such ideas emerge as new discourses in the environmental domain, and in that role brought about new processes of de- and re-institutionalisation (Hajer, 1995: 260). Indeed, we can observe the influence of the eco-modernist discourse on environmental policies all across the world. There is an ongoing process of de-institutionalisation and re-institutionalisation of environmental policies centred around eco-modernist principles and sustainable development, highlighting the importance of ideas in environmental policy.

As new institutionalists suggested, policy outcomes are not the same in every country because of their different institutional traditions. Recent studies on the impact of institutional factors on the environmental policy capacity of countries supports this thesis. For instance, in an article on the national variations in air pollution, Markus Crepaz discusses the impacts of political institutions on environmental policy-making. Crepaz's argument is that national variations in the pattern of how private interests are aggregated, funnelled, and shaped into public policies matter with regard to the levels of air pollution in industrialised democracies. According to Crepaz the success or failure of environmental policies is intimately connected to whether the system of interests representation is consensual and accommodative (corporatism) or whether it is adversarial and competitive (pluralism) (Crepaz, 1995: 393). The goal-oriented, accommodative, co-operative, and consensual style of corporatist policy-making results in lower emissions of traditional air pollutants than the process-oriented, competitive and disjointed form of pluralist interest representation (Crepaz, 1995: 407). Similarly, David Vogel claims that 'the characteristics of a political regime are more important than the nature of the particular policy area itself in explaining policy processes' (Vogel, 1986: 195). While a sound environment is a good equally desired by everybody, Crepaz argues, institutions present different filters through which preferences are channelled. Thus, political outcomes are not only a function of individual preferences but also of how these preferences are structured, shaped, and sculpted by different institutional frameworks. And variations in institutional structures account for differences in outcomes.

In a similar fashion, Martin Jänicke argues that the constitutional, institutional and legal structure, the routinised rules and internalised norms, constitute the framework of interaction in the field of environmental policy. Jänicke refers to three political-institutional framework conditions for environmental policy capacity: participative, integrative and strategic action capacities. Participative capacity relates to the openness of the input structures of the policy process, which is an important aspect of the opportunity structure of environmental interests. Decentralisation and strong local communities are seen as favourable conditions for participation. Sometimes the pressure from environmental movements is mentioned as a relevant factor for the general opening and modernisation of political systems. The openness of the legal system to 'protective' interests is also mentioned as a kind of catalyst for participation (Jänicke, 1995: 14).

Integrative capacity relates to participation and decentralisation, because environmental policies require a high level of integration. The literature generally stresses voluntary co-operation ('consensual capacity') as an institutional condition of success in environmental policy. Co-operation is usually seen as a superior approach and corporatism is seen as good for environmental policy. Integrative capacities are important at different levels. Firstly, intrapolicy co-ordination, i.e., the integral integration of the policy field, is important. This includes the co-ordination of environmental policy at different levels of the political system. The second field of integration is interpolicy co-ordination, the cross-sectoral integration of conflicting policies. Thirdly, the external integration of environmental policy institutions and non-governmental actors, including target groups is needed. Finally, a capacity for strategic action is seen as the highest stage of institutional capacity building in environmental policy and management, a factor that differs from country to country (Jänicke, 1995: 14).

As the new institutionalist analysis suggests, we see stability, continuity and path dependence. This implies that an analysis of the impact of national institutional contexts, an institutional analysis, will be unable to explain the changes that occurred in the past, because these institutions changed themselves as well. It uses the institutions as an explanatory factor, but in order to understand and explain recent changes in institutions we need to look at the role of new policy ideas. The perception of the analysts, the way problems are perceived and defined, has a crucial impact over the policy process. In other words, we need to look at the interaction of institutions and ideas in order to understand changes in environmental policy. The role of ideas will be a useful supplement to an analysis of institutions.

Finally, we can argue that both new environmental policy ideas and historical and institutional factors play a major role in the environmental policy capacity of an individual country. In that sense, there is a complex two-way relationship between ideas and institutions. New environmental policy ideas can influence the dominant ideas concerning the environment and development, and contribute to the establishment of a new breed of institutions for that purpose. In other words, new ideas contribute to environmental policy change. However, environmental policy change is also conditioned by and filtered through the already existing institutional and ideational contexts of countries, leading to a divergence in environmental policies. We cannot disregard the role of these two factors in environmental policy change.

As Weaver and Rockman suggested, institutional effects on government capabilities are not uniform, direct or unidirectional; nor are they non-existent. Institutional effects are real and significant, but often indirect and contingent. Indeed, the case studies suggests that terms like advantages and disadvantages are a misleading way of thinking about institutional effects on government capabilities. Political institutions are best thought of as creating risks and opportunities for effective policy-making. Whether these risks and opportunities are avoided respectively realised depends upon whether the specific conditions that facilitate or limit those institutional effects are present. In short, institutional arrangements that create opportunities for effective governance in one country may heighten the risk of governmental failure in another since the latter government faces different facilitating and limiting conditions. Moreover, countries face different policy challenges that make certain capabilities more or less important. Thus it makes little sense to speak of one set of institutional arrangements as inherently more effective than another, with respect either to any single capability or to the whole range of capabilities. Increasing a government's capability involves finding the best fit among three factors: the nature of its policy challenges, its institutional arrangements and the conditions that facilitate and limit institutional effects (Weaver and

Rockman, 1993: p 39-40). This is the dilemma confronting European environmental policy as much as other countries.

The European case

The European Union is something more than a collection of nation-states, yet it is still a union of nation-states since member states have not delegated their full authorities in several fields. On the one hand then, a European environmental policy is being developed at the Union level, while on the other there is the continuing impact of national environmental regulations. The question then surfaces how we can deal with the problems of institutional change in EU environmental policy and accommodate the impacts of the different national styles on the European environment. Is it possible to develop a European environmental policy to be implemented all around the Union, or will the strong national traditions of regulation and national priorities on environmental issues override the development of a European environmental policy?

Although EU environmental policy developed out of the preferences of member countries, it is something different from the individual countries' preferences. EU environmental policy is supposed to be implemented all around the EU in the same manner, but instead of a policy convergence there is a policy divergence with different practices in different countries. Yet it would be wrong to see the EU environmental policy process as one of incommensurable preferences and conflict between the national and EU levels of regulation. It is worth while to understand it instead as a process of learning from partners and experimentation, a process that can benefit from the richness of the policy diversity in EU member countries. In order to understand policy diversity and institutional context of the countries we need to understand institutions and ideas in that context.

Strategies of pollution control are deeply embedded in national traditions and administrative arrangements, and if we know anything about bureaucratic behaviour we know that old habits die hard, and it is difficult and time-consuming for established organisations to change complex routines. According to Weale, there are different interpretations that policy-makers in different countries give to – apparently – the same problem. More specifically, the balance of argument over the interpretation of policy problems varies from system to system, often meaning that policy-makers fail to understand what their counterparts elsewhere are saying (Weale, 1994: 78).

To illustrate this point, Weale argues that the whole philosophy behind the Dutch approach to environmental policy was a vision of the economy not as a production line but as a potentially circular flow of resources. The German Packaging Ordinance, which can easily be interpreted as a barrier to trade, was developed as a response to what was seen a policy failure in Germany in 1980s. The idea behind the policy was the need to create a circular flow of resources throughout the economy. The UK approach contrasts to these approaches. The most prevalent forms of environmental regulation in the UK are still dominated by an approach that stresses the need to understand the capacity of the environment to act as a receiving medium for wastes and the consequent need to achieve an optimal trade-off between environmental protection and the costs of regulation. This approach is buttressed by the intellectual and institutional standing of natural scientists in the policy process who have a tendency to stress to uncertainties surrounding the establishment of cause and effect relationship in the natural world. This, in turn, gives the regulatory system a bias against precautionary action (Weale, 1994: 78).

According to Weale, the contrasting development of environmental policies in Europe cannot be understood without reference to changing ideas about the character and scope of environmental concerns, differentially affecting the countries involved. However, he argues, to say that an adequate account of policy developments needs to make essential reference to intellectual factors is not to say that intellectual factors are sufficient, decisive or central to policy development, either (Weale, 1993: 196).

How we can relate this issue to the idea of learning from partners? Simply asserting that European environmental policy is an issue of the national domains or the European level does not provide us with a good tool for solving environmental problems in the European context. There is more than one way of doing things, including environmental policies. In the case of Europe, I shall argue for an experimental strategy, which does not stick to a single project imposed from above or to one highlighting national contexts. Obviously, environmental policy is a main policy field of the European Union and differences between the level of regulation that nation-states have will create a disparity between the member states and bring a comparative advantage to the states with less stringent environmental regulations. In that sense, there is not a single definitive answer to this question. However, if it is a question of change, we should understand the logic of previous changes to be able to propose further changes.

There are various approaches to pollution control in Europe. According to Weale, instead of trying to eliminate European variation in approaches to pollution control we should try instead to utilise such variation and learn from the diversity of experience. In other words, we can think of European environmental policy systems as a sort of natural experiment in institutional design. From this point of view, just as with laboratory experiments where we should spend a lot of time observing, so with institutional experiments we should observe more and tinker less (Weale, 1995: 24).

According to Weale, choice and diversity imply that different rule systems will suit different countries. Environmental standards may be higher in country A than in country B as a legitimate reflection of differences in collective preferences. Experimentation implies diversity, enabling policy-makers to learn about alternative effects and approaches, thus enabling them to select the best strategies on the basis of experience and systematic evidence. Experiments should come to an end when they have proved their worth; choice and diversity as expressions of differences in collective preference should remain. Successful experimentation will, ultimately, reduce choice and diversity as administrative systems learn from the experiment and move towards the best. But if choice and diversity are strong effects themselves, we would expect the amount of learning leading to convergence to be reduced (Weale, 1994: 77).

As we have mentioned before, bureaucratic structures have different attitudes to environmental problems. However, Weale argues, behind these bureaucratic structures, moreover, there lies the development of public opinion in the countries concerned. There is evidence that environmental awareness is differentially spread across European publics with the Danish, Dutch and German publics being among the most environmentally aware in the world, a fact reflected not only in their shopping behaviour but also in their willingness to engage in source separation for recycling. After all, the problems over the recycling of plastics that the German DSD scheme has run into arose because of a greater than anticipated public willingness to separate plastic wastes from other sources (Weale, 1994: 80).

Environmental awareness is too deeply entrenched within European populations and environmental bureaucracies are now more established than in the late 1970s, when the pressure for greater environmental regulation was last rolled back. What we may expect will happen is that these bureaucracies will increasingly come to explore new policy instruments, other than conventional regulation, as the limits of regulation are increasingly apparent. Eco-taxes, subsidies, the development of public transport, model cities, policy dialogues, voluntary agreements, education and other measures promise as much as regulation, however necessary the later may be (Weale, 1994: 86).

According to Weale, despite their problems, the combination of competition and harmonisation might serve as useful policy instruments for the setting and raising of environmental standards. Competition in itself is not sufficient. There are certain problems, particularly associated with the release of toxic chemicals into the environment, where harmonisation based on the principle of substance bans seem most appropriate. Moreover, competitive mechanisms work well, as is clear from the example of evolution, when there is a feed-back loop that selects the most successful experiments, and when we are comparing regulatory systems there is no such feed-back mechanism analogous to those that exist in nature. On the other hand, the use of the strong thumbs of harmonisation also has problems, most notably the fact that policy-makers lose the capacity to learn from diversity. Thus, where there is genuine uncertainty about how to deal with an environment problem, properly monitored and assessed diversity seems to be an appropriate solution. After all, the less you know, the more you need to experiment (Weale, 1994: 87).

Conclusion

What is the impact of this interpretation of changing ideas on our understanding of institutional change in the field of environmental policy? The changing perceptions of environmental problems contributed to institutional changes and policy changes that occurred in the past. Proposals for further environmental policy changes are related to changing values in the public at large as well. In other words, the way people, the academic community, bureaucrats, politicians and all other actors in the field interpreted the environmental problems had a definite impact on the way all these changes took place as well as on proposals for further changes. During the past three decades we saw a number of changes in the ideas that affected the key actors, and changes in the environmental policies and institutions which deal with environmental problems, and which were institutionalised within the current institutions.

Basically, we have witnessed some massive changes in the way environmental problems are tackled and the way institutions for environmental policy are established. The challenge now is to understand how these changes happened in the past and to make projections for the future. Of course, it is very difficult to come up with one recipe valid for all circumstances. However, we can identify under which circumstances change has occurred and again under which circumstances change will be possible. There are some changes internationally agreed upon and in the implementation of these changes the national institutional contexts matters. In this case, institutional analysis gives us a good tool in understanding the impact of domestic institutional contexts on the implementation of environmental policy. As we have observed in the past, although we had some global principles for environmental policy, a policy divergence occured for which national institutional contexts were responsible. However, institutions do not remain fixed or constant over time. Actually they have both influenced the process and changed themselves as well. In order to understand changes in institutions and policies, we thus need to focus on the role of policy ideas as well.

Finally, EU member countries have different positions concerning environment policy, and this is conditioned by their different institutional backgrounds and the way they perceive environmental problems. In order to develop a sensible EU environmental policy, we need to understand the background of the positions of member states, and for that we need an institutional-discursive analysis of their respective environmental policy positions. In order to develop a partnership and benefit from the experiences of different countries through experimentation, we need to understand the ideas and institutional configurations behind their positions. Only then can an EU environmental policy benefit through a learning process from the diversity and richness of the experiences of the individual countries. Overall, policy diversity has some further advantages. As Marcel Wissenburg has pointed out, there are three clusters of reasons in favour of policy diversity:

(1) Policy diversity has learning effects. One may expect diversity of policies to produce more knowledge about the effectivity and efficiency of policies, even if both means and objectives differs.

(2)   Policy diversity can contribute to sustainability on a far larger scale than ecological sustainability alone; in the given context of a region, nation, whatever, it is far more likely than uniformity to produce optimal strategies for cultural, economic, social and political sustainability.

(3)   There is also a moral argument for the policy diversity. It allows a multitude of conceptions of good life and of the good environment to be realised, thus offering room for the recognition of value pluralism and the realisation of individuals' equally worthy plans of life.

For Wissenburg, policy diversity enhances policy choice. Policy diversity is good because it contributes to developing optimal strategies for sustainability, both in terms of political sustainability and moral sustainability. However, it makes life more complicated and can counteract (or even contradict) other policies. Overall he argues that diversification is indispensable in the pursuit of knowledge and in the search for the best available environmental policies (Wissenburg, 1997:133-134).

In conclusion, we cannot defend a centralised and strict European environmental policy as a viable solution to environmental problems in Europe. Although a certain level of harmonisation is a necessary condition for the success of EU environmental policy, because of the interdependent and cross-boundary nature of environmental problems and the comparative economic advantages of less stringent environmental regulations, we should nonetheless recognise the differences and diversity in Europe and continue our search for the best available policies. We should try to accommodate these differences within Europe through a process of learning from partners. In order to do so, we should learn about the institutional traditions of the individual countries and their dominant ideas concerning environment and development.

Notes

[1]   An earlier version of this chapter was presented at the Third IRNES European Conference at the University of Nijmegen. I would like to express my thanks to Prof. Albert Weale for his support during the process of writing this chapter, and to Dr. Marcel Wissenburg for his encouragement and valuable comments on the manuscripts. I would like to thank to participants of the IRNES Nijmegen Conference for their contributions as well.

2 Although the post-positivist policy analysis has not yet developed into a unified and well defined whole, we can use the term to refer the critiques of the mainstream policy analysis.

3 Political Modernisation and the Institutionalisation of Environmental Policy

JAN VAN TATENHOVE[1]

Introduction

The institutionalisation of environmental policies is influenced on the one hand by changing relations between state, civil society and market, and is on the other hand the result of interactions and interdependencies between interdependent actors, such as politicians, bureaucrats, representatives of environmental movements, corporate executives, etcetera. In this process of institutionalisation specific environmental policy arrangements have been formed.

In this chapter the relation between the institutionalisation of environmental policies and political modernisation is studied from an institutional perspective.[2] Political modernisation refers to processes of transformation within the political domain of (western) societies. To understand the dynamics of the process of political modernisation I shall distinguish analytically between four phases of political modernisation (cf. Alexander, 1995): 'early', 'anti', 'post' and 'reflexive' political modernisation. Each of these phases can be characterised by specific relations between state, civil society and market and by dominant discourses on governance. The central question in this chapter is: in what way is the institutionalisation of environmental policy influenced by the process of political modernisation?

In the next section, institutionalisation and the phases of political modernisation will be discussed in general. Following that, the interrelation of phases of political modernisation and the institutionalisation of environmental policy will be studied. Special attention will be paid to new kinds of coalitions and environmental discourses[3] in the institutionalisation of environmental policies. The final section contains some concluding remarks about the institutionalisation of environmental policies in the nearby future.

Political modernisation and institutionalisation

Institutionalisation

Institutionalisation is a process of preservation of values and norms, in a structure of rules and resources. Institutionalisation, understood as a process of preservation, has its origin 'whenever there is a reciprocal typification of habitualised actions by types of actors' (Berger and Luckmann, 1966: 72). It is a general process of human action and refers to an ongoing (de)construction of day-to-day activity. More specific, policy institutionalisation is an ongoing process of transformation in which institutions are (re)produced in interaction. As capable and knowledgeable actors, policy-makers have the ability to realise policy outcomes and try to realise policy goals, in order to make processes of policy-making manageable. They make use of 'stocks of knowledge' (discourses), (policy) suppositions ('rules of the game) and resources both on a discursive and a practical level. By using these rules and resources, structures of domination, signification and legitimation[4] of institutions are (re)produced, which are both enabling and constraining. In other words, new possibilities for policy-making are created in interactions, while at the same time policy-making takes place in the context of existing institutions, that is a specific division of resources and more or less formalised rules.

Analytically a distinction can be made between internal and external institutionalisation of policy. Internal institutionalisation of policy refers to the process of (re)production of the structure (both content and organisation) of a policy domain by public actors (members of other policy domains, parliament, advisory boards, other governments, etcetera). External institutionalisation of policy refers to the process of (re)production of the structure (both content and organisation) of a public domain by both public and private actors. We have to keep in mind that the distinction between internal and external institutionalisation is artificial and only analytical, since institutionalisation is always the result of the interplay between public and private actors.

With the concepts 'structuration' and 'stabilisation' it is possible to conceptualise institutionalisation as a struggle for power (Van Tatenhove, 1993). As a result of interaction, structural properties of social systems are reproduced. This process of structuration is the result of struggle for power between public and private actors, within the context of existing structures. However, since structure is (re)produced in interactions, the conditions for action will be changing. The process of 'stabilisation' refers to the struggle for power in which actors try to maintain and continue the rules, resources and activities connected with existing structural properties. Institutionalisation, understood as the interaction between 'structuration' and 'stabilisation', depends on the involved actors, the resources they can mobilise and the rules they use in interaction. The interaction between 'structuration' and stabilisation' is influenced at a more general level by the relationship between state, civil society and market and discourses on governance. In the next subsection this complex of factors will be understood as phases of political modernisation.

Phases of political modernisation

Political modernisation refers to processes of transformation within the political domain of Western societies. The 'political domain of society' is the setting in which different groups (from state, civil society and market) produce and distribute resources (power and domination) and meaning (discourse) to shape public life (cf. Held, 1989).

To grasp the dynamics of the process of political modernisation we distinguish analytically four phases of political modernisation: 'early', 'anti', 'post' and 'reflexive' political modernisation (cf. Alexander, 1995). To typify the phases of political modernisation two categories are used. First, the relationship between state, civil society and market. Each phase of political modernisation can be characterised by ideal-typical relations between state, civil society and market. Special attention is paid to the changing role of nation-states. A second category is formed by central discourses on governance, more specific the organisation and structuration of processes of policy-making. It is important to understand that anti-, post- and reflexive modernisation are different reactions to early political modernisation. However, we do not want to suggest an evolutionary development. During the process of institutionalisation of environmental policies elements of different phases of political modernisation are emphasized.

Early political modernisation The phase of 'early political modernisation' is closely linked with the project of modernity itself. Giddens (1990) takes modernity as a cluster of institutional forms and processes, which came into being on the cross-roads of capitalism, industrialism and the nation-state.[5]

Central elements of the early political modernisation discourse are progress and control of nature and society. Although modernity itself is a permanent revolution of ideas and institutions (see Kumar, 1995; Wagner, 1994) these elements come together in the notion of the 'manageable society'. The 'manageable society' refers to the idea of the shapeability of the social and physical world. The increasing control and exploitation of the physical environment reveals itself in increasing amounts of withdrawals and additions, which results in a deterioration of the 'sustenance base' (Schnaiberg, 1980). On the other hand, the Modern project is characterised by rationalisation and control of human interactions and interdependencies, mainly through the institutions and policies of the (welfare) state. According to Albrow (1996: 189):

> Underpinning modern discourse was the assumption that there were rational ways to determine optimum arrangements of the elements and that these necessarily integrated the spheres of individual and state activity and all the intermediate instances of social activity, such as family, firm and community. The principle of hierarchy appeared in numerous ways, in decision-making trees, in relations of authority, in levels of abstraction or of jurisdiction.

Although the modernisation project was driven by different ideologies (Kumar, 1995), they shared the assumption that it is possible and recommendable to sketch the most desirable development of society. In the political domain this discourse of the constructed society is translated and reflected in models of synoptic rational policy-making, pluralistic conceptions of democracy and rational conceptions of steering (governability). A central role in models of synoptic rational policy-making is played by public actors within the domain of the state. The basic assumption is that public actors design – in a rational manner – a complex of coherent means and ends. The influence of private actors on the process of policy-making is underestimated. Policy-makers try to solve problems along the lines of scientific rationality; the policy-making process is organised around rational scientific principles. The conception of insulation of state, market and civil society also has an effect on conceptions of governability. Conceptions of monocentric steering dominate in the phase of 'early political modernisation'. Characteristic for this conception of one-way steering is the subject-object relation between state, civil society and market, which reinforced the belief in a 'constructed society' by policy-makers and politicians.

In general, in the phase of early political modernisation there is an insulation of the subsystems state, civil society and market, each having distinctive rationalities (respectively bureaucracy, solidarity and competition) (Leroy and Van Tatenhove, forthcoming). The insulation of subsystems, however, does not imply a fixed position of each subsystem in relation to others. On the contrary, specific interrelations between state, civil society and market in a certain era depend upon ideological and political preferences of a society of that period, and give rise to different institutional arrangements, such as statist, corporatist and liberal policy arrangements. Each of them implying specific conceptions of governance, governability and policy-making (Frouws and Van Tatenhove, 1993; Leroy and Van Tatenhove, forthcoming; Van Tatenhove, et.al., forthcoming; Williamson, 1989).

During the 1960s, the model of 'early political modernisation' came under fire. In the next subsections three kinds of alternative reactions to political modernisation are discussed.

Political anti-modernisation   According to Alexander (1995), modernisation theory died sometime in the later 1960s. Although others doubt that the project of modernisation really died (see Giddens, 1990; Bauman, 1992; Kumar, 1995), Alexander's conception of anti-modernisation theory offers an interesting way to describe one of the directions within the project of political modernisation. The 1970s show both a renewal of theories of modernisation and the formulation of radical alternatives such as theories of anti-modernisation. According to Alexander (1995), anti-modernisation is a reaction on the unsolved 'reality problems' in the modernisation model, such as poverty, dictatorship, post-colonial nations, and so forth. Theories of anti-modernisation were proposed as more valid explanations of these problems in the 1970s. Inequality-, conflict- and state-centred political theories were developed. They focused on issues such as inequality and emancipation, democracy and participation. Both the newly developing social movements and intellectuals inspiring them characterised the period of 'early political modernisation' as one-dimensional, materialistic, bureaucratic and repressive (Marcuse, 1964; Habermas, 1968). In their opinion, modern Western society was no longer rational, interdependent and liberating but backward, greedy and impoverishing.

Central elements of the political anti-modernisation discourse, such as politicisation and emancipation, were elaborated on in neo-Marxist, eco-socialist, counter-productivity, dependencia or de-industrialisation theories (Bahro, 1982; Huber, 1985; Keohane and Nye, 1989; Sachs, 1977; Ullrich, 1979) and by new social movements. These theories played a crucial role in the formulation of discourses in opposition to capitalism and the oppressing role of the state. The emancipation of deprived groups, the liberation of labour from capitalist alienation and oppression were defined and presented in terms of conflict, revolution and collective emancipation, and, according to anti-modernists, required a politicisation of the institutions of modern (industrial) society (compare Offe, 1986). According to Offe (1986) the politics of new social movements was aimed at the emancipation of (bourgeois) society from the state. Although in the phase of 'political anti-modernisation' the state is under attack, state, civil society and market are still considered insulated subsystems.

Although anti-modernisation theory is the anti-thesis of early modernisation theory, a central element remains belief in the grand narrative of the 'manageable society'. The ideal, however, was a free and emancipated civil society. Their normative and ideological criticism concerned the one-sided, one-dimensional and reductionist role of the state and the market, both reinforcing the social order for the enhancement of particular (capitalist) interests, both at the national and international level. As a consequence, proposals for alternative orders were formulated, in which the domination of the capitalist state and market over civil society was questioned, such as forms of radical democratisation, self-government and emancipation, which implied a reversal of the domination order at that time. Although such proposals for alternative societal orders were never (fully) implemented in the western world, these visions nonetheless influenced politics and policy-making on the ground. First, a change in the contents of politics was provoked, resulting in different forms of welfare policies, such as environment, community work, culture or education.

Secondly, new policy arrangements were created, characterised by participation, self-regulation and self-determination (Van Tatenhove, et.al., forthcoming).

Post-political modernisation Although post-modernisation takes, just as anti-modernisation, 'the modern' as its explicit foe, the contents of 'the modern' are completely different. According to some post-modernist theorists, contemporary societies show a new or heightened degree of fragmentation, pluralism and individualism, while political, economic and cultural life is strongly influenced by developments at the global level. Post-modernism proclaims multi-cultural and multi-ethnic societies and promotes the 'politics of difference' – linking the local and the global – in which identity is not unitary or essential, but fluid and shifting, fed from multiple sources and taking multiple forms (Kumar, 1995). The result is an erosion of the nation-state, a renewed interest for the local and sub-national and regional culture. However, 'the irreducible pluralism and diversity of contemporary society is not denied. That is what makes it modern as opposed to traditional. But that pluralism is not ordered and integrated according to any discernible principle'. There is no longer any controlling and directing force to give it shape and meaning – neither in the economy, nor in the polity, nor in history and tradition. 'There is simply a more or less random, directionless flux across all sectors of society. The boundaries between them are dissolved, leading however not to a neo-primitivist wholeness but to a post-modern condition of fragmentation' (Kumar, 1995: 102-103). Accentuating fragmentation, pluralism and the absence of a 'centralising force' has lead to a 'dissolution of the social', not in the sense of denying society as such, but in denying its power as an embodied collectivity (Kumar, 1995: 132).

Translated to political modernisation this means an erosion of the nation-state. Lyotard describes post-modern society as a network of loosely connected communities, inventing their own forms of life and finding their own means to express them. Not social systems governed by meta-languages, but the 'atomisation' of the social into flexible networks of language games (Lyotard, 1984). More permanent institutions and organisations are no longer encased within the framework of the nation-state. Social movements have also changed. In the 1970s the new social movements emphasized small scale initiatives and a collective emancipation. The accent of social movements in the 1990s is on interaction and the tension between the global and the local.

> In raising questions of ecology and of human rights, the new social movements aspire towards the universal. They stress what is common to humankind. At another level though the new social movements are about 'the politics of difference' so strongly featured in postmodernist writing. They stress plural and multiple identities, what divides us by gender, sexuality, ethnicity, locality. As against the universality and generality of ecology and the global environment, they draw our attention to the particularities of group, place, community and history (Kumar, 1995: 187).

The end of 'grand narratives', such as the emancipation of the rational, the liberation of the exploited, or the belief in progress, the deconstruction of the rational actor and the linking of processes of globalisation and localisation not only meant the erosion of the nation-state, but also the end of the idea that society could be constructed by policy-makers. According to Albrow, modernity is even supplanted by globality: 'a new level of organisation, to which any agent can relate, but which has no organizing agent' (Albrow, 1996: 121). Ideal-typically, in the phase of post-political modernisation the nation-state is vaporised and has merged into fragmented collectivities or networks of negotiating and calculating actors, with different definitions or social constructions of reality. Problems defined as policy problems are treated from different perspectives and attempts are made to remain in an 'perpetual dialogue' (De Wit, 1995). Policy-making takes place in networks, which are constructed around problems with different coalitions of public and private actors. Those networks are not governed by meta-languages or universal rules of the game; rules of the game have to be agreed on by its present players and any consensus can be subject to eventual cancellation.

Reflexive political modernisation   Reflexive modernisation takes up a middle position between early and anti-modernisation on the one hand and post-modernisation on the other. According to Giddens (1990, 1994) and Beck (1994, 1996, 1998), contemporary society is in the phase of 'high' or 'radicalised' modernity, which can be characterised by a high degree of reflexivity.[6]

Central in their analysis is the changing nature of global risk. It seems as though there is no way to negotiate global risks (like global warming, BSE, the E-coli virus), but at the same time the way we live with these unforeseen consequences of modernity will structure society and politics (see Franklin, 1998). According to Beck the project of modernity resulted in the *risk society*. The risk society is understood as a phase of development of modern society in which the social, the political, the ecological and individual risks created by the momentum of innovation increasingly elude the control and protective institutions of industrial society. Essential is the unintentional and unseen transition from modern industrial society to risk society. In other words, risk society is not an option which could be chosen or rejected in the course of political debate (Beck, 1996a: 27-28). Additionally, Giddens (1998: 25-26) characterised a risk society as 'a society where we increasingly live on a high technological frontier which absolutely no one completely understands and which generates a diversity of possible futures'. According to him, the origins of the risk society can be traced to two fundamental transformations which are affecting our lives today: 'the end of nature' and 'the end of tradition'. As a result of the intensification of technological change and the increasing influence of science we have started to worry increasingly about what we have done to nature – instead of worrying about what nature could do to us – and we no longer live our lives as fate.

The side-effects of modernisation, especially the emergence of the risk society, have become the pivot of governance. On the one hand new ways of governance have to be developed within and beyond the nation-state model, because the effects of risk society that cannot be dealt with and assimilated in the system of industrial society (Beck, 1994). On the other hand, the nation-state model seems to lose its exclusiveness and the relations between state, civil society and market are less clear:

> a whole arena of hybrid sub-politics emerges in the realms of investment decisions, product development, plant management and scientific research priorities. In this situation, the conventional political forces and representations of industrial society have been sidelined (Beck, 1998: 10).

According to Beck the essence of contemporary politics is (reflexive) sub-politicisation of society.

> Sub-politics (...) means shaping society *from below*. Viewed from above, this results in the loss of implementation power, the shrinkage and minimisation of politics. In the wake of sub-politicisation, there are growing

opportunities to have a voice and a share in the arrangement of society for groups hitherto uninvolved in the substantive technification and industrialisation process: citizens, the public sphere, social movements, expert groups, working people on site; there are even opportunities for courageous individuals to 'move mountains' in the nerve centres of development. Politicisation thus implies a decrease of the central rule approach; it means that processes which had heretofore always run friction-free fizzle out in the resistance of contradictory objectives (Beck, 1994: 23).

To understand sub-politics, that is politics outside and beyond the representative institutions of the nation-state, Beck makes a distinction between 'rule-directed politics' and 'rule-altering politics'. Rule-directed politics functions within the rule system of the nation-state. Rule-altering politics on the other hand concerns altering the rules of the game, self-confrontation and reflection on norms, rules and resources. In reflexive political modernisation 'rule-directed' and 'rule-altering' politics are mingled, overlapping and interfering with each other, resulting in a metamorphosis of the nation-state and a re-organisation of governmental tasks. One aspect of this is the constitution of a global civil society of *ad hoc* 'coalitions of opposites', in opposition to modern political institutions: its globality does not exclude anyone or anything. 'It is, in the end, a politics *without opponents or opposing force*, a kind of 'enemyless politics'' (Beck, 1996b: 19). However, this does not exclude opposing coalitions, but relations of opposition have become more fluid. In the Brent Spar case for example, Greenpeace opposed Shell, but in other cases these players may share the same negotiation table. Essentially, relations between state, civil society and market are exceeding the nation-state model, resulting in new coalitions between market en civic parties on a global scale. This is what Wapner (1995) calls 'World Civic Politics beyond the State'. In the words of Castells (1997:355): 'In this end of millennium, the king and the queen, the state and the civil society, are both naked, and their children-citizens are wandering around a variety of foster homes' (Castells, 1997: 355).

Institutionalisation of environmental policy

In this section the institutionalisation of environmental policy in some European countries is analysed as a result of changes in the process of political modernisation.

Structuration and stabilisation during phases of early and anti political modernisation

The end of the 1960s is a valid starting point for a description of institutionalisation of environmental policy. By then, there was considerable concern about the environment among scientists, and public debates about the seriousness of environmental problems were emerging. These debates were quickly followed by growing political and general interest in environmental problems. The first step in the process of political institutionalisation was made during the heyday of 'early' and political 'anti' modernisation. There was a great optimism that (urgent) environmental problems could be solved with technical measures and legislation. To clean up the most threatening environmental problems, such as water pollution, air pollution, waste and noise, end-of-pipe technologies were used. 'The policy response to this upsurge involved legislation specifying more stringent controls on pollutants and toxic substances, and regulating the use of the air and water' (Weale, 1992: 11). Examples of this kind of legislation are the 1970 Clean Air Act in the United States, the 1974 Federal Immission Control Act in the Federal Republic of Germany, the 1974 Control of Pollution Act in the United Kingdom, the 1961 Air Pollution Law and the 1964 Water Law in France and the 1969 Surface Water Pollution Act and the 1970 Air Pollution Act in the Netherlands.

The policy response also involved the creation of Ministries or administrative bodies dealing with environmental problems: the US Environmental Protection Agency (1970), the German Interior Ministry (1969), the Ministry for the Protection of Nature and the Environment in France (1971), the Department of the Environment in the UK (1970) and the Ministry of Public Health and the Environment in the Netherlands (1971).

A common feature of substantive environmental policy in different Western European countries in the 1970s was the use of traditional administrative regulatory strategies. Policy-making relied to a large extent on direct regulation: general standards were set at the national level and formed the basis of licenses for individual plants or activities (Van Tatenhove, 1993; Liefferink and Mol, 1996). Regulation by legal rule was the norm.

However, not only elements of early political modernisation, but also political anti-modernisation influenced the (external) institutionalisation of environmental policy. Whereas environmental pollution was seen as an expression of growing welfare before the 1970s, this changed radically when anti-modernist theories and the social movements of the 1970s formulated discourses in opposition to capitalism, technology and the oppressing role of the state. By redefining the environmental issue in the context of broader social developments, the environmental movement in different countries played a crucial role in getting environmental issues on the public and policy agendas. Different ways of politicisation and emancipation were presented, varying from establishing 'communal societies' (Illich), dismantling of the existing economic and technological systems of production (e.g. Commoner, Roszak, Gorz, Ullrich, Sachs) to the anarchistic renewal of society and politics (e.g. Bookchin). The environmental issue was an important example in the analysis of anti-modernist theories of the one-dimensional character and the neglected side-effects of the modernisation project. These initiatives were reflected in different environmental discourses, stressing specific relations between the environment and the society. Examples of environmental discourses in the phase of political anti modernisation were 'small is beautiful', 'eco-development' and 'political ecology'. These discourses referred to ideas, theories or programmes, to give meaning to environmental problems and to design solutions for the environmental crisis. Political ecologists, for example, believed that the ecological crisis was due to the capitalist economy and strove for a green-socialist society, while the supporters of the discourse 'small is beautiful' and 'eco-development' propagate a small-scale society, both in the North and the South. Because of their anti-statist and anti-capitalist nature these discourses only marginally influenced the institutionalisation of environmental politics. More important was the aspect of countervailing power of the environmental movement and their furthering the environmental concern among Western publics.

To summarise, organisational policy structures and a complex of sectoral environmental legislation were developed during the 1970s. The internal structuration of environmental policy was strongly influenced by 'early' political modernisation and the countervailing power of anti-modernist ecological discourses. On the one hand the governmental approach to environmental problems was by legislation and scientific techniques, while on the other anti-modernist discourses paved the road to a new understanding of environmental problems and issues in relation to societal changes.

Environmental policy-making from 1980 onwards: an interaction between reflexive political modernisation and environmental discourses

By the end of the 1970s, drawbacks of the legislative sectoral environmental policies became manifest, such as the 'implementation deficit'[7] (Weale, 1992), 'fragmented institutionalisation' of environmental policy[8] (Van Tatenhove, 1993) and problems of cross-media transfers.[9] Efforts to overcome these problems were influenced by discussions about the role of the state during the 1980s and new social, political and scientific constructions of the environmental crisis. As a result of the economic crisis in the 1970s, the idea that the state could blueprint societal developments gradually disappeared. The belief in planning and detailed regulations first came under scientific attack, leading to political discussions about the scope and the level of detail and complexity of governmental regulation. A process of political modernisation was set into motion to intensify the relations between state, market and civil society. At the same time there was a striking change in environmental discourses and politics in most Western European countries. The two most important discourses in the debate on the environmental crises in the 1990s are (1) the global and local construction of environmental problems and (2) the project of ecological modernisation.

From the 1980s on, the institutionalisation of environmental policies became influenced by the interaction between (reflexive) political modernisation and new environmental discourses. According to Jänicke (1993), reflexive modernisation was both medium and outcome of the ecological crisis. On the one hand, environmental policy-making was influenced by reflexive modernisation from the 1980s on. On the other hand, the nature of environmental problems was an important motor for reflexive modernisation. 'The fundamentally new double structure of the state as a bureaucratic intervention mechanism legitimised through majorities that now became visible, would have been incomprehensible without the ecological question' (Jänicke, 1993: 159-160; translation MW). In other words, reflexive political modernisation is also the result of the demands that environmental problems pose on the political system. Authors like Giddens and Beck also accentuate the relation between reflexive modernisation and the environmental crisis, and believe that the environmental crisis plays a vital role in the emergence of a new phase of reflexive modernity. In this phase of modernisation the side-effects of modernisation – especially global environmental problems – have become the pivot of societal development (Beck, 1994), and provoke a fundamental change in some of the basic institutions of modernity (Mol, 1995). Two hypotheses about the interrelations between reflexive political modernisation and environmental problems can be formulated:

(1) Processes of globalisation and localisation lead to a diffused negotiating nation-state. These processes are reinforced by the ecological interdependence between the global and the local.

Characteristic for contemporary environmental discourse is an increasing concern with environmental problems on different spatial scales, varying from global environmental problems, such as the hole in the ozone layer, global warming and the implications of decreasing biodiversity, to regional and local environmental problems, such as acidification, eutrophication, disposal of waste and disturbance (noise, smell, air pollution and so on). The construction of global and regional or local environmental problems will affect the position of nation-states in two ways.

First, in dealing with global environmental problems nation-states have to negotiate with other nation-states at a supranational level (Arts, 1998). For some nation-states sovereignty in the ecological field will be substantially limited as a result of for example EC environmental policy-making, while national sovereignty of other nation-states is hardly affected. In his study of EC acidification policy Liefferink (1995: 173) concludes that for countries like Germany and the Netherlands,

> the Europeanisation of environmental policy did not pre-empt or replace national policy in this field. It rather entailed the establishment of an additional level of governance, as it were 'on top of' domestic environmental policy-making and improving the control particularly of its economic aspects. Arguably, sovereignty in the ecological field was substantially limited in practice only in member states that followed the respective EC initiatives (...).

Secondly, there is a localisation of environmental policies. To overcome the drawbacks of fragmented institutionalisation for example, the integrated region-oriented approach was introduced in Dutch environmental policy (Van Tatenhove, 1993). This region-oriented policy meant a shift of administrative responsibilities from the national to local levels, reflecting changing relations between state, civil society and market. Although the initiative is in the hands of public actors, actual policy measures are developed together with private actors. In this process co-operation, negotiation and deliberation play a major role. By relocating administrative responsibilities through regionalisation and decentralisation the predicaments of national environmental policy are in fact passed on to local authorities (Frouws and Van Tatenhove, 1993: 227-228).

During the phase of reflexive political modernisation ever more coalitions of public and private actors are formed across the classical divisions and traditional boundaries of individual nation-states. This process concerns both the broadening of coalitions at different levels (horizontal linkages) and increasing interrelations between these levels (vertical linkages). The intensification of levels of interaction and interconnectedness within and between states and societies (Held, 1995), combined with the interdependence of the global and the local[10] (Robertson, 1995) will affect the institutionalisation of environmental policy within nation-states. For example, international actors, such as the World Bank and the global environmental movement, collaborate with actors at the national level (for example environmental policies in Mexico, Hoogenboom, 1998), while local actors such as farmers organisations or local authorities themselves appear in international policy-making at UN headquarters (see for the biodiversity case, Arts, 1998). As a result, nation-states – consisting of a diversity of actors – will be evolving into a collection of negotiating actors, who have to participate in a diversity of policy arrangements on international, national and local levels.

(2) An effective approach to environmental problems demands a reconstruction of production and consumption processes. Initiatives of the State depend on initiatives within societal subsystems, which result in reflexive policy-making and reflexive steering.

In contrast to the anti-modernist solutions, such as de-industrialisation of the economy and small-scale initiatives, positive-sum game alternatives were developed during the 1980s. Dominant anti-capitalist environmental discourses, such as political ecology, eco-development and 'small is beautiful', were replaced by all-embracing consensus discourses like ecological modernisation and sustainable development. An important trigger for this change in discourse was the World Commission on Environment and Development report (WCED, 1987). Its central concept of sustainable development not only integrates economy and ecology, but economic growth and technological development are no longer suspected and condemned as the main causes of environmental destruction. The environment is adopted by a diversity of actors, including industry and international institutions such as the OECD, the UN, the EC and even NAFTA.

> Global commitments were seen to be urgently needed, to mitigate global risks. This conjuncture seems to have created conditions for a paradigm shift in environmental discourse. In the new dominant 'greenspeak' of sustainable development following the 1992 Rio Earth Summit, eternally expanding technological-economic systems (...) are assumed to be compatible with environmental 'sustainability' – a term which accommodates ideas of growth, change and development much more easily than the earlier term of 'equilibrium' (Szerszynski et.al., 1996: 19).

Consonant with the primarily political concept of sustainable development is the more analytical and sociological concept of ecological modernisation (Spaargaren and Mol, 1992; Mol, 1995; Hajer, 1995; Spaargaren, 1997). The concept of ecological modernisation[11] is used both as a theoretical concept for analysing the necessary development of central institutions in modern society aimed at solving the fundamental problem of the ecological crisis, and as a political programme to direct environmental policy (Spaargaren and Mol, 1992; Spaargaren, 1997). As a theory of social change in industrial societies, ecological modernisation can be characterised by two main projects. The first project emphasizes technological transformations. First-generation technologies (end-of pipe) must be replaced by second-generation environmental technologies geared for clean production processes and products. In the end this must lead to an ecologisation of economy. The second project involves an 'economisation of ecology' by for instance placing an economic value on nature as a production force besides labour and capital. As a political programme, ecological modernisation focuses on altering processes of production and consumption by restructuring production processes or by a selective contraction of the economy.[12]

Ecological modernisation theory meant a break with some unrealistic expectations about the 'state' and its role in environmental policies. 'Curative and reactive policies turn into preventive ones, "closed", centralised modes of policy-making into participative, decentralised ones, and dirigism is being replaced by contextual "steering"' (Liefferink and Mol, 1996: 3-4). In this 'Huberian' variant of ecological modernisation theory, the emphasis is on economic mechanisms and instruments on the one hand and on decentralised and participatory policy-making on the other.[13]

To some extent this shift from 'early' and political 'anti' modernisation to 'reflexive' political modernisation has also taken place in the Netherlands. Policy-makers realised that without the help of private actors environmental policy-making could not improve. In Dutch environmental policy new relationships between private and public actors had been activated. The internalisation ('verinnerlijking') of environmental responsibility and target group policy are concrete elaborations of these changing interrelations between state, market and civil society. Although the concept of internalisation was first introduced to improve the enforcement of environmental legislation in the industrial sector, this concept soon evolved into a strategy to encourage the environmental responsibility of polluters. Internalisation refers to the need to raise the willingness of polluters to contribute to the solution of environmental problems by involving their sense of 'social responsibility' on the one hand, and it entails paying serious attention to the needs and wishes of groups affected by environmental policies, taking them into account in the design of measures (Liefferink and Mol, 1996). The concept of internalisation is elaborated in the target group policy. Target groups are defined as more or less homogeneous groups of polluters, such as agriculture, traffic and transport, industry and refineries, gas and electric supply. By contacting these target groups directly, an attempt is made to bring about an internalisation of environmental perspectives among them. Although target group policy has neo-corporatist elements, such as exchange relations between the state and functional interest organisations, there are also elements of reflexive policy-making. A crucial element of the interactions and negotiations between public and private actors is the accessibility of the 'network' and the possibility of actors of self-confrontation with and reflection on norms, rules and resources (cf. Pestman and Van Tatenhove, 1998).

Institutionalisation of environmental politics in the 21st century: some concluding remarks

The structuration of environmental policy was strongly influenced by 'early' political modernisation during the 1970s. To tackle environmental problems sectoral legislation and end-of-pipe techniques were used. Efforts to overcome the drawbacks of this approach, such as fragmented institutionalisation of environmental policy, problems with implementation and enforcement and problems of cross-media transfers, were influenced by changing environmental discourses and changing relations between state, civil society and market (political modernisation). This specific interaction offered policy-makers opportunities to look for new frameworks and solutions in the context of reflexive policy-making and steering. In the previous section two hypotheses were formulated. Translated to the institutionalisation of environmental policy in the nearby future, two related processes of institutionalisation can be distinguished: heterogeneous and homogeneous institutionalisation.

As a result of processes of glocalisation, environmental policy-making will occur in the context of policy networks on both the supranational and the local level. Representatives of nation-states are participants in these networks. Through this *heterogeneous institutionalisation* new political arrangements will be formed. These coalitions are not restricted to the contexts of nation-states only. Interregional coalitions and supranational coalitions – exceeding the boundaries of individual nations states – will also be formed.

The ecological restructuring of production and consumption on the other hand will lead to forms of more *homogeneous institutionalisation*. Because this restructuring is taking place within the institutions of modernity (capitalism and industrialism) the translation into the environmental policy of nations states will be more (western) universal. However, ecological modernisation as a political programme will always be translated and embedded in the context of already institutionalised national environmental policy.

Environmental policy-making in the 21st century will be influenced by the interaction between heterogeneous and homogeneous forms of institutionalisation, through which nation-states will be changing into diffused negotiating actors in supranational, national and regional policy arrangements. Although these arrangements still have to be anchored within historically grown political structures, legal orders and administrative bodies of individual nation-states, the processes of structuration and stabilisation of environmental policy will in the future be influenced more and more by the tension between homogeneous and heterogeneous developments on the supranational, national and local levels of policy-making.

Notes

1   This chapter is based on a paper presented at the Nijmegen IRNES conference of December 1996 and a paper presented at the 'International Conference 'Environment, Long-term Governability and Democracy: 21st Century prospectives for the Environment, Abbaye de Fontevraud, France, September 1996.

2   An institutional analysis focuses on institutions as chronically reproduced rules and resources (Giddens, 1984). Elsewhere I also elaborated on the impact of agency on policy arrangements, combining a strategic analysis of conduct with this institutional analysis (Van Tatenhove and Arts, 1998; Van Tatenhove *et al.*, forthcoming).

3   A (policy) discourse can be defined as: 'a specific ensemble of ideas, concepts, and categorisations that are produced, reproduced and transformed in a particular policy domain and through which meaning is given to the physical and social realities of that domain' (Hajer, 1995: xxx). Dryzek defines a discourse similarly as 'a shared way of apprehending the world. Embedded in language, it enables those who subscribe to it to interpret bits of information and put them together into coherent stories or accounts. each discourse rests on assumptions, judgements and contentions that provide the basic terms for analysis, debates, agreements and disagreements (...)' (Dryzek, 1997: 8).

4   Policy making involves the communication of meaning, the operation of power, and modes of normative sanctioning. In interaction, actors draw upon and reproduce corresponding structural properties of social systems: signification, domination and legitimation (Giddens, 1984 and 1985), by way of respectively rules (interpretative schemes and norms) and resources. In policy making the sanctioning of policy conduct takes place by using norms and the interpretation of reality by using interpretative schemes. Power in interaction involves employing facilities, which are (asymmetrically) divided within the current structure of domination.

5   See for extensive analyses of the characteristics of the early modernisation model for example Giddens (1990), Alexander (1995), Kumar (1995) and Albrow (1996).

6   Bauman also takes an alternative position between modernists and post-modernists. Bauman sees post-modernity as fully developed modernity 'taking a full measure of the anticipated consequences of its historical work (...). Postmodernity may be conceived of as modernity conscious of its true nature - *modernity for itself*

(Bauman, 1992: 187-188). Bauman, however, refers to the 'limits of reflexivity' or 'the lack of identity, and co-ordination, between the subjective capacity to reflect and the immunity of the world to the practical measures which reflection may suggest' (Bauman, 1993: 202).

7   An implementation deficit arises when legislative and policy intent is not translated into practice.

8   Fragmented institutionalisation means that the formation, implementation and enforcement of environmental policy is divided among different ministries or administrative bodies, all dealing with different aspects of the environment.

9   Since the sectoral legislation protected only a particular receiving medium, like the air, the solution of for example air pollution, created landfill or water pollution problems (Weale, 1992), problems of policy integration and problems of ecological integration became institutionalised.

10 According to Robertson (1995), globalisation and localisation are interrelated processes: 'it makes no sense to define the global as if the global excludes the local'. To accentuate the interdependence of globality and locality he introduces the concept of *glocalisation* as a multi-dimensional process.

11 A central idea of the theory of ecological modernisation is the pursuit of major transformations in modern society; 'an ecological transformation of the industrialisation process into a direction in which the maintenance of the sustenance base can be guaranteed. Ecological modernisation indicates the possibility of overcoming the environmental crisis while making use of the institutions of modernity and without leaving the path of modernization. The project aims at "modernizing modernity" by repairing a structural design fault of modernity: the institutionalized destruction of nature' (Mol, 1995: 37).

12 According to Spaargaren and Mol (1992: 339) the Dutch National Environmental Policy Plan is an example of ecological modernisation as a political programme. The core of the new approach is: (i) closing substance cycles; (ii) conserving energy and improving the efficiency and utilisation of renewable energy sources; (iii) improving the quality of production processes and products.

13 See Leroy and Van Tatenhove (forthcoming) for an analysis of the relation between political modernisation and ecological modernisation and the assumptions of the ecological modernisation theory about state, civil society and market.

PART II
STRUCTURE AND
BACKGROUND

4 Towards Sustainability in the European Union – Beyond the Rhetoric

UTE COLLIER[1]

Introduction

Since the 1992 Rio Earth Summit, sustainable development has become a buzz word, utilised by politicians, industrialists and environmentalists alike. Few governments and businesses now dare to ignore the principle and the pursuit of environmental goals. Yet, as the Rio follow-up in New York in July 1997 so aptly demonstrated, little progress has been made towards a more sustainable world since 1992. A recent survey of global environmental destruction carried out by the World Wide Fund for Nature (WWF) confirms this (WWF, 1998).

Amongst OECD nations, the EU and its member states usually are seen as more progressive in terms of sustainability and environmental protection than most other countries. At the Kyoto Climate Summit in December 1997, for example, the US emerged as the global villain, while the EU's negotiating position was welcomed by all but the most radical environmentalists. However, in the end, the EU's legally binding greenhouse gas reduction target inscribed in the Kyoto Protocol was only marginally higher than that of the US and much backpeddling on the original EU position has occured since. This and similar episodes indicate that the EU's environmental commitments can be little more than rhetoric.

Environmental policy is generally considered to be one of the EU's more successful policies (Haigh, 1992; Johnson and Corcelle, 1996; Krämer, 1995). Around 200 directives and regulations[2] covering areas ranging from drinking water standards to the protection of rare bird species are in force and five Environmental Action Programmes (EAPs) have been elaborated. Although environmental protection was not included as an objective in the Treaty of Rome, it has been a distinct policy area for over 20 years and was given a legal basis in the Single European Act (SEA). Yet, the 1995 report by the European Environment Agency for the review of the 5th EAP comes to the conclusion that:

> The European Union is making progress in reducing certain pressures on the environment, though this is not enough to improve the general quality of the environment and even less to progress towards sustainability. Without accelerated policies, pressures on the environment will continue to exceed human health standards and the often limited carrying capacity of the environment. (European Environment Agency, 1995: 1).

This is not entirely surprising in the light of a number of academic analyses of EU environmental policy which have shown that despite the large number of pieces of legislation, the policy process has not been without delays and obstacles (see e.g. Haigh, 1992; Hey, 1994; Hildebrand, 1993; Krämer, 1995; Liberatore, 1991; Liefferink, Lowe and Mol, 1993). Many legislative proposals have never been adopted by the Council of Ministers, or agreement was only reached after years' of negotiation and on a lowest common denominator basis. Not all directives have been implemented by the member states and enforcement has been difficult. Most activity has been in the area of water and air pollution, while other environmental issues such as nature conservation have seen little EU involvement and many member states have failed to effectively draw up and implement their own policy measures. Meanwhile, other member states have felt that the EU is actually jeopardising their efforts in the environmental field, and the negative environmental effects of other EU policies (especially the Common Agricultural Policy (CAP), the Structural Funds and the Internal Market) have become ever more apparent.

Nevertheless, the early 1990s promised improvements. With the ratification of the Treaty on European Union (hereafter referred to as the Maastricht Treaty), 'sustainable growth respecting the environment' became one of the Union's main tasks. Hildebrand (1993) describes this as a considerable 'greening' of the traditional growth ethos. Indeed, it seemed as if the 1992 Rio summit might mark the beginning of a new 'ecological era' (Ciuffreda, 1996). The 5th EAP entitled 'Towards Sustainability', put much emphasis on policy integration, the use of a broader range of instruments and the involvement of a variety of actors. Yet, the impetus for environmental protection in the EU appears to have slowed since 1992, casting doubts on the existence of such a 'greening'.

As a matter of fact, the adoption of 'sustainability' as a major principle in the EU has coincided with other developments which are having a fundamental effect on EU environmental policy. Firstly, policy-making has become increasingly influenced by the application of the subsidiarity principle. Subsidiarity, although already implicit in Article 130r of the SEA, only became a real issue with the signature of the Maastricht Treaty. While in principle a sensible idea in environmental terms, it can become an excuse for not taking action and raises issues of enforcement in the case of framework directives, which are becoming increasingly popular. Subsidiarity is particularly problematic in the environmental area as a number of member states are unlikely to take environmental action in the absence of EU legislation (Collier and Golub, 1996).

Secondly, the general climate of liberalisation and deregulation has influenced the environmental policy area. Some industrial lobby groups have long argued that tight environmental regulation is a hindrance to international competitiveness (see e.g. UNICE, 1995). In 1995, the Commission set up an expert group whose report comes to the same conclusion (European Commission, 1995a), although, to date, no major deregulatory drive in EU environmental policy has ensued. Nevertheless, pressure for a change in regulatory focus towards economic instruments and negotiated agreements will continue, despite many potential problems.

The aim of this chapter is to examine the current state of EU environmental policy in light of these challenges, putting particular emphasis on the juxtaposition between the issues of sustainability, subsidiarity and deregulation. Only the sustainable development concept originates from the environmental policy sphere, with subsidiarity essentially being a political principle, while deregulation primarily has an economic rationale. Yet, as this chapter demonstrates, there are some areas of overlap and compatibility between the three concepts and, taken together, they have the theoretical potential of strengthening environmental protection. However, this chapter will argue that, in reality, because of political and economic expediencies, a weakening is more likely.

The chapter examines the three concepts in turn and then uses the example of the climate change issue to illustrate their influence on a specific area of EU policy-making and to point at interlinkages between the three policy modes. Finally, conclusions are drawn about the future of environmental governance in the EU.

Towards sustainability?

The report of the World Commission on Environment and Development entitled 'Our Common Future' is generally considered as the catalyst for the sustainable development debate (Collier, 1994), with Agenda 21 agreed at the Rio summit then providing the basic framework for national sustainable development plans. The Commission has made sustainable development the central theme of the 5th EAP, entitled 'Towards Sustainability'. Within the programme:

> the word 'sustainable' is intended to reflect a policy and strategy for the continued economic and social development without detriment to the environment and the natural resources on the quality of which continued human activity and further development depend (European Commission, 1992a: 12).

The approach adopted is supposed to mark a new direction for EU environmental policy, focusing on target sectors (energy, industry, agriculture, tourism and transport), broadening the range of instruments and applying the principles of susidiarity and shared responsibility, involving all economic and social actors. Sustainable development thus implies a less state-centred perspective of environmental policy and, in this sense, also conforms with the principle of subsidiarity.

However, it is not clear whether the embracing of the sustainable development concept is very helpful for the development of EU environmental policy, at least not until it can be made more tangible. As has been discussed at length elsewhere, the concept is subject to a variety of interpretations (see e.g. Common, 1995; Jacobs, 1991; Pearce, 1993). Although environmentalists, policy-makers and industrialists all have embraced sustainable development as their main objective, deep divisions between their views of what the realisation of the concept actually entails exist. Such a division is reflected in the distinction made in the EU between sustainable 'growth' (as in the Maastricht Treaty) and sustainable 'development' (as in the 5th EAP). While these two terms appear sometimes to be used interchangeably, sustainable development as a concept is in principle much broader and includes quality objectives, while sustainable growth focuses on quantity (Bartelmus, 1994).

Baker (1996) has argued that the distinction between sustainable development and sustainable growth may not be so incidental, considering the long and protracted drafting of the Treaty. Certainly, the 5th EAP reflects mainly the thinking of Directorate-General (DG) XI (the Environment DG in the Commission), while the Maastricht Treaty is much more indicative of the general climate of opinion amongst policy-makers. However, in both cases, the EU interpretation of sustainability is in anthropogenic terms, i.e. protection of the environment for the sake of human welfare, rather than for the sake of ecosystem preservation per se.

The Amsterdam Treaty, which revised the Maastricht Treaty in 1997, does address this issue and now speaks of both sustainable development of economic activities and of sustainable growth. The Amsterdam Treaty also saw a move of the 'integration clause' from article 130r to article 6 (general objectives). However, it remains to be seen whether this change in terminology can help overcome the continuing divisions between different DGs or between industry and environmental non-governmental organisations (NGOs).

Implementing the sustainability concept

Notwithstanding the different sustainability paradigms, there is some consensus about the basic features of sustainable development. They include the following:

(1)   integration of economic, environmental and social policy objectives
(2)   greater participation of relevant actors (including NGOs, citizens, local authorities)
(3)   better internalisation of external costs, reduction of market failures

The second and third points in principle concur with the notions or subsidiarity and deregulation, although as later sections show, in reality this compatibility is not necessarily assured.

The lack of integration of environmental concerns into major policy decisions became very apparent with the Single European Market initiative, with a task force hastily assembled to report on the matter after most of the decisions had been taken (Weale and Williams, 1993). The Single Market was conceived prior to the EU embracing the sustainable development concept although the findings of the Commission's interim review of the 5th EAP, published in December 1995, show that the situation has not changed significantly since then. While it points to progress in some areas, it also observes that:

> There is insufficient awareness of the need and a lack of willingness to adequately integrate environmental and sustainable development considerations into the development of other policy actions. ... [W]hat is lacking are attitude changes and the will to make the quantum leap to make the necessary progress to move towards sustainability (European Commission, 1995: 3).

Three years later, the situation was still unsatisfactory, although at least there seemed to be high level recognition of the problem, by both the Environment and European Councils. The Commission presented an integration strategy to the Council in June 1998, although it was not clear how its implementation was going to be ensured, considering the absence of measurable targets and timetables.

The lack of progess is not entirely surprising. Lenschow (1995) has pointed out that while political elites may have subscribed to the sustainability concept, it must not be overlooked that most political decisions are taken with a short-term and sector specific perspective. Even if, in the long-term and at the aggregate level, environmental protection and economic development may be compatible, in the short-term and at the sectoral level, trade-offs have to be made. However, rather than expecting too much, one could concur with Lafferty (1996), who has argued that one of the values of the sustainable development idea is its ideological and mobilising function. While we can certainly not talk of a major value change in EU policy-making, a degree of mobilisation has occurred, with many more actors aware of and participating in the environmental debate.

A main priority for making the sustainability concept more useful in policy-making must be to improve its measurability by developing sustainability indicators. Suggestions have been made to make better use of the ecological concept of carrying capacity (Jacobs, 1991) or to quantify the 'environmental space' available, i.e. the total amount of environmental resources[3] that human kind can use without impairing the access of future generations to the same amount (Friends of the Earth, 1995). An important dimension will also be a departure from the use of narrow economic growth indicators (i.e. GDP/GNP) for measuring progress. The short-comings of the current economic accounting system have been widely acknowledged and the Commission itself has suggested to develop a European System of

Integrated Economic and Environmental Indices (ESI) which could then serve for defining sustainability targets (European Commission, 1994a). To date there is a lack of acceptance for this proposal, although work on sustainability indicators is continuing in the European Environment Agency.

The influence of the subsidiarity debate

In principle, the notions of sustainable development regarding greater participation and 'bottom-up' approaches could be assisted by the application of a principle which, since 1992, has become increasingly influential in EU policy-making, namely the subsidiarity principle. However, it must not be forgotten that this principle has always existed in EU environmental policy, although until recently more implicitly. The first Environmental Action Programme (EAP) for example referred to five possible levels of action and stressed the need 'to establish the level best suited to the type of pollution and to the geographical zone to be protected'.[4] The SEA for the first time incorporated provisions which would later become known as the subsidiarity principle, but only in Article 130r covering environmental policy:

> The Community shall take action relating to the environment to the extent to which the objectives...can be attained better at Community level than at the level of individual member states (EC, 1988).

In practice, these provisions had little influence on the development of EU environmental policy prior to the Maastricht Treaty. Krämer (1995) reports that between 1989 and 1991, the EU enacted more environmental legislation than during the previous 20 years. However, during the discussions surrounding the Maastricht Treaty, the subsidiarity issue was suddenly pushed to the top of the political agenda, not only in relation to environmental policy but for EU policy-making as a whole. The Maastricht Treaty then included the following requirement in article 3b:

> In areas which do not fall within its exclusive competence, the Community shall take action...only if and in so far as the objectives of the proposed action cannot be sufficiently achieved by the member states and can therefore, by reason of the scale or effects of the proposed action, be better achieved by the Community (EU, 1992: 9).

Different interpretations

The subsidiarity principle has been and continues to be subject to different interpretations. As Aquilar (1997) has shown, it has been promoted for three different reasons based on three fundamentally different interpretations. Some countries (especially the UK and Denmark) wanted to curb the powers of the EU and regain control over various policies. Others (Germany and Spain) saw it as a means to safeguard the powers of their regions. Finally, the subsidiarity principle also suited those countries which wanted to preserve different regulatory traditions, such as the Netherlands with its preference for 'self-regulation' (e.g. negotiated agreements).

In terms of environmental policy, the subsidiarity principle can also be interpreted in different ways. On the one hand, it can easily be used as a legitimisation for EU power by arguing that in some cases, and for a number of reasons, policy objectives can be better achieved at the EU level. Firstly, and most obviously, there is the transboundary nature of many environmental issues. This certainly applies to air pollution (with many pollutants travelling long distances and across borders), to some extent to water pollution, as well as to the protection of certain animal species (especially migratory birds). In these cases, national action is clearly insufficient, and there needs to be an EU level response, or even an international environmental agreement.

Secondly, EU environmental action can also be justified in terms of the need to harmonise various environmental standards applying to traded goods, so as to eliminate barriers to trade and to allow the smooth operation of the single market (see Liberatore, 1991). Golub (1997) also suggests several criteria for EU action on issues which lie more clearly within the national sphere, including financial shortages, legislative gaps and implementation failures, which mean that member states cannot 'sufficiently achieve' (in the words of the Maastricht Treaty) the objectives of the Treaties (in this case environmental protection). Furthermore, Wils (1994) argues for the consideration of what he terms 'psychic spill-over effects', relating to the integrity of nature.

To date, the debate surrounding the subsidiarity principle mainly has been couched in terms of EU versus national action, with some member states (with the UK in the forefront, but also Denmark) arguing for the repatriation of much EU legislation to the national level. However, as Golub (1997) has pointed out the intra-state aspects of subsidiarity must not be ignored, and in principle could imply a strengthening of regional and local actors. This is a very pertinent issue in environmental terms, linking in with the notion of shared responsibility. The 5th EAP strongly advocates 'a mixing of actors and instruments at the appropriate levels' (European Commission, 1992a).

The environmental dimension of subsidiarity

Obviously, environmental problems fall into different categories in relation to the scale at which they occur. However, in terms of measures to deal with such problems, even global problems have their local solutions, as the environmentalist campaign slogan 'think globally, act locally' so aptly depicts. In the case of climate change, for example, local authorities have competences in a number of important areas, such as public transport provision and local energy management. The local level is particularly important in that it involves 'decisions taken as close to the citizen as possible' (as required by the Maastricht Treaty), allowing scope for citizen participation in decision-making. Furthermore, the regions have in many member states important roles both in the definition and implementation of environmental policy. Jachtenfuchs, Hey and Ströbel (1993), for example, have argued that a more environmentally focused interpretation of the subsidiarity principle would require the financial and institutional strengthening of the regional and local levels of government, especially in the areas of energy, transport and agricultural policy.

The local and participatory dimensions of environmental problems have received renewed currency with the sustainable development discussion, prominent since the 1992 Rio Summit. Most countries signed Agenda 21, an action plan which sets out the principle guidelines for sustainable development and requires signatories to prepare national programmes in accordance with these guidelines. This document emphasizes that 'environmental issues are best handled with the participation of all concerned citizens, at the relevant level' and stresses the crucial role of local authorities, in particular because of their functions and ability to mobilise people's support (United Nations, 1992). As a part of this, local authorities are expected to draw up their own Local Agenda 21 in consultation with citizens, local organisations and private enterprises. As Voisey, Beuermann, Sverdrup and O'Riordan (1996) demonstrate, this is happening in some EU member states, although some local authorities are clearly more innovative than others.

However, while there may be a greater role for local environmental action, local authorities cannot assume all responsibility for environmental policy. Quite obviously, there needs to be a sharing of responsibilities between different levels, with measures ranging from international environmental agreements to local authority action plans. The exact allocation of responsibilities must depend on the specific environmental issue. Deciding which is the most appropriate level of action is not always straightforward, in particular when environmental criteria need to be balanced with political and economic ones. One problem is that local and regional authorities as yet have no voice in the development of EU environmental policy. The institution of the Committee of the Regions (CoR) is a first step towards a greater involvement of sub-national authorities in the EU policy process, and the CoR has already passed a number of resolutions on environmental issues, although to date its influence has been marginal. It has also argued at the Inter-Governmental Conference (IGC) for a specific mention of regional and local authorities in article 3b (Committee of the Regions, 1996).

Political realities

While, in principle, the subsidiarity principle thus can be either used as a means of legitimising EU environmental action, or of strengthening the role of sub-national actors, its immediate effect has been to limit EU action in this area and to reinforce national powers. This has mainly taken two forms:

(1)   a downgrading of environmental proposals (e.g. from directives to framework directives or even recommendations), so as to leave considerable scope for national interpretations;
(2)   the repatriation of proposed measures (in some cases existing directives) to the national level

As a result of the subsidiarity debate, several states compiled 'hit' lists of legislation which in their opinion interfered unnecessarily with national sovereignty by exceeding the legitimate scope of EU power. Environmental measures figured prominently in these lists. For example, the UK list of 71 pieces of legislation included 27 which pertained to the environment (Axelrod, 1994; Wils, 1994). Despite fierce resistance from the

European Parliament, the Commission eventually surrendered to pressure from several member states, most notably the UK, and removed or changed some proposals, although no existing directives of any significance have been repealed. Examples of the influence of subsidiarity vary from the directive on minimum standards for zoos, which was downgraded to a recommendation, to the demise of the proposals for a carbon/energy tax (see below).

If environmental objectives can be achieved at other levels of governance, may be this trend should be welcomed on environmental grounds. The potential demise, or at least scaling back of European-wide environmental standards might allow pro-active leader states or regions to forge ahead free from EU constraints, but it also poses a number of potential threats to environmental improvement, perhaps the greatest being the reliance on reluctant national and subnational government structures. In the past, EU policies have been important for remedying the dismal environmental record of many national governments, and many of the environmental achievements witnessed at the national level were the result of direct pressure brought through EU obligations. Returning control over environmental policy to these states, or their regional governments, does not bode well for the future (Collier and Golub, 1996). The problem is particularly acute in southern European countries, where economic disparity between sub-national regions results in fierce economic competition for employment and inward investment, leading to frequent agency capture and outright environmental policy implementation failure (Pridham, 1996).

EU level environmental measures are also important in view of the growing number of international environmental agreements. If the EU acts as a block, it should be able to exert more pressure on other countries than individual member states and can hence play an enabling role in international agreements. This was the pattern of thinking behind the initial proposals for a carbon/energy tax (see below) but in this case no progress was made.

Deregulation and the market doctrine

The subsidiarity issue has coincided with a growing concern about the negative economic effects of various forms of state intervention, especially on industrial competitiveness, which has resulted in pressure for deregulation and liberalisation. These issues are generally discussed totally separately from subsdiarity. However, while a repatriation of responsibilities to the national level does not necessarily have to mean deregulation, in some cases national member states will see it as a welcome opportunity to loosen regulatory intervention. Flynn (1996) cites the recent eco-audit regulation and the auto-oil programme as examples of this.

A number of member states have set up deregulation task forces and some, like the UK, have been very active in liberalising certain parts of the economy, especially those dominated by public utility companies. Although such activities have not been specifically concerned with environmental issues, in some cases, they have had a knock-on effect on the environment, as the example of electricity sector liberalisation in the UK shows (Collier, 1997a). Apart from liberalisation, deregulation has two other facets. One is legislative simplification and the withdrawal of certain pieces of legislation, the other should be more appropriately termed 're-regulation', i.e. the use of different types of instruments.

At EU level, the deregulation drive started with the Single Market programme but intensified subsequently, with environmental policy as one of the focal areas. In September 1994, the Commission established a high-level group of 'independent experts' to examine the impact of EU and national legislation on employment and competitiveness. The Molitor report, named after the chairman of the group, was published in 1995 and chose environmental legislation as one of only four sectors examined. The report advocates a new approach to environmental regulation:

> which stresses the setting of general environmental targets whilst leaving the Member States and, in particular, industry the flexibility to choose the means of implementation... (European Commission, 1995b: 54).

This echoes the calls for both subsidiarity and deregulation. At the same time, the group also advocates the use of market-based instruments:

> Any new proposal should be accompanied by a careful analysis whether or not market-based methods could be employed to achieve the same goals; where a market based approach is feasible, any departures from it should be justified (European Commission, 1995b: 57).

The report was heavily criticised for its methodology and narrow focus. According to the dissenting opinions of one of the members of the group, Pierre Carniti, the report treated environmental protection as an obstacle to economic aims, rather than understanding the interdependence between economy and environment (European Commission, 1995b: 64). Even though the report may not have been overly influential, and a number of conservative government with neo-liberal tendencies have demised since, pressure for regulatory changes in environmental policy is continuing, both at EU level and in the member states. At the same time, deregulation and liberalisation moves are continuing in various industrial sectors, in a number of EU member states, as well as in Eastern Europe. In both cases, economic and political issues dominate the discussion and the assessment of the environmental implications of deregulation has been rather limited.

Considering the implementation and enforcement problems which continue to prevail in EU environmental policy, as the 1996 Commission Communication on this topic demonstrates (European Commission, 1996a), 'deregulation' could actually be an attractive proposition. Market-based approaches such as taxes and 'self-regulation' imply 'automatic implementation', as it should be in the own interest of economic actors to act, whereas 'command-and-control' approaches involve coercion which needs to be monitored and enforced by often overloaded public agencies.

Taxes and self-regulation

To some extent, deregulation also concurs with the principles of sustainable development, which assume that economic development and environmental protection are inherently compatible (at least in the long-term) and that many opportunities exist for policy actions which make both economic and environmental sense. An obvious example here would be energy efficiency improvements, of which there are many cost-effective examples. Yet, because of the existence of a variety of market failures, such improvements are currently not being made. The solution is thus assumed to be a policy which is based on remedying such market failures.

The use of taxes, as a means of internalising the clear external costs associated with various economic activities, appears promising. However, the valuation of these external costs is far from straightforward. There are clear methodological problems and ethical questions arise about the intrinsic value of nature, as well as of human life. Further difficulties occur, in the case of a carbon tax, related to the high price elasticity of energy, as well as a range of other market failures (Jackson, 1992). To be effective, a carbon tax would probably have to be set at a level which would be highly socially regressive, economically damaging and politically unacceptable. Generally, there are suggestions that taxes are less reliable than regulatory tools (OECD, 1993) in that polluters may choose to pay the tax and continue to pollute. Despite these problems, a greater degree of internalisation of the external costs of production is clearly desirable, even though environmental taxes may need to be applied gradually and with compensatory measures.

One suggestion which has found increased support in recent years is that of integrating environmental taxes into a much broader environmental tax reform. At EU level, this idea was put on the agenda in December 1993, when the Commission, under the initiative of then President Delors, published the White Paper on Growth, Competitiveness and Employment (European Commission, 1993). The paper stressed the promise of the so-called double-dividend, i.e. the possibility of integrating environmental protection with economic growth through, reducing labour taxes as well as job creation in the environmental field. A supporting study was prepared by a team of consultants led by DRI and published in 1994 (DRI, 1994).

The study considered the integration of a range of mainly fiscal measures into sectoral policies, with a concurrent reduction of income or payroll taxes. Environmental externalities were thus supposedly integrated into other policies in a cost-effective manner, with a slightly beneficial effect on GDP growth (2.2% per annum compared to a predicted 2.15% in the reference scenario). This so-called 'integrated' scenario suggested substantial reductions in SO_2 and NO_x emissions, although it actually predicted a small increase (around 4%) in CO_2 emissions by 2010. From an environmental viewpoint, no real 'victory' can thus be claimed, as the 'win-win' approach still leads to increases in CO_2 emissions. Carraro, Galeotti and Gallo (1995) found in a similar analysis short-term emission reductions but long-term increases, as net wage increases stimulate the consumption of all goods including energy.

Recently, the tax reform issue has dropped off the political agenda, with little support in the Santer Commission. The idea of environmental taxes certainly has not found much favour with industry. At EU level, the use of economic instrument is also problematic for other reasons. EU intervention in fiscal policy has always been an area of contention, as the problems encountered during the tax harmonisation efforts of the 1980s exemplify. A number of member states, in the forefront the UK, have been very determined to preserve their sovereignty in the fiscal area, whether related to environmental protection or not. This is reflected in the specific exclusion in the Maastricht Treaty of fiscal measures from qualified majority voting under article 130r. The subsidiarity principle has strengthened the member states' scope for dissension, as the below discussed example of the carbon/energy tax shows.

Apart from taxes, a market-based environmental policy also includes instruments such as tradeable emission premits, negotiated agreements with industry, environmental management systems and labelling (often referred to under the term of 'self-regulation'). The EU has made some progress in this area with the regulations on eco-labelling and on eco-auditing, nothwithstanding some teething problems. Neither of these are compulsory, which renders their effectiveness rather uncertain. Meanwhile, experience with negotiated agreements in the Netherlands, the member state which makes the most intensive use of these instruments, is ambiguous, especially as far as implementation and enforcement are concerned (Liefferink and Mol, 1997). In general, market-based instruments might facilitate environmental policy-making, but should not be viewed as a panacea, nor necessarily as a means for reducing the regulatory burden. In order to guarantee pollution reduction, these instruments will have to be set within a regulatory framework which establishes quantitative goals, monitors progress and provides enforcement mechanisms. (Collier and Golub, 1996).

Climate change, a case study in 1990s EU environmental policy-making

Climate change abatement has to focus on reductions in greenhouse gas emissions. These cannot be achieved through environmental policy instruments alone, but require, in the case of the most important greenhouse gas, CO_2, changes in the direction of energy and transport policies. Climate change policy thus provides a classic case for the need for policy integration and sustainable development practices. A study of EU climate change policy also reveals how years of protracted discussions often yield few result and demonstrates the potentially negative impacts of the subsidiarity issue and deregulation moves.

The first significant event in the EU's climate change policy history occured in 1992, just before the Rio Summit, when EU member states agreed on a common stabilisation target for CO_2 emissions by 2000, based on 1990 level. Six years later, and one year after the Kyoto Climate Summit,

EU climate change policy still consists of little more than targets. After Rio, back in 1992, the Commission presented proposals for a climate change strategy which promised some real progress towards greater sustainability, providing for a carbon/energy tax, an energy efficiency programme, and a renewable energy programme (European Commission, 1992b). In reality, these proposals either came to nothing or where downscaled so much that the resulting policies and measures had little effect.

The carbon/energy tax faced the greatest obstacles, despite the general calls for more market-based instruments from various quarters, including industry. In this case, industrial opposition was strong from the beginning, resulting in some early concessions for energy-intensive energies. Despite these concessions, the proposals made little progress when discussed at various environment and ECOFIN (Economic and Finance Ministers) Council meetings.

As this was a fiscal measure, unanimous agreement was required. The main objection came from the UK, which was vehemently opposed to any European intervention in tax matters, invoking the subsidiarity principle. Furthermore, France favoured a pure carbon tax, so as to protect its nuclear industry, and the cohesion countries were only prepared to accept the proposal in return for additional structural funding (Skjaerseth, 1995). As no progress was evident, various new approaches were discussed, including a possible reform and harmonisation of current energy taxes. However, no agreement could be reached on this either. Finally, after four years of discussions, the idea of a common carbon/energy tax was all but abandoned at the Essen summit in December 1994. The Commission was asked to submit a new proposal outlining common guidelines for those member states who want to implement their own taxes. However, the amended Commission proposal[5] still left the member states divided and by 1998, and several proposal revisions later, no progress was evident.

The carbon/energy tax was expected to achieve the bulk of the emission reductions required to achieve stabilisation by 2000.[6] In its absence, the other measures of the strategy soon proved inadequate. The SAVE programme for energy efficiency consisted of financial assistance for some pilot studies and a framework directive, which left member states so much flexibility in its implementation that the Commission itself commented that the estimation of the effects of SAVE was highly uncertain (European Commission, 1994b). As Collier (1997b) discussed, the application of the subsidiarity principle was the main reason behind SAVE's transformation into a framework directive. A proposal for SAVE II was presented by the Commission aiming at energy savings of 60-70 million toe per year by the year 2000 and involving a budget of 150 million ECU between 1996 and 2000. However, in the Energy Council in May 1996, France, Germany and the UK refused to approve a budget any higher than 45 million ECU,[7] which makes SAVE II unlikely to become any more effective than SAVE I. Furthermore, the renewables programme ALTENER is also underresourced (40 million ECU for 5 years) and consists mainly of non-binding targets.

Meanwhile, other developments in the energy area demonstrate the failure to integrate environmental concerns into this policy area. Proposals for greater energy sector liberalisation, in pursuit of an Internal Energy Market, paid little attention to environmental concerns (Collier, 1994). Agreement on liberalisation was reached in the Council in July 1996 (with an initial opening up of 30% of the energy market), with the ultimate aim of achieving lower energy prices and improving industrial competitiveness. As liberalisation progesses in the member states, the disincentives to energy efficiency posed by lower energy prices have become increasingly evident. This result was supposed to be avoided through the imposition of the carbon/energy tax. A directive on Rational Resource Planning in the energy sector, published in 1995,[8] was a different approach to this problem but was vetoed by a number of countries. These developments are indicative of the existence of a separate, two track approach to energy and environmental policies, implying that a more sustainable energy policy, as referred to in the Commission's recent White Paper on Energy Policy (European Commission, 1995c), remains largely an illusion.

Paradoxically, CO_2 emissions stabilisation by 2000 would be achieved under current trends. However, this stabilisation would be due to the industrial collapse in Eastern Germany, as well as a coincidental move to gas-fired generation in the UK's electricity sector as a result of energy liberalisation. More importantly, stabilisation would likely to be short-lived, as neither the EU nor any of the member states have so far taken measures which lead towards longer term structural changes in the energy and transport sectors.

Post Kyoto, EU climate change policy is little more than an empty shell. The Kyoto Protocol requires the EU to decrease its aggregate greenhouse gas emissions by 8 per cent by the year 2012 (as opposed to a 15% reduction in the three main gases by 2010, as proposed in the EU's

Kyoto negotiating position). The EU and its member states will be jointly responsible for reaching this target as signatories of the protocol. It took the EU member states six months to decide how this 'burden' was supposed to be shared out and at the time of writing, an implementation strategy was being prepared by the Commission.

The only tangible measure on climate change agreed on recently has been a voluntary agreement reached with the Association of European Automobile Manufacturers (ACEA). Transport sector measures will be of crucial importance for the achievement of the Kyoto target, considering that CO_2 emissions from this sector have increased by 11 per cent since 1990.[9] Emission reductions will require a shift to public transport, a move from road to rail freight, as well as more efficient vehicles. For the latter, a directive imposing fuel efficiency standards on motor manufacturing was one avenue considered by the Commission but the Environment Council decided in 1996 (in the spirit of deregulation) that a voluntary agreement by the car industry would be the preferred option. An agreement was adopted by the Council in October 1998 but it contained figures significantly below the aspirations of the initial Commission proposals. Car manufacturers will have to achieve a fleet average of 140 g of CO_2 per km by 2008, as opposed to the Commission's proposals for 120 g CO_2 per km by 2005. Indications are that the the the EU's future climate change strategy will rely heavily on such voluntary agreements, as well as member state measures.

Returning to the issue of subsidiarity, the EU's failure in implementing an effective climate change policy would be irrelevant if the member states (or indeed regional or local authorities) were mounting comprehensive responses themselves. In principle, all 15 member states are committed to action through their signature of the 1992 Framework Convention on Climate Change and the 1997 Kyoto Protocol. However, a number of studies (e.g. Collier et al, 1997, O'Riordan et al, 1997) have shown that activities at the national level have to date been rather patchy and often incoherent. Some greater commitment can be found at the local level in some countries (especially Germany and Sweden) but local authorities are constrained in their scope for action due to an unfavourable national and EU policy context, especially as far as energy prices are concerned). The Collier et al study identified a clear role for EU action in a number of areas, in particular in relation to the integration of climate change concerns into specific EU policies, plans and operations (for example the plans for energy sector liberalisation, funding under the Structural Funds, as well as the Trans European Route Network plans) and the application of energy consumption standards for motor vehicles and electrical appliances. It remains to be seen what political will there is to implement such measures at EU level.

Conclusions: future prospects for EU environmental policy

The previous sections have aimed to shed light on the significance of the concepts of sustainable development, subsidiarity and deregulation for EU environmental policy. Only one of these concepts, sustainable development, originates from the environmental sphere, yet all three have significant implications for EU environmental policy. In principle, an environmentally-focused application of the two other principles could comply with the general principles of sustainable development and herald a fundamentally different approach to environmental protection in the EU. It could result in a new type of environmental governance, away from a heavily interventionist environmental policy, with decision-making mainly at the EU and member state level, to a decentralised approach, using the market and individual responsibility. Yet, at the same time, if political and economic priorities dominate developments, environmental protection is likely to be weakened.

This chapter has argued that the re-orientation of policy-making towards sustainable development has to date made little progress. Short-term and sectoral thinking prevails amongst policy-makers both at the national and at EU level, impeding the integration of environmental concerns into other policies. The vagueness of the sustainability concept and its various interpretations, including distinctions between growth and development, raise doubts about its usefulness. A way forward might be better quantification of the concept and the use of sustainability indicators, as well as targets. Participatory decision-making processes are important for achieving a consensus on such targets.

In principle the increased application of the subsidiarity principle should provide encouragement for a more 'bottom-up' approach. However, in reality, it has provided reluctant member states with new ammunition for the re-nationalisation of policy proposals. Currently, despite the increasing globalisation of environmental policy through UN conventions, high environmental standards cannot be assured without common action.

Environmental commitment still varies across the EU and certain member states lack the will and/or the capacity to design and implement effective environmental policies on their own accord, both at national and local levels.

Deregulation so far has had a limited effect on environmental policy and a more market-based approach has remained fairly elusive. Despite the promise for greater compatibility between economic and environmental objectives, economic instruments have not proved to be politically any more feasible than regulatory instruments. Fiscal instruments are likely to continue to be problematic at EU level because of the subsidiarity principle and industrial opposition, which has strong lobbying capacities both at EU and the national level. Because of different industrial structures, economic instruments will affect different member states in different ways and are thus not an easy option, especially where unanimity is required. Instead, there appears to be a growing reliance on voluntary measures by industry, the effectiveness of which remains to be seen.

Yet, we would like to finish this chapter on a positive note. In late 1998, the outlook for greater sustainability in the EU was better than it had been for a number of years. Efforts to implement the integration principle was gathering momentum. A number of member states (including Germany and the UK) had voted for governments with strong environmental commitments, in particular on CO_2 emissions. Thus, while post-Maastricht progress in EU environment policy had become somewhat elusive, the prospects for the Millenium appeared brighter.

Notes

[1] An earlier version of this chapter was published by Frank Cass as Collier, U. (1997), 'Sustainability, Subsidiarity and Deregulation: New Directions in EU Environmental Policy', *Environmental Politics*, Vol. 6, No. 2, pp. 1-23. The chapter was written by the author in a personal capacity and does not necessarily reflect the views of the World Wide Fund for Nature.

[2] Directives and regulations are the two binding legislative instruments that the EU has at its disposal. Regulations are binding in their entirety, whereas directives allow member states some flexibility on how to transpose them into national law.

[3] For example absorption capacity, energy, non-renewable resources, agricultural land and forests.

4   *OJ* No C 112 of 20/12/73.

5   *COM* (95) 172.

6   Emissions were expected to increase by 12% between 1990 and 2000, mainly due to increased energy consumption. Stabilisation thus effectively meant a 12% emission reduction.

7   *Agence Europe*, 6/5/96, p. 3

8   *COM* (95) 369 final.

9   *ENDS Daily*, 3/8/98.

5 Does Subsidiarity Make a Difference to the EU Environmental Institutions?

BRENDAN FLYNN

Introduction

While it may be a relatively unremarkable assertion to say that institutions 'matter' in policy-making, what may be less admitted or understood is how higher constitutional norms, which govern institutions, impinge on their substantive competence in actually influencing policy. In this short chapter I to hope argue that the introduction of such a higher norm, subsidiarity, has actually made a difference both to substantive policy-making and institutional competences. I will also suggest that looking at the question of subsidiarity and how the institutions have managed its discursive application, tends to reveal a balance of institutional power which favours intergovernmentalist interests.

However, such a conclusion does not come easily from a mere reading of the legal significance of the term, and in fact subsidiarity appears to be an elusive and slippery concept to pin down. For instance a close examination of the wording of Article 3(b) reveals a curiously worded Treaty provision whose immediate import is not clear:

> In areas which do not fall within its exclusive competence, the community shall take action, in accordance with the principle of Subsidiarity, only if and in so far as the objectives of the proposed action cannot be sufficiently achieved by the member states and can therefore, by reason of the scale or effects of the proposed action, be better achieved by the Community. (CEC, 1993)

Equally, as Anthony Teasdale would have it, if subsidiarity is 'the principle that decisions should be taken at the lowest level consistent with effective action within a political system' (Bainbridge & Teasdale, 1995:430-432), then what could this possibly mean for European environmental institutions? Does subsidiarity mean that the nation-states will do more not less and that they are serving notice of this intent?

In truth, if the term is so hard to define then a number of objections may be made to seeing subsidiarity as in anyway significant for the EU's environment institutions. The question might be put does subsidiarity actually make any difference to the environment institutions and how could such a higher norm impinge on their institutional interests? In this regard a number of possible hypothesis may put forward:

(1)   Subsidiarity is a principle which allows for 're-nationalisation' of environmental policy through acting as a 'brake' on the exercise of discretionary competences of the European environment institutions.

(2)   Subsidiarity is so vague as a concept and so open to subjective meaning that its does not really have any significance for institutional politics. As John Peterson describes it, subsidiarity suffers from the fact that its open to a 'definition to suit any vision' (Peterson, 1994). This approach would stress that subsidiarity is largely a rhetorical device used in the context of treaty negotiations to assuage the fears of some member states, but in practice its import may be little.

(3)   A third hypothesis may rest in the argument that as a Treaty provision, Article 3(b) is not amenable to judicial review by the Court. This is not a pedantic legal point. If the European Court of Justice (ECJ) cannot review subsidiarity based decisions then in an important sense the institutional balance of power may be upset, with actions not amenable to judicial scrutiny offering scope for the other institutions to abuse their discretion.

(4)   A fourth hypothesis may be to argue that while subsidiarity has been successfully defined and applied by the European institutions, this process has had little relevance for environmental policy considerations. This is the sense that subsidiarity is all very interesting as a question but it that dos not impact on the business of the EU environment institutions.

(5)   A fifth hypothesis, favoured by those who are unambiguously pro-integration in their orientation, would be to argue that Article 3b represents a properly 'federal' principle at the heart of EU affairs. By this conception subsidiarity is something of a 'two-way street'. It can both give and take away the right to act on the part of an institution. It can not only justify that institutional actors ought to cede certain policy matters to the national level, but it may also mean that certain topics ought to be the concern of the European Institutions by 'virtue of scale and effects.' (CEC, 1993,TEU, Article 3b).

As a result of these possible interpretations, some quite obviously different, many commentators and particularly the European institutions themselves have had to grapple with the task of defining just what subsidiarity means and of how it could be applied. This chapter is then largely an empirical description of how the various institutions have accepted the term and of what significance the working practice of subsidiarity has for them. Specifically it is argued that there is some limited evidence for seeing subsidiarity support an interpretation of 're-nationalisation' occurring in EU environmental policy. The other hypotheses are largely rejected in this analysis.

Whatever happened to subsidiarity?

The murky starting point of beginning to actually see what subsidiarity would mean in practice was skilfully lead by the Commission in the historic summit of the European Council at Edinburgh in December 1992. One must emphasize the backdrop of a profoundly downbeat mood which the heads of government/state of the 12 Members found themselves in late 1992.

With in most cases fairly sharp domestic recessions biting, and with the Danish *'No'* and French *'petit oui'* raising fundamental question marks over the pace of future integration, subsidiarity became in the memorable words of Leon Brittain, 'an ugly word, but a useful concept'. In short it was grasped at by all-comers in the post Maastricht doldrums as something of a panacea. Yet most of all it was for intergovernmentalist critiques seen as the 'steady as she goes' brake which would curtail the adventures and ambitious of an out of touch Commission, and thus keep integration on a 'reasonable' level. In particular it entered into the political lexicons of domestic European politicians, particularly Danish and British ones, as they tried vigorously to square rhetorical circles with sceptical public opinion, about just where they stood on the benefits and cost of 'ever closer union' (Grant, 1994:220). As Grant memorably puts it, subsidiarity became the buzz word of the moment, and 'opposition to [it]...had become no more acceptable than the slaughter of baby seals.' (Grant, 1994:217)

It was precisely in this context then that Delors secured a number of fundamental procedural approaches which defused the Commission's own fear that the provision would be use to cap legislative proposals in a crude and restraining way. This was achieved with a neat side-step manoeuvre tactic which expanded on the meaning of subsidiarity as originally contained in the Delors report on the principle that was presented to the Edinburgh summit.

The tactic was to present to the heads of state/government, a vision of subsidiarity which was less a demarcator of competences, but instead as a new way of developing proposals and determining what direction or regulatory style they ought to take. In doing this, the Delorist Commission of the early 1990s brought subsidiarity down from the lofty heights of constitutional theory and possibly even avoided distressful explorations of a quasi-federal debates proper. Instead, the subsidiarity issue was decanted into the much more stable 'vessel' of a discussion about a new form of regulatory intervention, one redolent of neo-liberalist, anti-bureaucratic imagery and language.

A three stage test procedure was laid down which breathes considerably more certainty into the procedure than was known before. In the first stage, whenever the Commission has to consider a proposal, it must determine with precision whether it has an exclusive competence. Even where a proposed environmental law is based on such an exclusive competence, then it must still apply the second test of subsidiarity to its proposals, that of proportionality. Presuming the competence under which a proposed new environmental law is however a shared one, then the Commission must first really determine whether action is necessary. If the answer to that is yes, then as always the third and in many ways the penultimate stage must be entertained: this is simply that any action taken to fulfil an objective must be proportionate to the aim sought to be achieved. In Duff's view of the Edinburgh Annex, all of this can be reduced to a more simple set of propositions. He sees a three fold test procedure which asks the following. (1) Is the action proposed proportionate to the scale of the problem involved? (2) Is there a trans-national element to the problem? (3) Can the EU act efficiently in solving the problem? (Duff, 1994:28)

One might say here that the shrewd move on the part of the Commission has been to link the question of subsidiarity to the idea of proportionality, a principle which has a long standing pedigree with the Court of Justice. In this instance proportionality is a starting point for a discussion about the choice of instruments and the achieving of an optimum balance between reaching a given goal with what is in effect the least cumbersome, costly or interventionary instrument that the Commission can find. The whole focus is to move away from the simple choice of old, between largely either the directive or the regulation. Instead the application of subsidiarity demands of the Commission that they consider an arena where these latter instruments have merely become but one choice among many others; fiscal incentives, education, exchange of information flows, voluntary agreements, etc. Under this schema where measures need to be binding to secure a common mandatory goal, an even broader instrument is conceived than the directive of old, namely the 'framework directive'.

This is touted as something of a qualitative step forward in terms of being likely to be highly 'proportionate'. In this concept 'framework directives' largely concern themselves with just setting objectives, which may even be just guideline objectives expressed in ranges of minimum permissible measures of ecological harm/improvement.

Arguably, in conclusion then, there is a very strong sense in which the Commission has offered up this style of working, precisely in order to sate intergovernmentalist concerns which demand less interference and much more discretion from Brussels. The mantra rings loud and clear in the 1995 report of the application of the principle of subsidiarity: 'do less but do it better.' (CEC, 1995:3)

At this stage it may be worthwhile to take stock of the significance of this new working practice which the Commission has ordained as the single most practical manifestation of the subsidiarity principle.

The 1994, 'Report to the European Council on the Application of the Subsidiarity Principle' (CEC, 1994) tells us more about how the practice is being used. This basically involves a screening process whereby all new proposals are examined for proportionality and subsidiarity concerns. There is also of course the related commitment to a soft regulatory culture where fewer laws are devised but they are supposed to be 'qualitatively better.' The Commission has become more open and communicative we are told, informed by subsidiarity and proportionality concerns. Now it is supposed to seek out and consult the views of all relevant partners. White papers and Green papers are innovations which are designed to facilitate this and special meetings can even be arranged with member states, either solely or bilaterally on subsidiarity grounds. Both Britain and Germany have demanded and held such meetings (CEC, 1994:2).

Interestingly, the Commission does make a point of distinguishing between subsidiarity and recasting and/or redrafting legislation to root out inefficiency, etc. Presumably this is to reassure us that subsidiarity is a more fundamental concern that just 'good housekeeping' (CEC, 1994:2).

One thing the 1994 report does admit is that it may not be that easy to draw the line between what policy enjoys an exclusive competence and what does not. Guidelines have been developed to help in this and again extensive discussions with the other legislative partners are used to facilitate the ready application of the principle. However, clearly the picture that emerges is of a treating of the subsidiarity issue in very practical terms. The Commission have tactically avoided the dimension of subsidiarity that tackles the hard question of who does what in environment policy with rather one of how should the Commission act with what has already been agreed to by the member states, in the environment field. This new 'soft law' regulatory style then is about selectivity, about trying to exhaust alternatives to traditional legislation where possible and above all, continually communicating and 'sounding out' the relevant legislative partners (Snyder, 1994:83).

Perhaps the worrying thing in all of this though is that by some accounts the community are interpreting proportionality as meaning that they give priority to measures which are not legally binding. In other words, we are seeing with subsidiarity not just a move towards soft law, but one that is being undertaken at the expense of traditional forms of intervention, a viewed shared by Synder (1994:84)

In this regard it may be worthwhile to quote directly from the Conclusions of the Presidency, European Council in Edinburgh, 11-12 December 1992, Annex I to Part A, 'Overall Approach to the Application by the Council of the Subsidiarity Principle and Article 3b of the Treaty on European Union':

> The form of action should be as simple as possible, consistent with satisfactory achievement of the objective of the measures and the need for effective enforcement. The Community should legislate only to the extent necessary. Other things being equal, directives should be preferred to regulations and framework directives to detailed measures. Non-binding measures should be given where appropriate to the use of voluntary codes of conduct. (CEC, 1994:22-23)

Also in line with this is the withdrawal of legislative proposals, of which some nine were removed in 1993 and a further 66 were offered up on the altar of subsidiarity in 1994. Most sources suggest these were relatively minor and insignificant proposals rather than anything substantive. Time and space precludes a more complete examination here.

However, with regard to the environment the Commission has proposed 'simplification' of a competition policy regulation with regard to environmental protection considerations and domestic competition policy. The 1994 report notes the prime effect of this 'simplification' process has been to ensure greater certainty but also 'the details of aid are left to the discretion of the national authorities.' (CEC, 1994:24) While theoretically such 'simplification' should not allow much scope for re-nationalisation or 'watering down' of EU environment laws, that may be not as true for the whole- scale revision promised in 1994 of the following environmental measures.

(1)   A revision of the Directive 76/160/EEC on the quality of Bathing water (CEC, 1994:24).

(2)   A Proposed new Directive on ecological quality of surface water. (*ibid.*)

(3)   A Proposal to amend Directive 80/778/EEC on drinking water. (*ibid.*)

(4)   A Proposal to introduce a framework directive that will simplify air quality legislation. The report tell us; 'this seeks to establish a framework for the harmonisation and evaluation of air quality standards within the Union, while leaving Member States the responsibility for taking specific measures to reduce levels of pollution in their territory.' (*ibid.*)

(5)   A proposed revision of the Seveso Directive 82/501/EEC, so that 'Member States [can] choose the ways and means of achieving a high level of safety at major industrial plants and is thus fully in keeping with the spirit of the Fifth Community Environment programme.' (*ibid.*)

(6)   An amendment planned to directive 90/219/EEC on the contained use of genetically modified micro-organisms. (*ibid.*)

(7)   A re-evaluation of directive 90/220/EEC on the deliberate release into the environment of genetically modified organisms was also planned for 1995. (CEC, 1994:25)

Subsidiarity and the problem of 're-nationalisation' of European environmental policy

One of the most telling recent critiques of current EU environmental policy is that contained within the European Environmental Bureau's[1] recent 'Memorandum to the Irish Presidency and the EU Member States' (EEB, 1996). Their report is interesting not least because it paints a picture of an EU which is increasingly choosing to downplay its environmental responsibilities but that also this is being done as part of the shift to the new 'soft law' regulatory culture, a move which is fully in keeping with the subsidiarity principle.

For instance, the EEB specifically allege that this new working practice amounts to a 'cave-in' to the more recalcitrant member states on a variety of issues. Waste policy is now dispensing with a clear waste hierarchy such that the EU is 'giving the principle of flexibility priority over the principles of prevention.' (EEB, 1996:13) The revision of a directive on Biotechnology (91/219) is suggested as being brought forward too early such that a de-regulation emphasis in its recasting will only further undermine its already weak structure (EEB, 1996:12). Also, more concerns are voiced about the EU's auto-oil programme which was a classic manifestation of the new regulatory style. In this instance, rather than resort to old 'hard law' approaches, the Commission has allowed the Auto and Oil industries to come up with their own, essentially voluntary agreement. The EEB view this as a de facto abdication of responsibilities, having 'left it to the Commission to distribute to the European citizens the air quality the two industries are willing to pay for, thus giving the absurd interpretation of the polluter pays principle.' (EEB, 1996:13) Of even greater concern is their view on the whole scale rewriting of old water pollution legislation. Here the risk is a more explicit one of 'repatriating European environmental legislation ...especially in the field of water policy.' (EEB, 1996:12)

In conclusion, there is a general tone of hostility towards the new style of regulation which the Commission seems to be adopting with vigour. In this the EEB note that while this current penchant for neo-liberal soft regulatory styles may mimic developments in the USA, nonetheless US environmental policy also has a solid track record in old style 'hard law' regulation and good enforcement (EEB, 1996:8)

What of these fears then? Is there evidence that such a new regulatory style is leading to a re-nationalisation of environmental policy, a weakening of standards, and a reduction in the scope of action for the environment institutions?

As I am unable to develop a comprehensive empirical legal examination here of the re-drafted laws as yet, due to the obvious limits of the scope of a chapter such as this, one can nonetheless offer two conclusions. First, that the subsidiarity 'process' certainly displays greater opportunities than ever before for the member states to secure a re-nationalisation of environmental standards. There can be little doubt that it will mean a greater say and discretion in key areas of implementation than before.

Secondly, we may take it that there is much more evidence of intent on the part of the Commission and the member states to produce a more minimalist and less interventionary style of environmental policy. In many ways the fears of European environmentalists, that subsidiarity would prove to be a force for retrenchment by weak willed nation-states in environmental policy, has a certain body of evidence in elite politics accounts which sustains this suspicion.

There is for instance Grant's intriguing account, styled in the manner of 'high politics' and elite biography, of how Carlos di Ripa Mena (the famous activist Environment Commissioner of DG XI) fought with Delors over the subsidiarity principle in the field of environmental policy (Grant, 1994:218-219). A number of examples are offered by Grant.

The first relates to a seemingly unlikely move, by Michael Heseltine, then the Environment Minister in the British Government and wearing unsteadily on his head the 'cap' of the rotating presidency of the Council of Environment Ministers (*ibid.*) Heseltine in January 1992 suggested a proposal that the planned EC environment agency would actually take onboard serious trans-national inspectorate capabilities, or more especially that it would regulate the regulators in the member states and ensure that they were doing their job as best as was possible.

The fascinating thing here was that Delors rejected Heseltine's proposal, apparently on the grounds that it would violate the principle of subsidiarity regarding Britain's own prerogatives? This is indeed a reversal of what one might expect, whereby a Commission President sees fit to reject a Community proposal in the interest of the subsidiarity function of a given Member State. One would imagine such would be more the prerogative of the member state to decide and protest?

Grant specifically alleges that by the end of his last Commission term, relations with the head of DG XI and Delors were strained, precisely because Delors viewed Ripa as over zealous and creating too many directives which could never perhaps be properly enforced. Much of this tension spilled out over debates about subsidiarity. He further suggests that using the principle, Delors was able to frustrate the impact and content of a number of new key proposals, of which the first was the proposal to create an environmental inspectorate which would examine national environmental authorities and how good of a job they were doing (Grant, 1994:108) This was slowed down and altered so that in effect it was not until 1994 that the new European Environment Agency was set up in Copenhagen, and at that, its brief was strictly circumscribed as being concerned with the collection and transmission of environmental information only. It has no inspectorate powers in the sense in which Ripa and Heseltine thought it would and should.

More evidence comes in the form of the Spring 1992 'witch-hunt' of environmental measures which Delors eagerly pursued and which Grant details. When it came to examining a particular directive, that on hunting birds, it was found to be in Grant's own words 'a model of subsidiarity'. (Grant, 1994:220). All that it did was list certain species which ought not be hunted at certain times of their life cycle. How to achieve this was as ever left to the member states. Furthermore, by virtue of the scale of the environmental problem, depletion of migrating bird stocks through heavy hunting, the problem was objectively one which has transboundary implications. If the birds covered under the directive were under threat in one southern member state, then due to the migration patterns the bird life was diminished in a number of other north European ones as well. The fact of bird migration makes any environmental policy on birds a fundamentally transboundary issue, although Golub for one has argued that bird migration alone may not be enough to mean that the Birds Directive does not offend subsidiarity (Golub, 1996b).[2] In any event according to Grant, the Danish position over this issue appeared to precisely suggest that subsidiarity could not be used as a pretext to rewrite or even remove the Hunting of Birds directive on these grounds. (Grant, 1994:220)

Another example where Delors thought that there was an overintense use of EC law was with regard to the very popular and widely publicised Blue Flag clean beaches award scheme (*ibid.*). For Delors an equal effect could have been achieved through recommendations and awards and thus he seemed to suggest, that there was no need for infringement proceedings. What perhaps he forgot however, is that one clear virtue and appeal of the scheme was that because it was backed up by EC spot checks and other forms of validation, citizens in each member state felt they could trust the 'Blue Flag' status as it was more independently arrived at than if national authorities had a free hand. In other words, it is precisely the high level of involvement by the Commission in the scheme which has enabled its veracity for the public to be ensured.

Yet another area which was completely transformed lay with regard to a proposal that an eco-audit should be carried out as mandatory by certain companies (large ones and those engaged perhaps in particularly sensitive environmental processes). Under subsidiarity concerns this was whittled down to a mere voluntary scheme which would be administered by the Member States (Grant, 1994:108). Some commentators miss perhaps the dynamic substance of the effect of subsidiarity concerns as seen in this watering down of Ripa's intended eco-Audit proposal.

Butt-Philip for instance remains puzzled that although the eco-audits regulation is touted as a classic effect of subsidiarity in environmental policy it nonetheless takes the form of a regulation which is more binding, more stringent and leaves the member state with less room for movement (Butt-Philip, 1994:134). However, this misses what is suggested here throughout this chapter: that subsidiarity empirically is more a practice determining the content of legislation, rather than a filter deciding who does what. It is important for what the regulation says, not that whether what it says will be more binding. This is because if the details of future directives are very flexible and minimalist, then of course it matters little to the nation-states, and it costs them little, to rigorously implement an empty shell law.

Likewise, from interviews with Ripa, Grant maintains his proposal for a CO_2 tax as a key component of the EU's stance at Rio was undermined and effectively downplayed, again due to subsidiarity concerns. (Grant, 1994:108-109). While another clear example of subsidiarity being used in a manner which suggests it was attempted to claw back some innovations in environmental policy is the case of the proposal from Delors at the Edinburgh Summit (1992) for a whole-scale devolving of responsibilities for administration and monitoring of environmental policy back to the member states (Butt-Philip, 1994:134)

Again this fits in with the thesis that Delors viewed environmental policy as expendable and a key area where he could placate member states. What was interesting was that his idea was rejected by them, possibly more of out a reluctance to get caught up in yet more environmental bureaucracy which the shrewder states might have foreseen as certainly not cost-free. Equally important was the protest from European environmental groups who feared that the subsidiarity principle, once a source of hope for them, was now turning into a negative instrument in the hands of a frantic and panicky Commission, that was jettisoning all non-essentials overboard as the Danish 'No' crisis blurred into the ERM currency crisis.

Authorities other than Grant also suggest there is *prime facie* evidence that some member states were looking at the principle as a means to securing a recasting of environmental provisions which may be important. Butt-Philip suggests that both Britain and France are worried about their financial cost implications under the Urban Waste Water Directive (Butt-Philip 1994:135).

As a result of this necessarily brief discussion, a tentative response to some of the hypothesis set out in the introduction can be made. First, it appears that there is at least a *prime facie* case for seeing some 're-nationalisation' of environmental policy occurring, if we consider the intentions of the actors and the character of the new soft regulatory style it has engendered. Secondly, this must mean that those who view subsidiarity as having no tangible effects in the substantive process of integration would appear to be quite wrong. Subsidiarity clearly does matter. If it were not a concern and a key theme one would not see all the new legislative activity that is detailed above. More fundamentally such a dismissive view of the import of subsidiarity may miss the significance of this shift to a new regulatory style.

Equally such a finding, that subsidiarity is being fleshed out into a 'soft law' regulatory style means that it cannot be criticised as being a purely discursive domain. Subsidiarity is not mere rhetoric, it does matter for the institutions. It is true in this that while subsidiarity may not yet be seen as a causal variable, nonetheless as an 'effect' in its own right, it is clearly worth study as its implications are not clear-cut by any means.

The more substantive point of whether this new style has lead to a reduction in environmental standards requires a much more detailed empirical evaluation of the legal instruments in question, which is clearly beyond the scope of this chapter.

Evaluating the significance of the move towards 'soft law' for the institutions – who wins, who loses?

In the light of the above discussion, in this section the focus is more specifically on the impact of subsidiarity for the six institutions described. In particular in relation to examining its importance for the ECJ, the hypothesis on justiciability is addressed, as is the idea of subsidiarity being a 'federal' principle. However, more generally speaking it is possible to sketch out below institutional 'winners' and 'losers' under subsidiarity. Equally it is clear from the above considerations that subsidiarity directly affects some institutions more than others, for instance as it is chiefly concerned with justifying legislation and action, its main target is clearly the Commission who alone enjoys the right of initiative. Yet what of the environment directorate-general, DG XI, then? Is it a winner or loser, and what would that mean?

Winner and loser? Directorate General XI of the Commission

Arguably if the aim of subsidiarity has been to clip the wings of the Commission generally, or more likely those directorates whose output is regarded as less welcome from the member states, then DG XI has been a 'loser'. In this regard what is interesting is how subsidiarity concerns have been used to water-down key components of policy emanating from DG XI, such as the EEA policy and the Eco-audit scheme (see above). However, without being trite, in general the Commission has played a 'blinder' in fielding the whole question of subsidiarity. The strategic move in institutional terms has been to avoid an inflexible and legalistic definition which would have irrevocably frozen the borders of Commission competence, through treating Article 3b as a higher constitutional provision. By responding to Article 3b in terms of a new style of institutional working and a new style of policy, in many ways such a potential unhappy outcome has been avoided. Therefore DG XI and the College of Commissioners may have offered up some ambitions and freedoms to the high altar of subsidiarity, but there has been no whole-scale limit set on their power, as was feared.

Two final observations are perhaps useful here; The first is to say, that the new soft law style may still afford considerable scope for DG XI's ambitions. It is not yet clear if within this soft law regulatory style DG XI cannot yet still continue to exercise a formidable influence. Practically its work programme for the next few years will be cut out for it, in terms of redrafting, simplification and re-casting. One can say in this regard that it is doomed to consolidate what has gone before and continually muddle over 'more of the same'. Yet while we can expect the pace and sheer number of environmental laws to drop, DG XI's institutional style will likely expand more than ever in the direction of being an opinion leader and maker. Increasing emphasis will likely merge on 'consultative' voluntary projects where key epistemic and business communities are brought inside the policy network and canvassed extensively. The key idioms of EU environmental policy for the next decade within this interpretation then, may then be those of 'partnership', 'negotiation' and 'flexibility'. Paradoxically then for those who though subsidiarity would reduce the visibility of the Commission in environmental policy, DG XI may appear actually more visible, accessible, and tangible than before through greater emphasis on communication, and the use of persuasive force to secure action, rather than law. Such a social 'engagement' at the heart of policy may well bring DG XI into an institutionally closer relationship with its target groups than straightforward hard law approaches.

The second point is to more bleakly observe however, that with regard to institutional dynamics within the College of Commissioner, when 'push comes to shove' and some member states demand an effective reduction in the level of EU 'interference', DG XI is invariably weakly positioned to resist being forced to sacrifice its own projects. While one may suggest this was more a feature of the Delors Commissions, due to his personal views, there is a clear sense that some of the newer components of the environment action projects are not viewed as central to the Commission's collective interests. Why is it that subsidiarity seems rarely used within the context of debates on priority areas such as CAP (although now beginning), and EMU for instance? Does the way in which subsidiarity was used to undermine DG XI projects (outlined above) not suggest that it is a more marginal institution than heretofore there may have been evidence for assuming?

Clear winners? The Environment Council (Council of Ministers) and The European Council

If one accepts that much of the practice of defining and applying Subsidiarity has involved paying homage to member states' concerns about the growing power of the European institutions generally, then it seems to me that subsidiarity can only be viewed as a principle which supports intergovernmentalist concerns. Certainly the way in which it has been used to date would suggest a picture of a relatively 'bullish' European Council demanding from the Commission substantive proposals to show that it was more sensitive to member states interests. In the environment field what emerges was something akin to a mini-witch hunt of environmental measures which the Commission in a submissive and tactical way sought to offer up for sacrifice. Certainly all the major considerations of subsidiarity have involved the European Council, particularly at Edinburgh, setting the agenda in a very clear manner. Inexorably as a result there is a growing strategic 'steering' influence on the part of the European Council over the substantive work of the environment institutions. In fact the close attention and interest with which some member states expend on the subsidiarity issue continues. The UK for instance has submitted in 1996 a proposed amendment on the application of the principle of subsidiarity to the IGC.[3]

One might however argue the case that in the longer term subsidiarity may well prove to be a more generous principle which can act like a two way street in both granting a sphere of competence to the European environmental institutions and the member states as the case may be. Duff for instance argues that

> The writing-in of Subsidiarity to the Treaty is likely to be one of its lasting and most valuable achievements. Already, the Commission is being more circumspect in proposing and in accepting the proposals of other for yet more EC law. Some minor and superfluous legislation (actual and draft) will be dismantled. But there will be no wholesale rolling back of the powers of the Community. In fact, Subsidiarity is clearly a two edged sword which will strengthen the argument for EC action in appropriate cases. It is not a mathematical formula, but a logical one. By using its discretion about states' rights, the court of justice will be acting more and more in the role of a federal supreme court. (Duff, 1994:29)

Unfortunately for such adherents this interpretation was explicitly rejected through the Edinburgh consultative process.

Indeed this process has in fact made a number of points of application much clearer. For instance a UK proposal whereby a subsidiarity hearing would be held before a legislative proposal was debated in Council, was not accepted by the other heads of state and government. In fact, there is now agreement that subsidiarity concerns will be looked at the *same* time in which any legislative proposal is substantively discussed. Otherwise this could have been used to slow down and filibuster legislative proposals.

It has also been affirmed that subsidiarity will not alter existing *acquis communautaire* nor shall it alter existing administrative procedures. Therefore any challenge brought before the Court will be left until the legislation has run its course. Member states, it appears, have agreed that they will refrain from ambushing legislative proposals through subsidiarity-based court cases. Instead, their concerns will be worked through legislation. (Duff, 1994:28)

However, for those who think there is sufficient room for a federalist interpretation of subsidiarity from a future Court, this view has been explicitly denied by two developments. At Edinburgh it was agreed that, (1) questions of subsidiarity shall not entertain sub-state allocations of governance unless the national capital agrees to such, and (2) the idea that it could represent some embedding of a hierarchy of norms was rejected. The virtue of the latter argument was that such a hierarchy would replace the various jumble of acts, etc. which form a proto-constitution by default for the EU. Thus subsidiarity would be binding in its entirety over all EU actions and directly applicable for citizens, irrespective of who was supposed to do the implementation regarding a policy. The chief benefit of this would be clarity and transparency (Duff, 1994:28-29). However, this idea has been expressly throttled at birth by the member states.

Therefore at least the consensus was that there was no difficulty in deciding what subsidiarity did not mean. The implication of this administrative ruling is that Article 3 provisions of and in themselves *cannot* grant new competences to the Commission, nor for that manner in particular to sub-state authorities regarding their role in any EU policies at that level. Note that this does not mean that sub-state bodies (such as the relevant Bavarian environment ministry) cannot claim in future that the Commission is overstepping the mark with some proposal in a non-exclusive environmental policy area. This line of defence is obviously open to them. In any event, the Commission could still expand its scope for action by using Article 235 and Article 100/100a provisions where the member states agree to such. Yet what is vital here is the unanimity that would be required to act under Article 235 whereas federalists may have held out hope within the wording of Article 3b for a formula that grants a general technical test for competence 'by virtue of scale and effects.' That this has been explicitly rejected clearly shows which institutions are in the driving seat; the Environment Council and the European Council. I submit these administrative 'decisions' are very likely to be taken into account persuasively by the Court in any future case, a theme expanded on below.

There are three more fundamental institutional perspectives which should be remembered when discussing the Environment Council in particular. The first is to note that with the extension of qualified majority voting (QMV) into Environment Council decision-making after Maastricht there is more of a chance that a member state could find themselves on the losing side of a vote for a particular environmental measure. Arguably, subsidiarity thus offers such a disgruntled state potential redress, first in the form of putting the Commission on the defensive about justifying why a measure is needed, and secondly in securing a more flexible discretionary style of regulation from the Commission in the first place. As a result such a member state can perhaps be more secure knowing that the form of intervention will be less invasive and objectionable than perhaps traditional 'hard law' would be. Lastly, it gives a member state a 'nuclear option' of a legal challenge which may be loaded in favour of the member state to begin with (see below). However, one must emphasize, subsidiarity's chief effect is proactive and preventative. It has created an institutional sensitivity on the part of the Commission to member states, informally and in the working practices of policy-making, rather than serving to create a solid legal veto.

A related point to this is that with the extension of the European Parliament's co-decision procedure to in particular 'general action programmes setting out priority objectives', in environment policy (see Article 130S(3)), this too is a concern which might exercise the minds of reluctant member states. However, if subsidiarity serves to introduce more 'soft law' rather than formal hard law, then Parliament's impact may be muted or even circumvented. Will a voluntary agreement on the environment be amenable to co-decision and Parliament's scrutiny for instance? Does it matter if the Parliament does have a power of co-decision, if all that the Commission is proposing for legislation, as a result of subsidiarity, is framework legislation or even mere re-casting of earlier provisions?

Finally, the move towards 'soft law' may be fundamentally a move which is internationally being experienced within national environmental regimes. If this is so, and if such an approach is more approximate to the interests of the members of the Environment Council, defining subsidiarity has served to importantly imbed institutionally this 'regulatory style' for them and thus to afford greater harmonisation with national regimes.

Clear losers? The European Parliament's Committee 11 on the Environment. and the European Environment Agency

One clear loser and indeed early victim to subsidiarity type concerns must be seen to be the European Environment Agency (EEA). As was noted above one of the early critical aims of creating such a body was to provide an agency which could impartially regulate the various environment agencies of the members states and evaluate their programmes of compliance with Community policy. This key goal for the EEA stands all the more central if one accepts that implementation is one of the key problems with environmental policy to date. Indeed in the UK, parliamentary debate focused on this puzzling feature that the EEA's present remit of collecting information and ensuring technical veracity may actually be done already by the Commission (see House of Commons, 1989). What was missing of course was the role of an agent of enforcement – an environmental policy policeman – something which the UK, like many member states were keen to specifically prevent (House of Commons, 1989:vi). One might say that with this decision in some ways the EEA is a duplication of the statistics collecting and communicating duties which the Commission was already doing. Indeed the European Environment Bureau, one of the most authoritative and well respected NGOs, actually explicitly has called for the creation of a 'proper' environmental inspectorate by the year 1999 (Van Ermen and EEB/BEE, 1996:23. Although the Regulation setting up the EEA allowed for a review of whether it would expand ist power into the 'inspectorate of national environmental inspectorates' role, this review has not concluded with expansion in this direction.

One of the other institutions which arguably stand to lose out as the new subsidiarity culture manifests itself is Committee 11 of the European Parliament, an institution which counters the usual characterisation of the Parliament as something of an outsider in policy-making. In the past, through own-initiative reports and through some MEPs mastering their briefs exceptionally well, this committee has been able to secure a level of expertise in environmental matters which makes the Commission take notice. Equally they have been quick to start legal proceedings in the environment field where they feel that the Commission puts through legislation on a shaky legal basis, as they did in relation to basing legislation related to the Chernobyl disaster using the Euroatom treaty provisions (Jacobs, Corbett and Shackleton, 1992:188).

The main ways in which the Parliament could lose institutional power would be with regard to the move towards non legislative instruments, such as voluntary agreements and partnership 'education and learning' exchanges where the Commission would not be as amenable to scrutiny. This would in effect bypass the Parliament in some ways. More especially if one considers the way in which the Commission, Environmental Council and European Council are primarily discussing subsidiarity themselves and deciding what laws to recast, simplify or otherwise amend, then it is a process to which the Parliament can only incrementally respond. Perhaps the only concession which the Parliament has won is a key agreement, in the Inter-institutional Agreement on procedures for Implementing the Principle of subsidiarity, whereby there is acceptance by the Commission and Council of Ministers that questions of subsidiarity will be decided alongside as substantive discussion on a legislative proposal. If this were not the case it is possible that the member states could have used subsidiarity to choke off proposals using Article 3b, before they ever emerged into the legislative process, the only realm where the Parliament has at least some formal powers of opinion and amendment.

Subsidiarity and the 'strange' case of the European Court of Justice

Many legal authorities have been perplexed about the legal significance of subsidiarity and more particularly whether it is justiciable or not (see e.g. Dehousse, 1994 and Toth, 1992). One might say this is not just a moot point. For if decisions which have been taken on the basis of Article 3b, are not amenable to judicial review, then in some sense at least the institutional balance of power is upset, and baring in mind what has been said above, it would appear the member states embedded in the Environment Council could ride rough shod over the other institutions, in particular the Commission. While I think for many reasons this is an unduly alarmist and unreal fear, that is not to say that subsidiarity does not raise serious questions for the ambit of the Court. A Court, I might add, which has traditionally been seen by environmentalists as a guardian of the Treaties and a key agent in securing good environmental protection through infringement proceedings for lack of national implementation of directives, and especially through creative legal decisions which have developed concepts like 'direct effect' and 'proportionality.' More fundamentally it can be argued that it is the very law-based nature of the EU which breathes life into its supranationalist ambitions and moves it beyond mere intergovernmental diplomacy.

In this regard what is perplexing for anyone trying to get to grips with the elusive subsidiarity term is the perhaps interesting fact that the definition of subsidiarity offered in Article 130r(4) is more generous than that offered in Article 3(b). In the case of the former, the Community

> shall take action relating to the environment to the extent to which the (environmental policy) objectives.....can be attained better at Community level than at the level of individual Member States. Without prejudice to certain measures of a Community nature, the Member States shall finance and implement the other measures. (Butt-Philip, 1994:127-128)

In the Article 3b(2) expression of subsidiarity this single test of action being shown to be better achieved at community level, is seriously qualified by a prior demand that it be ascertained that national action is insufficient to tackle the given problem. This, it can be argued, is somewhat qualitatively more demanding than Article 130r(4), insofar as there may be many cases in environmental action where one could show Community action might be better, but not that national action was somehow insufficient as the text of Article 3(b) suggests (*ibid.*).

The two words in English are not synonyms and clearly while a state of affairs may be sufficient it may not be qualitatively superior or 'better'. Thus whereas Article 130r(4) seems to asks the intriguing and deep penetrating question as to whether Community action is an improvement (i.e. better), in contrast Article 3b(2) merely requires that nation-state action be adequate?

Arguably, as a result we are deprived of a debate about a more fundamental question; who ought to do what? Moreover there is also the question: 'what is it, that they ought to do to make environment policy better?' It is suggested that these are the two critical points. A sensitivity to the intergovernmentalist voice has rendered subsidiarity more semantically challenged as a legal concept than practically far-reaching in its power as higher norm that could inform environmental policy. However, to say that the principle is not readily applicable, may be not yet to deny it cannot permit a test of objective criteria nor that it will hold up in a court of law. These points are considered in a brief discussion of the question of 'justiciability' below. The reader will appreciate being spared the full scope of a legal argument. I have opted for just a few brief statements about what is perhaps a reasonable question which has spawned such a massive and patently 'unreasonable' literature, at times bordering on the verges of legal sophistry.

Simply put, it is logical that the subsidiarity principle was intended to be justiciable; if not one has to answer the question, why else would the drafters have put it into the EC Treaty which is explicitly open to judicial review, unlike other chapters of the Treaty of Maastricht? In John Pinder's opinion the terms of article 3b(2) tend to suggest that it was clearly designed to be operational legally; why bother otherwise formulating a test in such detail if it were not meant to be applied by a court like body? In doing this he refutes Bradely's thesis that Subsidiarity is more amenable to purely political language and should not be subjected to a legal scrutiny (Pinder, 1994:280)) Pinder suggests that if this proves a problem then a future way around this would be to specifically delineate the powers that are reserved to the Member States, as Australia and Canada actually do in their constitutions. In any event the Commission can still make environmental policy with the full force of law in a way which avoids Article 3b(2).

This is because one of the key thresholds regarding the drafting of Article 3b(2) is the qualification that it only applies to areas outside of the Community's exclusive competence. One should note that this does not mean that subsidiarity concerns are absent from other types of competences, as even other articles of the Treaty of Maastricht come under Article 3b(3)'s test for proportionality. Indeed, as per the Edinburgh Summit Protocol, all proposals must actually be tested for this.

Nonetheless, it is hard to demarcate which competences are exclusive and which are shared (or concurrent). Alan Butt-Philip makes a brief stab at it, in suggesting that agriculture, transport, Common Commercial Policy, management of the single currency, the Single Market and Customs Union provisions would all be exclusive to the EC. Newer areas such as Culture, Public Health, etc. are by virtue of their status in the TEU, clearly designed to be shared (Butt-Philip, 1994:128). Yet what of the environment?

Its clear that an activist Commission could perhaps legislate for environmental measures under Article 100a provisions which would link their objectives with the smooth working of the Single Market. There is after all the fundamental sense that environmental externalities if not properly controlled and regulated for in a single market will create dislocative effects and competitive advantages and disadvantages. In many cases it is clear that a majority of environmental directives has emerged under such a legal basis rather than merely Article 130r (4), which may be more open to interpretation as 'concurrent' competence area (Golub, 1996a).

Finally a few points about legal arguments for and against the 'justiciability' of subsidiarity. First, its not an argument against the concept to suggest that it is controversial and will create political 'heat' should European Judges decide on the issue. Judges in all jurisdiction have strayed into contentious policy areas if they see fit; witness abortion. Similarly the ECJ has not shied away from making decisions which are profoundly politically unpopular with a member state – witness the recent ruling on social legislation which the UK government lost to its bitter embarrassment. The ECJ is a powerful independent court, perhaps in some ways more independent that national courts, chosen as they usually are by national executives. The uniformity of a national interest in some way gets reduced in the background mix of the Court's composition and independent legal tradition.

Secondly, if it may be admitted that lawyers, particularly constitutional lawyers are fundamentally creative nowadays in their approach to argument, through doctrines such as implied rights and 'natural law', one should not perhaps worry too much for now whether we can construct a case of seeing subsidiarity as justiciable. Would it not be rather better to leave it to the lawyers to 'drive a coach and four through the laws of the land'? We can perhaps rest assured that when 'the' subsidiarity case comes, all legal parties will deal with it. As Koopman concludes after a survey of case law to see whether there may be any line precedent which might inform the Court, despite a paltry array of such evidence, he can still nonetheless take hope in the fact that 'the Court's case law gives a tiny indication in the direction of Subsidiarity.' (Koopman, 1994:55)

Thirdly, if we can think of the so called 'added value' test within Article 3b(2) as being applied in its most restrictive sense, to mere economic considerations of effectiveness which pervade issues of scale and predictability of effects, then it would nonetheless appear that environmental policy would fare at least as well as other regulatory policy areas. Indeed with the growth in the whole environmental economics school, this may allow for objective comparison in terms of economies of scale, etc. While we might say ideally that pure economic language would not be the most favourable one by which to compare the relative merits of environmental criteria (cf. Bercusson, 1994:167), it may nonetheless invite an approach which is not impossibly incompatible with securing comparative evaluations which in many cases could well validate the Community's role. In this regard at least one writer (Joerges, 1994) has made the obvious link with the American literature on comparative efficiency of different regulatory regimes, and its focus on economies of scale and dis-economies of scale, etc. (Joerges, 1994:58). Even critics such as Dehousse admit the possibilities of certain legal directions which the court could take, in his suggestion that the court in a line of cases where they have examined the 'statement of reasons' requirement for action, under Article 190, in a way which has not merely questioned whether the correct procedure has been established but also delved into substantive considerations as to whether these reasons are technically plausible (Dehousse, 1994:116).

To conclude: it is too early to tell as yet how the Court will view subsidiarity, however it would appear to be a relatively alarmist position to take to suggest the principle is at heart non-justiciable. For these reasons it does not seem that subsidiarity has altered the institutional basis of the Court.

Conclusions – understanding the EU's environment institutions after subsidiarity.

A number of brief conclusions may be offered at this stage, bearing in mind the above discussion. What has been attempted here has been to capture the reader's attention to the fact that subsidiarity does matter, and is not just 'pie in the sky' theoretical posturing. Secondly, it is important to state that subsidiarity as a higher constitutional principle is impacting on environmental policy and the environment institutions. Not only that, there is also *prime facie* evidence to suggest that the effect is one whereby a subtle 're-nationalisation' has emerged. This is at once a trend which may call into question the coherence of environmental policy but also the competences and effectiveness of the environment institutions themselves. In fairness we must await more detailed empirical studies before one can be substantively sure that EU environmental laws are being reduced in scope and vigour as a result of subsidiarity.

In terms of institutional dynamics, the fact that the member states have secured a shift to a fundamentally more acceptable form of environmental regulation, namely that of 'soft law' cannot be underestimated. While also in this light, those first crop of commentators who viewed subsidiarity as a vague and relatively insignificant concept, have proven perhaps misplaced in their dismissal of its power to govern institutional action in some important ways.

In practical terms the Edinburgh rules of application for subsidiarity are now also important 'meta'-rules governing the conduct and competence of the environment institutions. For this reason alone we must surely expand the brief sketch of a study of their impact on those institutions, which has been offered here.

As regards the substantive question of this chapter however, whether subsidiarity has made any difference to the EU's environment policy, the question is not merely an empirical one, but also a normative one in some ways. There is sense after all in asking whether it has as a principle made a difference or impact, if we can say it is one that is for the better or the worse. All too briefly perhaps, in the final sections of this chapter, ways have been tentatively suggested in which subsidiarity could affect the way the environment institutions work. What this has revealed, as much as insights on subsidiarity, is the fluid balance of institutional power between the various environmental institutions. In that regard the picture painted here confirms a view of those institutions with an intergovernmentalist orientation being clearly ascendant. One can draw one's own conclusions about what this augurs for substantive policy outcomes, depending upon one's perspective, but it is suggested that 'doing less, but better' may actually just mean that the EU's environment institutions end up doing less.

Notes

1   The EEB is not just 'any' environmental lobby. It was founded in 1974 and remains one of the best organised, widely supported and most respected of the various transnational European Environmental NGOs which have developed. Therefore its views must be arguably accorded at least some weight in the policy process.

2   Indeed provocatively, he cites the limitations of a transboundary test is the case of bird protection. Cleverly, Golub argues that some commentators such as Grant, have seen in the fact of European wide bird migration, a rationale for Commission involvement in what should otherwise be a local issue. However, if as he suggests only some half of the birds covered by the Birds Directive are actually migrationary, then this logic would fail to cover the non-migrationary birds under a right to EU level legal protection. This is however, a little bit too clever by half. For it ignores the fact that migrating and non migrating species may be interdependent upon each

other in terms of an overall habitat and ecosystem perspective. For example some non migrating birds of prey feed on migrants, and vice versa. If one is therefore interested in protecting a given species which migrates one must do so with reference to its overall relationship with other species, who perhaps do not migrate. To give a concrete example, where two bird species lived in proximity in the south of France with each other, and one was a migrant species, it would be a nonsense to permit national authorities allow hunters to shoot at the neighbouring domestic species just because they were not migrants and thus not protected by EU law. Such would be likely to led to accidental deaths of the protected migrant species, if not the complete end of a feasible protected status for the other birds. This is because hunters could falsely claim protected kills were accidental. More probably though there would be at least disturbance of nesting and reproductive cycles of the migrating species. Therefore what Golub seeks to take away from the transboundary test in terms of its utility, ornithology can actually defend. In conclusion this suggests the transboundary test is more robust than Golub would have us believe.

3   See: Proposal at the 1996 Intergovernmental Conference, On the Application of the Principle of Subsidiarity, submitted by the UK delegation' reproduced in *The European Review*, Volume 3, Number 1, October 1996. Centre for European Studies at the University of Essex, pages 40-42.

6 The Mobilisation of Ecological World Views in a Post-corporatist Order

DETLEF JAHN[1]

Introduction: ecological discourse in Sweden and Germany from the early 1970s until the mid 1990s

Over the last two or three decades environmental issues have received increasing significance on the political agenda of most industrial societies. This debate is very well reflected in the social sciences in the growing literature on the emergence of (new) environmental movements, Green and Left-Libertarian parties, the responsiveness of established political actors such as political parties, interest groups, bureaucracies and administrations as well as public opinion and the mass media.[2] However, very few studies attempt to analyse changes in the perception of environmental issues in whole societies.[3] And studies which do aim to move whole societies into the centre of their analysis focus in fact on media discourse (Gamson and Modigliani, 1989; Djerft, 1996; Brand et al., 1997). However, as I will argue in this essay, the media discourse may be of a different sort than more institutionalised discourses of collective actors.

In recent years, several authors (Hajer, 1995; Dryzek, 1997) use the analysis of environmental discourses in order to demonstrate the degree of 'greening' of modern society. These discourse analyses often have a comparative approach. The shortcoming of these studies is that they focus primarily on abstract discourses without clear reference to empirical evidence (Dryzek, 1997) or they concentrate on a specific issue and only the actors that take part in the issue-specific discourse (Hajer, 1995). Although both methods of analysis give ample evidence of important learning processes they neglect the institutional power struggle in society.

In order to overcome this limitation I would like to combine a discourse analysis with an institutional approach to the political process in modern society (Easton, 1979). An empirical analysis focusing on whole

129

societies has to face substantial analytical and methodological challenges. In this article I take a constructionist view by focusing on the shifting world views of collective actors as the basic actors of the political process in modern society.

However, the political process in contemporary society has changed fundamentally over the last decades. Well-structured interest aggregation and intermediation has been replaced by disorganised forms (Offe, 1985; Lash and Urry, 1987, Jahn, 1998b). One aspect of this has resulted in the political process becoming increasingly influenced by the definition of social issues. In social theory this transformation of society has been explained via the term 'reflexive modernisation' which implies a permanent confrontation of society with itself (Beck, Giddens and Lash, 1994). In particular, political communication receives a higher status in the field of social analysis (Habermas, 1981, 1989; Eder, 1996). However, even if the political process is more confused than before, it is possible to focus research on relatively stable factors within this fluid process. Collective actors are such stable factors which take part in a symbolic struggle over competing definitions of reality. I use the standpoints of collective actors because of their societal importance. This is particularly true for an analysis that focuses on cognitive aspects since collective actors '... stabilize themselves by referring to rules that carry in themselves legitimacy and consensus.' (Eder, 1993: 4, see also: Gamson, 1988; Sztompka, 1993: 221-222). In order to overcome the issue related bias I will focus on major actors of the political process in industrial society: the interest groups of Capital and Labour, the representatives of various ideologies in society which are organised in political parties, the mass media and indicators of public opinion as institutions of the public discourse, and finally different shades of the environmental movement.

I will focus my empirical analysis on Sweden and Germany. These two countries are especially instructive examples for use in the analysis of ecological discourse. While Sweden was particularly receptive to environmental concerns during the 1970s (Lindberg, 1977; Kitschelt, 1986), West Germany has an outstanding record concerning the strength of its movement sector (Frankland and Schoonmaker, 1992; Markovits and Gorski, 1993). Comparing these two countries enables me to deduce hypotheses about the effectiveness of ecological protest in two different settings. In Sweden ecological protest was quickly incorporated into established politics (Jamison et al., 1990) whilst in Germany it took some time for established political actors to respond to the ecological voices. This led some authors to conclude that Sweden, in sharp contrast to Germany, has detached itself from a productionist path where material aspects and economic growth are the principle imperatives for political action (Kitschelt, 1986). However, as recent trends document, Sweden is more pronounced in its productionist path than Germany and most of the other highly industrialised nations (Jahn, 1992; 1998a; 1999a). This leads us to the conclusion that structural explanations are insufficient for an understanding of political outcomes. The basic assumption in this essay is that the character and changes of the national ecological discourse of relevant collective actors provide a better understanding of social developments in both countries than the analysis of the political opportunity structure. As the results of this investigation show, the situation in both countries today is quite the reverse of the starting point in the early 1970s even if German unification has altered the intensity of the ecological discourse.

Interest mediation in a post-corporatist order

How new ideas enter into society and by doing so alter established world views is not very thoroughly analysed in empirical social sciences. As a starting point, for the analysis of interest intermediation in a post-corporatist order, a classical model of the political process can be employed (Easton, 1979) which distinguishes three spheres: First, the private sphere where interests and concerns are generated. Second, the political-administrative sphere (or the state) where decisions are taken and implemented and, finally, the public sphere or civil society where the interests and concerns are aggregated, articulated and negotiated by different actors.

Three types of actors can be distinguished which intermediate the interests in society and which hold various functions and status in this process: (new) social movements, political parties and interest organisations. New social movements are more embedded in the private sphere than the other organisations but they have no direct influence in the political-administrative sphere. In contrast, political parties are less strongly embedded in social milieus than new social movements. Instead, most notably through their representation in the parliament and in governments, they are deeply involved in the political-administrative system. Interest groups have a status between new social movements and political parties, although there is a huge variation between different organisations. What they share with new social movements, is their ability to articulate interests. However, due to their close contact with parties and administrations, most of them also have a greater influence on state decisions. This is especially true in countries with corporatist arrangements such as Sweden and Germany (Katzenstein, 1985). The parliament is often considered as the addressee of the struggling collective actors. Although its function has changed in recent decades, it is still an important institution for the translation of interests between civil society and the state. The mass media finally, receive a high status in new studies that focus upon the communicative aspects of society (Eder, 1995; Kriesi et al., 1995). They are able to influence public opinion on important aspects. However, as will be outlined below, the mass media has another function in civil society compared to the other collective actors. The following figure summarises the argument so far.

Figure 6.1   Collective Actors and the System of Interest Intermediation

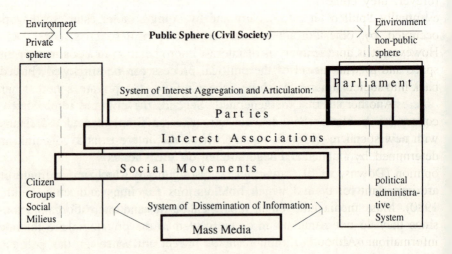

Source: The figure is based on the work by Easton (1979: 374). However, it has been modified by analysis by Katz and Mair (1995) and above all Rucht (1995: 108).

In a dynamic model it is possible to consider social movements as driving forces for social change. In his classical study, Herbert Blumer (1951: 54) describes social movements as '... one of the chief ways through which modern societies are remade.' Alain Touraine (1977: 298) sees in them 'historical actors,' Ron Eyerman and Andrew Jamison (1991: 26) label them as 'transforming agents of political life' or 'carriers of historical projects' and Piotr Sztompka (1993: 274-300) analyses them in terms of 'forces of change.' Social movements are therefore 'messages' (Melucci, 1989) and actors that redefine special issues and reality in general (Halfmann, 1989). New social movements act as 'forces of definition' (in reference to Karl Marx's term 'forces of production') by opening up a space for alternative interpretations in which interaction between different collective actors and world-views can take place. They carve out an actual societal space for possible versions of the future (Eyerman and Jamison, 1991: 4).

This perspective on social movements implies that they are neither permanent or long-lasting collective actors. Their life span is directly dependent on the symbolic struggle in a society: '... movements do not last forever, they come for a time, carve out their movement space, and get eventually "pulled" back into the society, as the space they create gets occupied by other social forces.' (Eyerman and Jamison, 1991: 65) However, it is an empirical question how deep they carved out a movement space and to what degree they bring societal change when they are pulled back into society again.

Another societal sector which remains relatively open to ecological concerns is public opinion and the mass media. However, even more than with new social movements, the representation of concerns in this field is determined by fluctuation. Media attention shifts quickly, as does public opinion (Downs, 1972). Nevertheless, public opinion and media discourse are important for the making and breaking of movement concerns (Gitlin, 1980). Mass media are not as institutionalised as other collective actors since they do not articulate and aggregate interests but rather disseminate information: 'Although the mass media play a crucial role in framing the themes and counter-themes of public discourse, the actual formation and transformation of collective beliefs take place in exchange within the groups and categories with which individuals identify.' (Klandermans, 1992: 89)

Established political parties are much more institutionalised in society than the former actors and areas. According to Seymour Lipset and

Stein Rokkan's thesis (1967) they are the institutionalised organisations of social cleavages which were once, or are currently, of predominant importance for Western societies. Given this perspective Green parties are an expression of the relevance of an ecological cleavage in society. Green parties in Sweden and Germany are important advocates for ecological concerns although they differ in ideology and status (Jahn, 1993b).

The responsiveness of established parties to ecological concerns is dependent on intra party coalitions, external pressures and party competition. These complex relationships cannot be discussed here in detail (see Jahn, 1999b: chapter 4), however it is important to mention that parties are important because they are well established in the political-administrative system through their activity in parliament and government. Nevertheless it would be wrong to conclude that other actors such as interest groups have no influence in a post-corporatist order. Some of these interest groups have gained a quasi public status (Offe, 1981). Within industrial society, influential interest groups focus on economic aspects so that it is fair to say that productionist world-views have an overrepresentation in modern society. Above all, the interest groups in the production sector (this term encompasses producing as well as service activities) are of outstanding importance because of their high societal status, on the one hand, and because this sector needs to be most directly transformed if ecological concerns are to achieve a higher status in society, on the other. In order to speak of a fundamental institutionalisation of ecological concerns the collective actors even in this societal sector must have been open to at least some of these concerns.

The argument so far can be summarised as follows: The degree of societal institutionalisation is dependent upon the mobilisation of ecological world views in different arenas and by specific collective actors in society. Social movement and protest activities may be considered as a distinctly superficial level of institutionalisation. The institutionalisation of environmental associations and Green parties is already one step further along the scale of societal institutionalisation. If ecological concerns become common issues in public opinion and the mass media they leave the 'ecological milieu' and enter into larger sections of society. However, this process does not imply that ecological concerns are stabilised. Ecological concerns penetrate a society when established political parties integrate ecological concerns in their party ideology and programme. Most importantly, the societal institutionalisation becomes deeply rooted when these parties express ecological concerns in parliament. However, the toughest test case for the societal institutionalisation of ecological concerns lies in the arena of industrial relations. This arena is the centre for production and, hence, the centre for a society which builds its identity upon growth and progress. If the collective actors in this field integrate ecological concerns in their programmes it is possible to speak of a high level of societal institutionalisation.

Another aspect of institutionalisation is *cognitive institutionalisation*. This aspect focuses upon the extent to which ecological concerns are expressed. It is possible to distinguish between, on the one hand, the established ideology of economic growth, technological development and expansion – this ideology I will term productionism since wealth production is at the centre of its orientation – and on the other hand the alternative-ecological positions such as small-scale production, decentralisation and a strong skepticism towards economic growth. This dichotomy of social orientation has been analysed via the concept of competing social paradigms (Cotgrove, 1982; Milbrath, 1984). However, instead of a dichotomy, it is possible to analyse the stands of political actors along a continuum.

Of course, the analysis of the ecological discourse(s) is complex and a dichotomy is without any doubt a simplification. New discourses have emerged such as 'ecological modernisation' and 'sustainable development.' These discourses aim to overcome the dichotomy between what I have called here productionism and ecology. However, what they do is to disengage the ideological core of political ecology such as the concern about self-determination, decentralisation of decision-making and reversibility etc. from environmental issues. Even more, they aim to connect environmental protection with the core ideological elements of industrial society such as economic growth and progress. If one accepts this argument then it is possible to judge these concepts on the continuum between productionism (without any environmental consideration), eco-productionism in various forms where ecological aspects are connected to the productionist ideology, and ecologism where the treatment of environmental issues is connected with ecological ideology. Similar attempts have been conducted recently where the continuum reaches from a treadmill approach of industrial society to an 'ideal model' of sustainable development (Baker et al., 1997: 8-18).[4]

The findings which will be presented in this essay later on are based on a much more complex analysis of various 'packages' (Gamson and

Modilgiani, 1989) which have been used in the ecological discourse in Sweden and Germany. However, in order to keep the analysis in focus for the developments of two countries over three decades I will report here the results in a graphic form without referring in further detail to the empirical part of the study (for further details see: Jahn, 1999b). Figure 6.2 summarises the nature of the two dimensions of institutionalisation of ecological world views in modern societies.

Figure 6.2   Dimensions of the Institutionalisation of Ecological Positions in Modern Societies

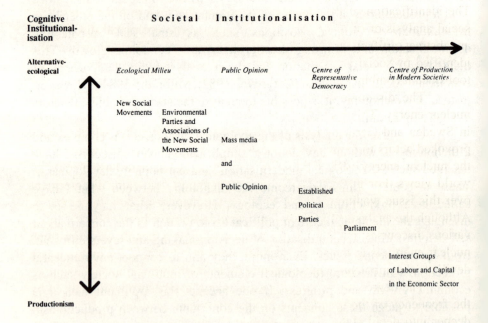

The more the ecological discourse is conducted in the upper half of the figure the stronger is the institutionalisation of the ecological political ideology. This is especially true when we move to the right part of the figure.

Discourse competition and discourse coalitions

Discourse analysis is one of the growing fields in environmental politics (see for instance: Litfin, 1994; Hajer, 1995; Eder, 1996; Dryzek, 1997; Jahn, 1999b). Most of these studies would probably agree that a discourse is a verbally expressed way of seeing things by a relevant groups of society. Of course, this definition is not without problems. For instance what are the 'things.' There is no ecological discourse as such but rather different discourses on various environmental issues such as acid rain, the ozone layer, nuclear energy, etc. The perception of environmental issues is largely dependent on scientific knowledge because they cannot – except from acute crisis or catastrophes – be directly experienced (Brand et al., 1997: 307). The identification of the underlying common themes are often a result of social analysis or of theoretical considerations. The ecological discourse is an abstract artifact, created by public and political communication and identified by social analysis. Nevertheless discourse analysis is a powerful tool since it combines aspects which are not immediately obvious.

The discourse analysis in this study refers to the perception of nuclear energy. This issue has been chosen because it is a politicised issue in Sweden and Germany over the last two or three decades which always provoked actors to express their views on it. The controversial character of the nuclear energy issue leads also to the expression of a huge variety of world views. For instance, nobody would support acid rain; disagreement over this issue would be mainly between the manner of how to combat it. Although the analysis of such an issue would also have been able to identify various discourses, nuclear energy provokes this in a clearer way. For some nuclear energy is at the top of technological development for others it is a devil's tool symbolising environmental destruction through human action.

The degree of the cognitive dimension has been operationalised by the frequency of the mentioning of specific views (*packages*). I cannot go deeper into detail (Jahn, 1999b: chapter 2) but these packages go from an uncompromising support of economic growth and technological progress to a reconstruction of current society according to the principles of no-growth and decentralisation. In between there are discourses which fall between these two extremes.

The second element in the definition of discourse above refers to 'a relevant group of society.' While most studies define this implicitly by including the actors which participate in the interpretation of an issue at a certain moment in time or over a time period, I include those actors in my empirical study which are key actors for the interest intermediation in modern society as mentioned above. Even if this approach may neglect some variation of the ecological discourse it includes those actors which may not be involved in the interpretation of the issue in a policy area but which may have 'veto power' on the societal level because of their important roles in society. However, I had to be selective in the inclusion of actors because of the huge empirical effort which this implies for a systematic analysis over three decades.

The (new) environmental movement can be considered as *forces of definition* as described above. Therefore I included the grass roots organisations MF, MIGRI, BUND and BBU in Sweden and Germany (see explanations in figure 6.3 for abbreviations). In particular in the 1970s these grass roots organisations introduced a new discourse to environmental issues. However, as has been pointed out, the discourse over environmental issues is not dominated by the environmental movement anymore but other actors, often the opponents of the environmental movement, which have conquered this terrain (Eder, 1996). This competition may have also occurred in the environmental movement sector which is composed of traditional, grass roots and other environmental organisations and which in sum may define the degree of the challenge for a given society (Diani and Lodi, 1988; Rucht, 1989; Jahn, 1996). Therefore I have included the traditional environmental associations in both countries (SNF for Sweden and DNR for Germany). However, a new challenge for the grass roots organisations are pragmatic, managerial organisations. A typical example of a managerial environmental organisation is Greenpeace (Jamison, 1996).[5]

Other interest organisations may represent other ideological aspects of industrial society which try to establish different discourses around environmental issues. The employer associations for instance may be the major actor for the productionist discourse oriented at economic growth and technological progress. Trade unions are another group of interest organisation which has been included in this study. While employer associations are representatives of Capital, trade unions are representative of Labour. But the labour movement is not a coherent actor (Touraine et al., 1987). The analysis of various trade unions (and left parties) here is also very illuminating in discovering the responsiveness of the labour movement to the new politics which some authors consider a necessary condition for the success of the new political actors (Offe, 1985). However, trade unions differ in respect to various cleavages (Jahn, 1993a). While the major difference between Swedish unions is between the blue collar, explicitly social democratic trade union (LO), on the one hand, and the white collar unions, organised under the umbrella of the politically neutral confederation TCO, on the other, in Germany the major differences are ideological. On one side there is the Metal workers' trade union (IGM) which represents the left wing of German unions (Markovits, 1986). On the other, the group of moderate or accomodationist unions, epitomised by the Chemical workers' union (IGC) and the Mine worker' union. The confederation of German trade unions (DGB) is often described as a weak confederation in comparison to its member unions and it often takes a stand between the two camps outlined above.

Political parties represent the relevant cleavages and ideologies of a given society (Lipset and Rokkan, 1967). The Social Democratic parties represent another branch of the Labour movement. Conservative and Christian Democratic parties often act in the interest of industry and may be considered as the party political wing of Capital. The same may be said for Liberal parties which may be, however, more open for new discourses and ideologies through their liberal attitude. Green parties, in contrast, are the party political wing of the grass roots movement and may promote the alternative-ecological discourse.

In the Swedish party system there are two further parties which I would like to call 'secondary environmental parties' (Jahn, 1999b: chapter 4). These parties put environmental issues high on their political agenda but they have non-environmental historical and ideological roots. This circumstance may lead to the situation whereby secondary environmental parties do not promote ecological world views to the same degree as Green parties and that they subordinate environmental aspects when they conflict with the primary ideology. In concrete terms these parties are the Centre Party and the Left Party. The former party has agrarian roots and promotes decentralisation and environmental aspects from the point of interest of the rural population and farmers. The Left Party in Sweden has a Communist tradition and turned to environmental attitudes in the early 1970s after it became politicised.

Even if parties may be divided in their ecological attitudes according to various dimensions which cannot be analysed here (Schmitt, 1987), one important aspect should be taken into account. Is the parliamentary group of a party less open for an ecological discourse than the extra-parliamentary party? If this is so than we could conclude that the ecological concerns are originating from the private sphere and enter through parties into the public sphere and finally into the political administrative system.

The mass media and public opinion is another actor in the public environmental discourse. As mentioned above, although mass media and public opinion may be highly relevant agents in the public sphere they have only indirect impact on the political administrative system and therefore on the degree of societal institutionalisations. The information of the position of the mass media and the public opinion is taken from longitudinal analysis of the media in Sweden (Djerft, 1996) and Germany (Kepplinger, 1988; 1989; Brand et al., 1997) and public opinion polls in both countries.

The above mentioned collective actors may differ or coincide in their ecological discourses. The more collective actors agree on one ecological discourse the more valid is this discourse in a given society at a given point in time. In order to make one discourse dominant various actors form 'discourse coalitions' (Hajer, 1995: 58-68) or 'advocacy coalitions' which are made up of people from various organisations '... who share a set of normative and causal beliefs and who often act in concert.' (Sabatier, 1987: 652) The approach of my investigation differs from the above mentioned approaches in that it focuses on collective instead of individual actors (see also: della Porta and Rucht, 1995).

In order to provide an overview of the changing positions of collective actors over three decades I distinguish only between two discourses. The productionist discourse which is supported by the 'Economic Growth Coalition' and the ecological discourse which is made up by the 'Eco-Coalition.' Of course, a more fine grained analysis would discover important variations of discourses within the spectrum of ecological discourses (Jahn, 1999b).

The making and breaking of discourse coalitions is a result of competition. Even if competition has an important status in modern approaches (Sabatier, 1987) no modern author is so explicit and elaborated in their analysis than the classical study of Karl Mannheim on 'Competition as a Cultural Phenomenon.' He (1952: 196-7) starts out by saying that '... from a view of the social sciences, every historical, ideological, sociological piece of knowledge (even should it prove to be Absolute Truth itself), is clearly rooted in and carried by the desire for power and recognition of particular social groups who want to make their interpretation of the world the universal one.' However, the '...struggle between different primary paradigmatic experiences peculiar to various concrete groups ...' (Mannheim, 1952: 198) is a dynamic process where actors change their attitude: '... whenever groups compete for having their interpretation of reality accepted as the correct one, it may happen, that one of the groups takes over from the adversary some fruitful hypothesis or category – anything that promises cognitive gain.' (Mannheim, 1952: 222) As has been mentioned above this adaptation of various discourse elements cannot be analysed here in detail. However, I will focus on shifting priorities in the context of the continuum between productionist and ecological world views.

Two dimensions will be used to clarify the position of the collective actors in the ecological discourse. First, the degree to which they refer to the productionist and ecological extremes as described above. This qualitative aspect of the ecological discourse is supplemented by the extent to which these positions are expressed. Both dimension together constitute the degree of the mobilisation of the competing world views.

The ecological discourse in Sweden and Germany from the early 1970s to the mid 1990s

In the following section I will analyse the stands of the above mentioned collective actors in the early 1970s, the late 1980s and the mid 1990s. These three periods are especially important in both countries. An analysis of the early 1970s reveals the situation at the beginning of the ecological protest. The 1980s can be described as the decade where environmental issues and concerns have been established in public debates. No matter how ambiguous concepts such as 'ecological modernisation' or 'sustainable development' may be, they demonstrate the penetration of ecological aspects into other areas of politics. The reactor accident at Chernobyl in particular, re-mobilised the anti-nuclear power movement and in this analysis it is possible to identify the extent to which political stands have changed during the decade. The 1990s are relevant for both countries because the continuity of development was harshly interrupted. German unification is known to most and needs no further explanation than to say that this event changed German politics. Regarding the ecological discourse it is fair to presume that it has been pushed from the political agenda by economic and national issues. But the Swedish development was also interrupted in the 1990s. The Swedish welfare state had been questioned and unemployment rose

Figure 6.3   Discourse Coalitions in the early 1970s in Germany

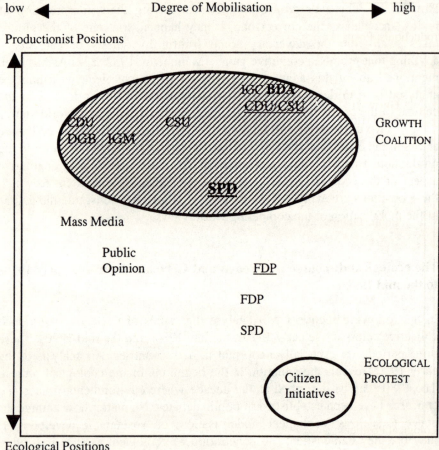

Explanations for this and the following figures:
- Environmental Associations:
(a) Traditional environmental organisations: SNF (Sweden), DNR (Germany);
(b) Managerial environmental organisations: Greenpeace (GP) in Sweden and Germany;
(c) Grass Roots organisations: MF and MIGRI (Sweden), BBU and BUND (Germany).
- Political Parties:
(a) Social Democratic parties: SAP (Sweden), SPD (Germany);
(b) Liberal parties: FP (Sweden), FDP (Germany);

Figure 6.4   Discourse Coalitions in the early 1970s in Sweden

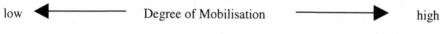

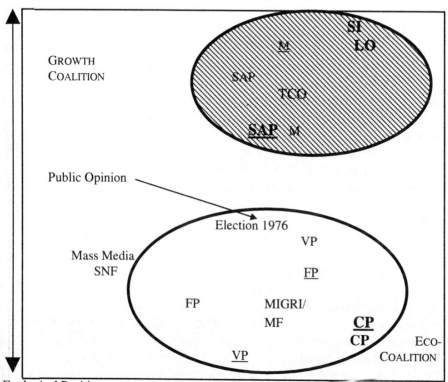

(c) Conservative parties: M (Sweden), CDU/CSU (Germany);

(d) Green parties: MP (Sweden), GRÜNE (Germany);

(e) Secondary Environmental parties: Centre Party (CP) and Left Party (VP) in Sweden.

- Interest Groups of Capital and Labour:

(a) Employer Associations: SI (Sweden) and BDA (Germany);

(b) Trade Unions: LO (Confederation of blue collar workers) and TCO (Confederation of white collar workers) (Sweden); DGB (Confederation), IGM (Metal workers union), IGC (Chemical workers union) (Germany).

dramatically. This was initiated by the right wing government under the leadership of the Conservative Party which came to power in 1991 but following the change of government the Social Democratic Party also subscribes to some essential elements of neo-liberal politics.

Figures 6.3 and 6.4 show the noticeably different starting points in both countries. The size of the labels of the different collective actors reflects their importance, and the depth of shading of the discourse coalitions represents the relative significance of the two discourse coalitions to each other. The darker the areas, the more dominant was the respective coalition at a certain time. The standpoints of the parties have been analysed in both the parliament (underlined) and at the party congresses.

For Germany, it is easy to see that the 'growth-coalition' promoting productionist politics clearly dominates the discourse in the early 1970s. This coalition includes protagonists from the political left and right, as well as 'progressive' left and more moderate forces. The major actors of an alternative world view can be found in the local citizen initiatives. Of the established political actors, the German Liberal Party (FDP) and the rank and file of the SPD were most open to ecological ideas. However it would be premature to suggest that these established parties would have joined the ecological camp.

The situation in Sweden was quite different to that in Germany in the early 1970s. Since the 1960s the former agrarian Centre Party (CP) had adopted an environmental policy by linking agrarian concerns over regionalism with ecological claims of decentralism. In the 1970s the CP successfully incorporated the nuclear power issue into its discourse and in the 1976 election this issue was a key factor in the change of government. From 1976 until 1982, though with significant interruptions, Sweden had a Prime Minister from the CP and the CP was the strongest party in the non-socialist bloc in the early 1970s. Through the CP the Swedish environmental movement had an established ally who represented their interests.

The CP even had an ecological complement on the left, the Left Party (VP). However, even if the VP was even more radical in its ecological stand it mobilised the ecological world views to a lesser extent than the CP. Furthermore the ecological profile of the VP was mainly expressed by the top of the party (in parliament) and much less so among the rank and file (at the party congress).

By and large the discourse coalitions of the early 1970s conform with the political opportunity structures described by Kitschelt (1986).

However, some aspects need to be mentioned because they are essential for an assessment of the openness of the political opportunity structure in both countries. First, the liberal parties were rather open to ecological concerns in both countries. The youth organisations especially, were important for the recruitment of new political activists. Furthermore, the mass media clearly contributed to the image of Sweden as an open society for ecological concerns. However, other factors do not conform to Kitschelt's conclusions. Above all it is important to note that, despite the greater challenge of ecological concerns, the mobilisation of productionist world views dominated in Sweden. Kitschelt painted a picture too favourable to ecological concerns. First of all the important collective actor of corporatism (trade unions and employer associations) remained firmly committed to productionist attitudes. Second, the ecologically open actors are extremely heterogeneous, stretching from the communist party, to agrarian interests, liberal attitudes and grass-roots activities. For Germany, Kitschelt neglects some substantial openness for ecological concerns within the FDP and SPD. Even if this influence has not been strong enough to change the policy of these parties it may have nevertheless fertilised the ground for fundamental opposition. This impression is justified when we turn our attention to the late 1980s.

In both countries the ecological discourse reached a new climax in the second half of the 1980s. One important factor was the reactor catastrophe at Chernobyl which, especially in Germany, had a tremendous impact (Koopmans and Duyvendak 1995). In Sweden environmental issues received top priority on the political agenda. The death of seals along the West cost of Sweden in particular, touched the hearts of many Swedes and the 1988 election has been labeled the 'ecology election' with the Swedish Green Party managing to enter the Swedish Riksdag; an achievement no other party had accomplished since the early 1920s (Bennulf and Holmberg 1990).

Figures 6.5 and 6.6 clearly document the differences between the ecological discourse in the late 1980s in both countries. In Sweden, the main protagonists of the ecological discourse were the mass media and the general public. The collective actors were rather moderate in their expression of ecological or productionist statements. In the growth coalition the Liberal Party (FP), shifting sides from the 1970s, was now most clearly expressing productionist standpoints. More important, however, is the increasingly heightened position of the Conservative Party elite (M). This

Figure 6.5   Discourse Coalitions in the late 1980s in Germany

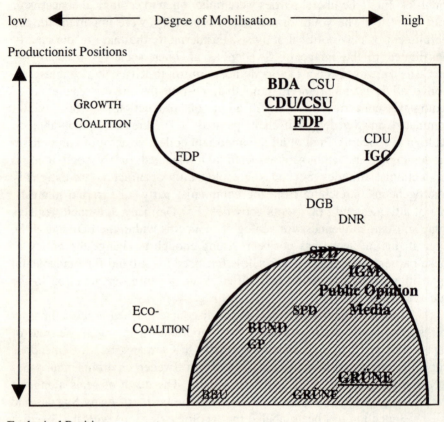

Ecological Positions

Figure 6.6   Discourse Coalitions in the late 1980s in Sweden

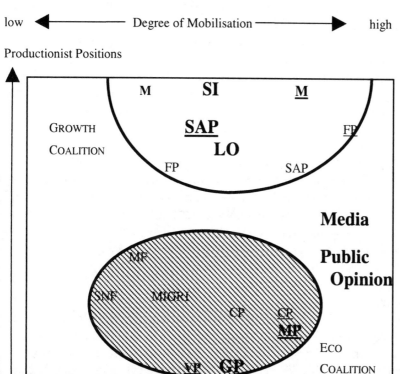

development went hand in hand with the electoral success of the (M). The (M) has become the strongest party within the bloc of the right of centre parties in Sweden, taking over this position from the CP. In this period it was the political parties in particular, rather than the employer association, which dominated the productionist discourse. On the other hand, there were also important changes in the eco-coalition. The Centre Party lost much of its ecological profile, whilst also experiencing a severe electoral decline. The movement organisations became almost invisible in the ecological discourse of the late 1980s and were hardly distinguishable from the traditional conservation association (SNF). In contrast to these actors, the Green Party, the VP and above all Greenpeace increased their activities in the ecological discourse in Sweden. As mentioned above, the Green Party (MP) succeeded in entering the Swedish parliament for the first time and the action and propaganda of Greenpeace resonated with the high media attention of environmental issues. However, the ecological discourse in Sweden was less radical and only very limited politically. It was 'pure' environmentalist.

The late 1980s were very different in Germany. Representation in the *Bundestag* since 1983 and increased participation in Länder-government made the German Greens leading figures in an important political discourse in Germany. Even if the mass media had a much less dominating role in Germany than in Sweden they also joined the ecological discourse (Kepplinger 1989; Brand et al. 1997). Ecological journalism became increasingly established in Germany during this period. More important however, was the changing attitude of labour. The SPD confirmed the view of Hanspeter Kriesi (1995) that social democratic parties may change their position towards ecological standpoints and become an alliance partner for new social movements when they are in opposition.[6] While Swedish labour remained productionist, the SPD increasingly joined the eco-coalition and the activist trade unions also emphasized their solidarity with ecological demands. This change, however, resulted in a deep split between the ecologically active camp within labour and the moderate wing which still adhered to productionist politics.

Even if the grass roots organisations also lost influence in Germany, they remained important figures in the eco-coalition and distinguished themselves from the traditional conservation association DNR. Greenpeace similarly did not play such a dominant role in the eco-coalition in Germany as it did in Sweden. It is fair to say that the ecological discourse was dominated by eco-political positions in Germany at the end of the 1980s. However, with German unification and the changes in Europe, the ecological discourse changed once more.

The primary change in Germany (see figure 6.7) concerned the diminishing level of mobilisation. Other discourses such as those of nationality and economy dominated the ecological discourse. However, the relative positions of the collective actors and coalitions remained stable even if the position of labour was less clear than in the late 1980s. The activist trade unions turned away from more radical ecological positions. On the other hand, the SPD elite increasingly became a member of the eco-coalition. The Green Party lost much of its influence at the national level by failing in the first all-German election. However, after re-entering the German Bundestag in 1994 they are again able to participate in the ecological discourse and they appear to be a strong political force.

The new German coalition government of Social Democrats and the Greens may foster an environmental policy more in line with the ecological political ideology than in any other country. However, as the position of collective actors show there is still a strong opposition to such a policy in Germany. Very important is also the split of the German labour movement. While there are some forces in the SPD which support the ecological ideology there are also some others which are more critical towards it. The new German Chancellor may be an ecological modernist quite reserved towards more radical changes.

The weakness of the eco-coalition was not counter-balanced by an increased radicalism and mobilisation of the growth-coalitions in Germany. Individual enterprises and firms as well as the CDU/CSU introduced environmental programmes. In sum, the ecological discourse in Germany in the first half of the 1990s had a low profile but displayed similar power positions to those of the late 1980s. Once the problems of unification and economic crisis are overcome there might be strong potential for an increasingly important ecological discourse. So far however, the 'cognitive infra-structure' has been preserved.

In this respect the situation in Sweden is completely different. The growth-coalition started an offensive which has no parallel in the last three decades. The Conservative Party and organised capital are the spear heads of this productionist attack. The emphasis upon productionist elements is embedded in the neo-conservative attack in Sweden which placed the Conservative Party as the strongest force within the non-socialist bloc. This

Figure 6.7   Discourse Coalitions in Unified Germany

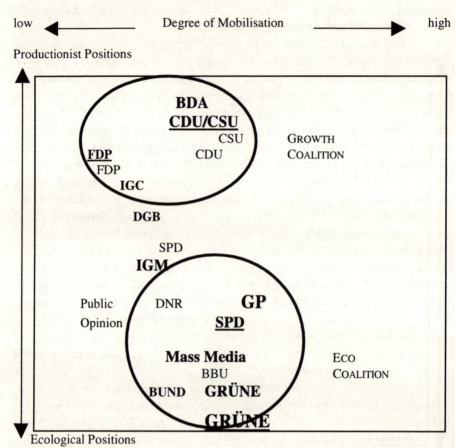

low ◄─────────────   Degree of Mobilisation   ─────────────► high

Productionist Positions

Ecological Positions

Figure 6.8   Discourse Coalitions in the 1990s in Sweden

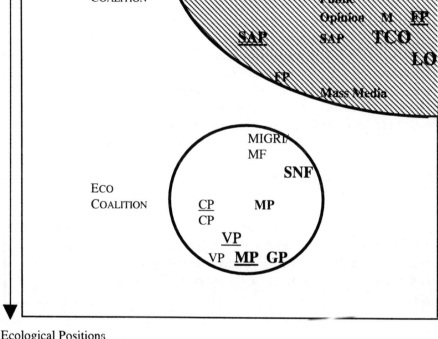

policy aims to dismantle the Swedish welfare state and to stress the economic aspects of policies. This radical market oriented approach gives little space for deep ecological aspects. This involvement of conservative forces even had fundamental effects on the media discourse and public opinion. Organised labour, especially the trade union wing, is clearly embedded in the growth-coalition. The SAP which returned to government in 1994, also prefers productionist solutions, although it is less clear on this position than the trade unions. This situation makes it very difficult for the environmental actors. The decreasing involvement of the two secondary environmental parties in the ecological discourse fundamentally weakened the eco-coalition. The development of the CP and VP clearly demonstrates that secondary environmental parties do not support environmental ideology to the same degree as genuine environmental actors (Flam 1994: 188). The same is true for managerial environmental organisations such as Greenpeace in both countries. The bleak picture for more radical changes in Sweden is complemented by the fact, that the grass roots organisations do not possess sufficient resources to re-vitalise the ecological discourse again. The major protagonists in the eco-coalition are the relatively moderate Green Party (Jahn 1993b) and above all Greenpeace. All in all it is fair to conclude that the ecological discourse is clearly dominated by productionist positions in Sweden in the 1990s.

This situation may not fundamentally change after the 1998 election when the Green Party (and the VP) support a Social Democratic minority government (see figure 6.8). The new Swedish government already pointed out that economic growth will be the major aim of its policy for the years to come.[7]

Conclusion

The mobilisation of world-views is a crucial factor in the interest intermediation of a post-corporatist order. A cognitive approach is superior to a structural approach. This could be demonstrated using the example of the ecological discourse in Sweden and Germany over the last two decades. Although the political opportunity structure is important for the initial period of the mobilisation of world views it does not determine the outcome of a protest cycle. Instead this is dependent on discourse coalitions which modify the degree of institutionalisation of ecological concerns in modern society. The processes of defining issues and reality depend on the mobilisation of cognitive resources and is more a question of the power relations between various collective actors than of structural conditions. According to the two dimensions of institutionalisation which have been employed to assess the changes in discourse coalitions, the findings of this empirical study clearly show that ecological positions are more strongly institutionalised in Germany than in Sweden. In reference to the outlined model, more fundamental ecological concerns could never penetrate Swedish society. The major obstacle has been the productionist stand of the labour organisations and the low key profile of environmental actors. In sharp contrast, in Germany the labour organisations carried the ecological position into societal arenas such as industrial relations which are highly relevant to industrial societies. However, the driving force of this development was the strong challenge of the grassroots movement which mobilised ecological world views much stronger than its Swedish counterpart and which was much later and less complete pulled back into society. Clearly the analysis supports the importance of cognitive alliances.

The findings of the analyses presented here appear to provide also a better explanation of the policy outcomes of the nuclear power conflict in Sweden and Germany than the political opportunity structure approach in this field. While the latter approach postulates a greater success for anti-nuclear positions in Sweden than in Germany, the former would suggest just the opposite. Although the anti-nuclear protest did not succeed in either country, it is clear that the nuclear power programme in Germany remained at an average level in relation to other western industrial societies. In sharp contrast, in Sweden the nuclear power programme is one of the largest in the western world. Together with France, Sweden has the highest proportion of nuclear electricity production and, in terms of nuclear energy production per capita, ranks as the leader among western industrial societies.

The analysis of policy regimes in environmental politics of the OECD-countries also demonstrates that Sweden, in contrast to Germany and other countries, pursues a productionist path, relying on high tech and an expansionist policy (Jahn 1998a).

In order to elaborate our knowledge of the political process in a post-corporatist order, more empirical studies, on various issues and in different areas are needed which combine a structural and cognitive approach and which consider the relations of actors promoting different world views. Such analyses would also qualify statements of conservative approaches which see no great changes in the process of interest intermediation and those who believe that modern society has already entered a qualitative new age of postmodernity.

Notes

[1]   The essay discusses some results from the research project "The Institutionalization of Ecological Issues in Modern Society" supported by the "Swedish Council for Planning and Co-ordination of Research" (FRN, *Forskningsrådsnämnden* (FRN): grant: 890721:2 A 8-5/105) in the framework of the "World Commission on Environmental and Development," the "Minister of Research and Technology of the Federal Republic of Germany" (BMFT, grant: SWF 0048 0) and the "German Research Foundation" (DFG, grant: Ja 638/2-1). A more detailed analysis can be found in D. Jahn (1999b) *Zur Institutionalisierung ökologischer Standpunkte in modernen Gesellschaften*. Baden-Baden: Nomos.

[2]   The literature in these areas is substantive and cannot be summarised here. For instance major current publications with a comparative perspective on environmental movements and organisations: Dalton and Kuechler 1990; Dalton 1994; Kriesi et al. 1995; Green and Left-Libertarian parties: Müller-Rommel 1993; Kitschelt 1988; political parties: Dalton 1991; interest groups: Siegmann 1985; Jahn 1993a; Hildebrandt and Schmidt 1994; bureaucracies and administration: Lundqvist 1980; Vogel 1986; Paehlke and Torgerson (1990); public opinion: Hofrichter and Reif 1990; Inglehart 1989; mass media: Eder 1995.

[3]   Partial exceptions are the studies of Jamison et al. (1990) focusing on the ecological debate in Denmark, Sweden and the Netherlands in the form of comparative narrative country case studies or Eder (1993) who analysed key mass media and the environmental discourse of collective actors. More formalised studies relying on public opinion and questionnaires are the study of Kriesi (1993) on the Netherlands and Laumann and Knoke (1987) on the USA.

[4]   However, in the above mentioned continuum the authors use the concepts anthropocentric versus ecocentric as the two extremes. These more philosophical standpoints, mainly from the Anglo-Saxon tradition of ecological thinking, may be differently applicable than the reference to political ideology of empirically existing ecological movements (summarising overviews over the ideological aspects of ecology are supplied by Cotgrove 1982; Paehlke 1989, Goodin 1992; Milbrath 1993).

[5]   A managerial environmental organisation is characterised by a hierarchical organisational structure without a great degree of grass root participation and an action repertoire which is in accordance with an *adhocracy*, i.e. to fuse experts into smoothly functioning ad hoc teams (see Jahn 1999b: chapter 3).

[6] However, this hypothesis does not work in all the aspects. The Swedish SAP was in opposition between 1976 and 1982 and did not change its productionist stand. The same is true for their opposition period in the early 1990s. In fact only the German SPD confirms the thesis when they changed positions in the early 1980s.

[7] The moderate position of the Swedish Green Party can also be seen in the fact that their anti-EU stand created more difficulty for an arrangement with the SAP than the claim of a more profound change of the productionist policy of the government. Even the Swedish Green Party seem not to challenge the growth oriented policy of the SAP.

PART III
IMPLEMENTING
ENVIRONMENTAL POLICY

7 Negotiated Science – The Case of Agricultural Biotechnology Regulation in Europe

SUSAN CARR and LES LEVIDOW[1]

Introduction

For decision-making about environmental risk, politicians rely increasingly on scientific advisers, yet their expertise is increasingly challenged. These challenges come from scientists as well as from environmental pressure groups. Given the unknowns in anticipating environmental impacts, there are various possible ways to generate and interpret scientific knowledge for decision-making. These differences often become the focus of disputes and protests.

In such circumstances, negotiated science offers a means to democratise risk assessment, through new forms of precaution and participation. Precaution allows time to gather more scientific information, encompassing a broader range of cause-effect models, while involving a wider constituency in discussion. Through such participation, scientific evidence and expertise can be scrutinised for their value-laden aspects, which can then be held publicly accountable.

Negotiated science is illustrated here by the regulation of agricultural biotechnology in Europe. Although an EC directive established a common basis for regulating the release of genetically modified organisms to the environment, member states have interpreted and implemented the directive in quite different ways, influenced by their domestic context. In response to public debate, some have developed new forms of precaution and participation, from which other European countries may learn. Such attempts have relevance to any environmental dispute over how to frame scientific unknowns.

Managing environmental uncertainty

Environmental questions do not have simple answers. Indeed, any answer depends on how the question is framed. Often, decision-makers downplay environmental uncertainties by treating the issues as if they were easily resolved by scientific methods and objective analysis alone. This approach only serves to heighten disputes.

Central to the complexity of environmental issues is the way in which biophysical causes are entwined with social and political ones. In addition, the cause-effect links may not be readily apparent. Feedback loops may reinforce or dampen anticipated effects. The problems fall untidily across disciplinary boundaries. Sub-division into component parts to make the problems easier to investigate may mean that researchers neglect important interactions, including synergistic or antagonistic effects. Research findings depend upon how the questions are asked.

Environmental problems often involve risk and uncertainty, again with social and political aspects intertwined. As with the pressures to frame all complex problems in terms of questions amenable to scientific measurement, so there are similar pressures to represent all forms of uncertainty as risks. As Wynne (1992) argues, such an approach can lead to poor decisions with potentially serious consequences. He distinguishes between four different types of unknowns: risk (where the odds are known); uncertainty (where the odds are currently unknown but the data needed to determine them are known or may be eventually obtained); ignorance (where we don't know what it is that we don't know); and indeterminacy (where behaviour is unpredictable, and thus outcomes open-ended; and/or where the validity of our present knowledge depends upon specific conditions). Wynne suggests that indeterminacy is embedded within the definitions of risk, and pervades even apparently technical questions. How, then, can these diverse unknowns be acknowledged and evaluated in decision-making?

The twin concepts of participation and precaution have been suggested as means to handle complexity and uncertainty, and thus to improve the resilience of environmental decision-making. Wider participation has been proposed as a means to evaluate different accounts of science. O'Riordan and Cameron refer to this democratic process as 'civic' or 'negotiated' science:

[A concept of science-democracy partnership] raises the issue of civic science, or a negotiated science in which participation becomes a means of brokering knowledge and valuation between scientific processes and public opinion. Precaution opens up the scope for this, because precaution encourages thoughtful and creative dialogue between an activated citizenry and the wider scientific community (O'Riordan and Cameron, 1994: 66).

In elaborating on this process, Hunt (1994) has proposed that there should be wider participation in groups providing scientific advice, with all participants having equal status, and all procedures being accessible. Through a 'democratisation of science', its status could be shifted 'from being the objective, final arbiter to a more conditional and consensus seeking knowledge form, which allows other forms of knowledge equal standing'. By acknowledging the inherent uncertainties of science, 'advisory groups might manage them to produce consensus rather than to utilise them in conflict' (Hunt, 1994: 123-24). In this way, decision-makers might gain greater public trust.

That argument has been made most forcefully for decisions which involve high stakes and uncertainty. Particularly in such circumstances, supposedly objective criteria should not be the only basis for judging the usefulness and validity of knowledge; rather, an 'extended peer community' can provide relevant 'extended facts', including anecdotal evidence (Funtowicz and Ravetz, 1992: 254).

Although participation and precaution may seem simple, neither concept is easy to implement in practice. Both are subject to widely differing interpretations. For example, participation may mean simply informing the people affected only after a decision has already been taken, or interactive joint analysis, or people themselves taking the initiative and only turning to external institutions when they need resources or advice (Pretty, 1995, Table 1).

Precaution has equally varied meanings. In a limited version, precaution means adopting a cautious approach until more scientific data are gathered. In a stronger version, precaution means acknowledging the indeterminacy of scientific knowledge, while linking potential harm with the question of who needs the hazardous activity -- who will be the beneficiaries and who the losers (Hunt, 1994).

Both these concepts, participation and precaution, meet resistance from traditional institutions. Even when the principles are formally adopted, there is a tendency to develop minimalist versions. There is concern that the precautionary approach will unduly restrict research and innovation, and that participation will delay decision-making. Although participation and precaution may have such results, equally the traditional approach may leave decisions vulnerable to further protest and delays.

Negotiated science offers a potential means for eventually achieving a legitimate and stable decision. Scientific expertise can be supplemented by public input, in the form of locally relevant knowledge and social values. For incorporating such values into expert decision-making, European countries offer various models from which others may learn: 'Diversity is the strength of Europe, not its weakness or problem' (Renn, 1995).

As an example, we examine the regulation of agricultural biotechnology in the European Union under the Deliberate Release Directive. We identify the lessons to be learnt from the experience of member states in devising various forms of precaution and participation for that purpose. In so doing, we illuminate the concept of 'negotiated science', that is, a democratic process for generating and evaluating scientific knowledge for decision-making.

The Deliberate Release Directive

The Deliberate Release Directive (90/220/EEC) was enacted in 1990 in response to public controversy in Europe about the potential impact of genetically modified organisms (GMOs). The wording of the Directive was admirable in its precautionary intent and scope. Before any evidence that GMOs could cause harm, it set the basis for a cautious stepwise procedure and case-by-case approval system. To oversee the notification and approval system, each member state is required to designate a 'Competent Authority', which has the responsibility to ensure that GMO releases do not cause 'adverse effects' on the environment or human health.

Anyone intending to release GMOs into the environment is required to notify regulators in advance and to submit a risk assessment, including any measures necessary to avoid harm. Controls can be gradually relaxed only after earlier steps, such as confined or small-scale releases, have shown that the next step can be taken. Each different combination of crop and genetic modification requires separate notification and assessment (EEC, 1990).

Applications for placing a product on the market, originally envisaged as the final step, involve an EU-wide approval procedure. After a member state has considered an application for commercial release and decided to recommend approval, other member states have the opportunity to respond. Objections are discussed at a formal meeting of all the Competent Authorities and are ultimately resolved by a qualified majority vote if necessary. By linking precaution with commercialisation, the Directive aimed to 'establish harmonised procedures and criteria' across Europe, and thus 'to complete the internal market' for genetically modified products.

The Directive requires public access to information before decisions are taken. Each member state must establish a public register of GMO release applications and may not withhold details specified by the Directive. It also suggests that member states may want to consult with the public. A more general requirement for information to be made publicly available was established by the Directive on the Freedom of Access to Information on the Environment (EC 90/313).

The Deliberate Release Directive established a common basis for GMO regulation throughout the EU, while leaving room for flexible interpretation.Such flexibility has been a key strategy for achieving agreement in international negotiations (Birnie, 1992). In the late 1980s model of harmonisation, Europe-wide safety approval was to be achieved through a 'mutual acceptance of data' among countries, rather than by establishing a new bureaucracy to set Europe-wide standards (e.g. Pelkmans, 1987). As examples of flexible interpretation that relate to precaution and participation, we analyse how member states defined the expertise to evaluate the risk assessment, the 'adverse effects' to be prevented, and the role of the public in the decision-making procedure.

The Competent Authority: defining expertise and risk

As each member state interprets the Directive, a key element has been its choice of ministry to be the Competent Authority, as well as its selection of advisers who may share responsibility for decisions. The choice affects how regulators define the risks, seek additional scientific information, and provide public access to decision-making. In the survey of member states below, the risk assessment of herbicide-tolerant oilseed rape serves as a case study for comparison (see also Levidow et al., 1997).

In Germany, which has had intense social conflicts about biotechnology, regulation has had the explicit aim of promoting biotechnology as well as preventing hazards. The government appointed the Health Ministry as the Competent Authority, because it was seen as more sympathetic than the Environment Ministry to the biotechnology industry. The German Competent Authority has considered only the most severe, immediate and clear-cut risk scenarios -- for which it was criticised by the Environment Ministry.

In Germany, administrators expect their decisions to be accepted by virtue of having followed the formal regulations, backed up by scientific expertise (Gill, 1996). They presume that there is only one correct interpretation of the law and only one rational outcome, so that objectors must be irrational. The narrow focus of their risk assessment excludes all the broader political and ethical issues that are central to the public controversy, thus precluding meaningful dialogue with environmentalists. An environmentalist representative originally joined the advisory committee but soon left, seeing little role to play. In addition, Germany has blamed the Directive for restricting biotechnology activities there, thus blaming EC law for its own domestic problems (Gill, 1996). Germany has thereby become somewhat marginalised in EU level discussions about the Directive.

In Denmark, where there have also been fierce social conflicts about biotechnology, the government developed a quite different approach to implementing the EC Directive. Each release application is considered through an open dialogue between the Ministry of the Environment and a parliamentary sub-committee, which raises concerns from environmental NGOs. Thus, by acknowledging the value-laden character of risk assessment, the government implicitly defines the relevant expertise to encompass all citizens. Under such pressure, Denmark has taken a broad view of the 'adverse effects' that should be considered. For example, for herbicide-tolerant oilseed rape, Denmark has criticised risk assessments for ignoring the inadvertent development of herbicide-tolerant weeds, which could preclude some environmentally preferable weed-control options and thus adversely affect overall herbicide usage.

Both the Netherlands and the UK have selected their environment ministries to be the competent authority. Each has a broad-based advisory committee that includes an environmentalist, industrialists and various scientific disciplines, including ecologists. This mixture facilitates consideration of ecological uncertainties. For the herbicide-tolerant oilseed rape, Dutch advisers emphasized the potential effects on biodiversity, while signalling the herbicide implications for the Environment Ministry to consider. The UK advisers and regulators did consider the weed-control implications but concluded that herbicide-tolerant weeds would be acceptable because they could still be controlled by using existing herbicide treatments. Neither the Dutch nor the UK procedures considered wider uncertainties such as the impact of the crop on overall herbicide usage.

In France, the competent authority is the Ministry of Agriculture jointly with the Ministry of the Environment, though the latter generally played a deferential role until the late 1990s. The government advisory committee is composed predominantly of molecular biologists. They perceive any risks as resulting mainly from genetic imprecision. Implicitly, they assume that if the precise genetic construct of the GMOs is known, then the risks are known too. This perspective provided little scope or interest to explore ecological uncertainties. As in the UK, the inadvertent development of herbicide-tolerant weeds was viewed as an agricultural-economic problem, outside GMO regulation. Although the committee included an environmental NGO, this representative rarely challenged safety claims.

After public protest intensified in 1997, however, the French advisory committee found that its earlier advice came under challenge from other scientists as well as from environmentalists. Such critics cited new scientific evidence, for example, that herbicide-tolerance genes can escape to weedy relatives and persist in the environment. Subsequently, a ban was imposed on commercial crops of herbicide tolerant oilseed rape, even though France had originally advocated its approval. Monitoring was required for commercial use of insect-resistant maize, even though this requirement had not been advocated by France at EU level (EC, 1997). The French Environment Ministry has now established its own advisory committee, whose membership includes environmental NGOs (Roy, 1998).

In various ways, then, some competent authorities more carefully consider environmentalist concerns, more thoroughly explore scientific uncertainties, and more actively involve other interested parties in the decision-making process, for example, within advisory committees. Environment ministries have gone further to accommodate precautionary perspectives than have agriculture and health ministries. Moreover, the competent authorities of the UK, the Netherlands and Denmark have been able to exert relatively greater influence in EU-level discussions, perhaps because their precautionary approach has given them greater opportunity for constructive discussion, critical reflection and learning in their domestic regulatory environment (Levidow et al., 1996).

Information disclosure and public participation

Member states vary widely in the extent to which they meet the Directive's requirements for disclosing information about release notifications. Apart from the type of representation within advisory committees already mentioned, few countries include public participation in the decision-making process, although some have encouraged public discussion of the issues. The various forms of public access can be analysed as part of state strategies for managing public debate (Boehmer-Christiansen, 1995; Levidow, 1998).

In Germany (and Belgium), NGOs have more easily obtained information from the notifiers themselves than from their governments; such access belies government excuses for withholding information, such as commercial confidentiality or avoiding procedural delays. Under general environmental law in Germany, citizens are permitted to obtain information on hazardous activities in their own locality and to challenge such decisions in public hearings. In effect, this law does not entitle them to obtain information on commercial release applications, since these are not location-specific.

Initially, Germany's 1990 Genetic Engineering Act provided mandatory public hearings for each field test consent. These hearings became lengthy set piece confrontations and were abolished when the law was amended in 1993. Deprived of any meaningful opportunity for constructive involvement, opponents expressed their views more by direct action, for example by disrupting field trials.

In response to the controversy, the German government sponsored a technology-assessment exercise on herbicide-tolerant crops in the early 1990s. Environmental NGOs argued that the technology assessment should compare biotechnology products to other potential weed-control methods, as alternative solutions to agricultural problems. However, the organisers rejected the NGOs' proposal; they restricted the remit to a risk-benefit analysis of herbicide-tolerant crops as such. Finding themselves in a 'participation trap', the environmental NGOs withdrew before the exercise could report its conclusions (Gill, 1993).

In the UK, the UK Department of the Environment adopted the view that 'secrecy breeds fear'. Early on, it established a public register with summaries of the information about each release. It tries to persuade notifiers to minimise the amount of information to be kept confidential. However, NGOs rarely sent comments to the advisory committee, partly because the regulatory procedure excluded important environmental concerns.

Although the UK government itself has not stimulated public debate on biotechnology, indirectly through its research councils it has helped fund initiatives aimed at 'promoting public understanding'. For example, in 1994 the Biology and Biotechnology Research Council funded a National Consensus Conference on Biotechnology, organised by the Science Museum, in which a lay (non-expert) panel put questions to experts. According to the organisers, the panel's report gave 'qualified support' for biotechnology. However, the report questioned who benefits from the present research and development priorities. It emphasized deficiencies in risk regulation, in ways similar to criticisms by environmental NGOs. Some critical views were omitted because the panel was required by the organisers to present a single 'consensus' report, without any minority views (Purdue, 1995). More recently, the government initiated a public consultation exercise by first setting up a steering group with representatives from academia, industry and consumer organisations (Goddard and Patel, 1998). However, this got off to a bad start when a government press release ignored the views expressed by the committee at the first meeting (Hill, 1998).

The Netherlands' competent authority places the entire dossier for each GMO release notification, including any associated correspondence, on shelves in their library, to which the public have open access. A leading environmental NGO, which also has a statutory representative on the advisory committee, regularly challenges permits for GMO releases through the administrative court, although this considers only technical-legal objections, not substantive risk assessment issues. The competent authority has developed an open negotiating attitude to all relevant parties, funding workshops on unresolved risk assessment issues and inviting various groups to help develop risk-assessment criteria (von Schomberg, 1996).

In Denmark, Parliament funded environmental NGOs to raise public debate on biotechnology as early as the mid-1980s, to ensure a well-informed public involvement from the outset. It then funded a consensus conference, which defined the risk issues to include sustainable agriculture. These events indirectly influenced legislators and regulators to frame risk assessment broadly, thus maximising scope for public participation (Toft, 1996).

Denmark routinely circulates summaries of notifications to a list of interested organisations, and supplies the full dossier on request. The public is granted access to every aspect of the regulatory discussion. Such information is then used to prepare for the Parliamentary hearings on each case. That procedure exemplifies the Danes' long tradition of developing policy by consensus, by involving all the main interested parties in negotiations to reach an acceptable solution. Despite early public opposition to GMO releases, the consultation process has allowed Denmark to reach consensual decisions to approve trial releases, as well as to oppose some marketing applications on grounds that the risk assessment ignores wider effects, for example, the implications for herbicide use if farmers grow herbicide-tolerant crops.

Initially France provided no detailed information on release applications, despite the requirements of the EC Directive. Such secrecy exemplified the French regulatory culture of centralised administrative control. Eventually this strategy collapsed in the face of growing opposition to biotechnology in 1997. In 1998 the government held a citizens' conference to consider all potential effects of genetically modified crops in France. Citing the report of the lay panel, the government reiterated its earlier decision to ban commercial use of herbicide-tolerant oilseed rape (Roy, 1998).

Harmonisation pressures

Soon after the 1990 Directive was enacted, it was attacked as irrational by some sectors of industry and government. Critics argued that it unjustifiably discriminated against GMOs on grounds that they result from a particular technique, thus implying that genetic modification makes organisms more risky. There were political disputes about the need to change or replace the Directive, even before it had been implemented in most member states.

In subsequent policy documents on biotechnology, the European Commission emphasized the need to enhance industrial competitiveness. It distinguished between 'science-based' safety regulation and the 'value-laden issues' surrounding biotechnology, thus implying that risk assessment is free from value judgements. The Commission sought to ensure that the regulatory requirements are 'commensurate with the identified risks', thus implying that any risks are readily identifiable (see references in Levidow, 1994).

In the early 1990s the Commission promoted harmonisation by asking CEN (the Comité Européen de Normalisation) to help establish a 'standard technical environment' for GMO regulation. According to some promoters of CEN, it should decide which GMOs require safety regulation and how safety standards should be set. However, this task proved to be impossible because member states did not agree on what 'adverse effects' must be prevented. CEN accepted the more modest role of providing advice on the technical aspects of satisfying data requirements.

The divergent stances of member states, especially in defining which 'adverse effects' must be prevented, have led to political pressures on regulators to harmonise their regulatory criteria. Regulators have been put on the defensive to demonstrate that their risk assessments are objective and soundly 'science-based'. Such pressures have threatened to weaken the precautionary nature of the regulations, to restrict opportunities for addressing wider environmental concerns, and even to deter regulators from acknowledging the practical difficulties of risk assessment.

As another subtle pressure on regulators, the 'step-by-step procedure' was generally cited to mean that environmental uncertainties would be progressively resolved with each step. Certainly the intermediate steps have allowed regulators some time and opportunity to think through the various uncertainties and to clarify regulatory terms in actual cases. Some regulators emphasize that field trial releases have shown no untoward effects, implying that commercial approval is a definitive final step. However, few claim that these have provided significant knowledge about the possible impact of large-scale commercial use.

Market-stage precautions

Facing increased public protest in the late 1990s, some regulators and companies began to treat commercial approval as a larger experimental step. They developed plans to minimise and/or monitor undesirable scenarios which were not officially regarded as 'adverse effects' when market approval was granted for EU-wide commercial use. These plans both accommodated public concerns and provided additional opportunities for public involvement.

For example, in the UK, opposition intensified during 1997-98, with widespread demands for a moratorium on the commercial use of genetically-modified crops. For oilseed rape, the debate focused on two related scenarios: the inadvertent generation of herbicide-tolerant weeds, and the destructive effects of broad-spectrum herbicides on wildlife habitats in or near fields. Such scenarios had been officially regarded as not 'adverse effects' when commercial approval was granted (EC, 1996). Even so, the Agriculture Ministry was already funding large-scale trials to research both issues and provide management guidelines for growers (Sweet et al., 1997).

Given that herbicide-tolerant weeds could jeopardise the efficacy of the product, the UK agricultural supply industry prepared management guidelines of its own. These are intended to prevent the spread of herbicide-tolerant pollen and volunteers (crop plants that persist to become weeds). Preventive measures include labelling, segregation of seeds, spatial separation of crops and monitoring. The guidelines state that 'Failure to comply will result in sanctions' by supply companies against negligent farmers (BSPB et al., 1998).

To take another example, insect resistance management (IRM) has now become quasi-mandatory for cultivating 'insect-protected maize' in Europe. This maize contains toxin genes from the naturally occurring microbial pesticide *Bacillus thuringiensis*. There has been concern that long-term exposure to such insecticidal crops could intensify selection pressure for toxin-resistant insects. If so, then this effect could reduce the utility to farmers of the naturally occurring microbial pesticide, thus eliminating an alternative to chemical pesticides. However, EU-wide market approval was granted to the first such product on the basis that reduced efficacy of the insecticidal agent would not be an 'adverse effect' (EC, 1997). Nevertheless, the relevant companies have undertaken to implement IRM plans for their products (for example, see EC, 1998).

Further precautionary measures have been introduced under the procedures for adding new plant varieties to the National Lists. For insecticidal crops, France and Spain require monitoring for various environmental effects, including insecticidal efficacy, insect resistance to the toxin, and harm to non-target insects (for references, see Levidow and Carr, in press). In France, the monitoring is to be evaluated by the new, broadly-based advisory committee of the Environment Ministry.

So, although market-stage precautions are not a general requirement of the Directive, moves are already underway to establish special protocols and monitoring measures for the commercial stage. There has been some discussion about whether the Directive should be changed along those lines, for example, to require monitoring during a seven-year conditional consent for marketing products (CEC, 1998).

Policy opportunities and dilemmas

As shown by these international comparisons of biotechnology regulation, public debate offers regulators some opportunities. Wide-ranging risk debates have stimulated regulators to reflect more carefully on the justification for their own views, and to consider a wider range of potential impacts than they might otherwise have done. Environmentalists have challenged the inadequacy of available knowledge and so stimulated further research on unknowns relevant to risk assessment. Citizens' conferences have made proposals to strengthen the precautionary controls.

However, public debate also presents regulators with dilemmas. If they adopt a narrow definition of 'adverse effects' and/or of 'expertise', then they can more readily carry out risk assessments to approve GMO releases as safe. Yet such an approach does little to accommodate public concerns and gain public legitimacy for the decision-making procedure. Moreover, if new scientific evidence strengthens the plausibility of undesirable effects, then regulators further lose credibility.

By contrast, if regulators define 'adverse effects' and expertise more broadly (as in Denmark and latterly in France), then they have a stronger basis to encourage and accommodate a wider public debate within the risk-assessment procedure. This approach may mean opposing or delaying commercial approval until more scientific information is obtained about the effects of a product, as in the case of Denmark and France opposing commercial use of herbicide-tolerant oilseed rape). Such participation and precaution is important for the legitimacy of decisions.

Negotiated science

The case of biotechnology regulation illustrates conflicts around negotiated science, that is, about how scientific knowledge shall be generated and evaluated for decision-making. Regulators face pressures to approve genetically modified products as speedily as possible so that they can be commercialised and cultivated just like their conventional counterparts. From other sources, they face pressures to adopt further precautions or even to impose a moratorium on commercial releases. One response is to promote harmonised regulatory criteria, which means downplaying unknowns and/or restricting the range of undesirable effects which must be prevented. An alternative response is to acknowledge unknowns and to evaluate a broader range of undesirable effects.

The alternative response offers greater opportunity for precaution and participation. Unknowns are investigated by continued research to support risk-assessment, by field trials designed to simulate commercial use of genetically modified crops, and by special management protocols to guide commercial use. Scientific evidence and expertise are scrutinised, for example, by parliamentary hearings in Denmark, by a new advisory committee in France, and by citizens' conferences in several countries. These experiences offer diverse models from which other European countries may learn.

Such measures can be understood as democratising risk assessment, through new forms of precaution and participation. Unfortunately, the consequent delays or special restrictions are often labelled as 'political', that is, as diverting risk assessment from its proper basis in science. However, public debate has already challenged some value-laden aspects of safety judgements, such as the acceptability of particular adverse effects. Given these disputes, negotiated science offers a means to hold such judgements publicly accountable, thus facilitating robust decisions which can eventually gain public legitimacy. In this respect, negotiated science has relevance to any environmental dispute over how to frame scientific unknowns.

Note

1   This essay arises from two studies: 'GMO Releases: Managing Uncertainties about Biosafety', funded by the European Commission, DG XII/E1, during 1994-95; and 'Safety Regulation of Transgenic Crops: Completing the Internal Market?', funded by the European Commission, DG XII/E5, during 1997-1999.

8 Policy Learning within and between Countries – Waste Policy and Policy Styles in the Netherlands and Bavaria

JAN EBERG

Introduction

Environmental problems are unstructured political problems, and the field of environmental policy is dynamical and refractory. One way to deal with this, is to improve our understanding of the problem context and the range of problem perceptions. This means we should investigate both the institutional and constructivist factors that influence environmental policy changes over time. From that, we can draw lessons to enhance the implementation and internationalisation of environmental policy. This chapter concentrates on the role of policy oriented learning in environmental management. Policy-oriented learning involves relatively enduring changes of thought as a result of analysis, experience, and public and political debate. Two kinds of policy learning are distinguished: (1) learning within and across advocacy coalitions *within* a country, and (2) learning *between* countries. The promotion of learning processes creates possibilities to structure political problems and to explore new problem-solution combinations. This central argument will be illustrated with data from a comparative research on waste policy and waste incineration management in the Netherlands and Bavaria. A reconstruction of the Dutch and Bavarian waste policies revealed different learning processes and learning styles. It also showed the impact of a specific policy style or characteristic way of policy-making, and points to the constraints and opportunities for learning between countries.

Waste problems and waste policy

Waste problems are part of environmental problems, which have become urgent social problems. Generally, environmental problems arise when larger societal units (groups of individuals, as well as organisations or institutions) consider a certain environmental effect caused by a certain activity as negative, and therefore start a debate about this activity, the level or scale of exertion and/or the technology employed. Put otherwise: Environmental problems are the consequences of human influence on the physical surroundings which people experience as problematic. Hence, environmental problems are societal problems. Perceptions and experiences involved, depend on norms and values, time and place, as well as the associated technical, economic and political contexts.

Waste problems are primarily related to pollution, which can be defined as the introduction in the environment of chemical compounds and physical phenomena, in amounts larger than normal background levels, and in such a way that damage is done to people, animals, plants, ecological systems, and cultural properties. *Waste* consists of restproducts of production, services, consumption and processing activities, and all other substances people want to do away with. Often, part of the waste can be re-used or recycled. As Gourlay (1992: 19) properly observed: 'Waste is more easily recognised than defined'. Wastes could be all kinds of emissions, effluents, remains, left-overs, or left-behinds, and what is eventually called waste will depend on the actual context.

Besides physical, chemical, biological and geographical factors, there is a social side of environmental and waste problems. On the one hand, social structure and cultural patterns will influence the extent to which waste problems occur. On the other hand, the degree of effects caused by the amount, toxicity, dispersion, or concentration of wastes will be assessed and experienced differently by individuals and groups. These differences depend not only on the specific situation people are in, but also on their cognitive involvement. Information is limited and often not widely available or understood, and perceptions are biased. Consequently, people's concerns are often diverse.

Waste policy, by definition, addresses the waste issue, whenever and wherever this arises. Basically, two main waste policy objectives are conceivable. First, to arrange a waste management structure that deals with the existing wastes and the additional daily produced waste streams in an efficient and effective way. Second, to adjust the waste management structure and the behaviour of people in order to ensure a reduction of the total waste volume and to establish safer conditions regarding waste treatment and disposal (T&D). These objectives point to ideal situations for the present and the future, respectively. Corresponding strategies and instruments would be to respond to the situation that is perceived as problematic and anticipate improvement, whereas supportive instruments would be drawn from either existing sets of regulations and technologies or new sets to be developed.

The waste issue can be typified as an *untamed* or *wicked* problem (cf. Rittel and Webber, 1973; Douglas and Wildavsky, 1982). It means that consent is contested and knowledge about the future is uncertain. Of course there are some rough ideas about the nature of the policy problem and possible problem-solution couples. But when it comes to detailed policy planning and implementation, there is no consensus about the problem definition and policy objectives, nor about the kinds and use of strategies and instruments. Furthermore, expertise is ambiguous. Waste policy faces just this kind of problems. Many different actors all have their specific responsibilities, rationalities, interests, and 'positions' in the waste T&D sector. Besides, the waste management structure is in a constant state of flux. Conditions are continuously changing, and 'solutions' may be the sources of new problems. This may impede co-ordination, planning, and implementation of the relevant tasks. Waste management is not just another public policy issue. It is a refractory policy field where predicaments prevail.

Policy analysis of waste management: the Advocacy Coalition Framework

The study of waste policy dynamics implies several analytical choices and considerations. Some general observations, however, should be borne in mind. First, as mentioned, the waste issue is an untamed policy problem. Second, policy processes are inherently dynamic. Many modern as well as classical policy scientists have pointed at the existence and influence of a variety of aspects that are connected with policy development and policy change. Numerous studies looked into policy change as a dependent variable (e.g. Lindblom, 1968; Heclo, 1974; Kingdon, 1984; Sabatier and Jenkins-Smith, 1993), and several new or changed subjects still need to be explained. In addition, today's politics are 'on the move', not only in terms of administrative decentralisation and internationalisation, but also in terms of 'sub-politisation of society' (Beck, 1992), that is the shift of political action from the traditional power centres to uninstitutionalised actors (e.g. consumers, marketers). Third, policy change involves learning processes. Processes of policy change are influenced by power struggles, conflicting interests, political pressures, political choices, changing discourses, and also by the improvement and exchange of knowledge and beliefs. In policy-making, learning is an appropriate strategy to deal with intractable policy problems (cf. Argyris, 1976; Schön and Rein, 1994; Hisschemöller and Hoppe, 1996). In policy analysis, learning is a supplementary perspective from which to study policy change (cf. Bennett and Howlett, 1992; Eberg et.al. 1996). And fourth, learning processes are context-bound. Both the policy-maker and the policy analyst will notice that learning processes are bound up with short-term and long-term constraints. This refers to all kinds of situational and specific conditions (cf. Rose, 1993). In the short run, it mainly concerns the presence and rates of information and communication. More sustainable constraints can be summarised as institutional and cultural factors. This also means that, depending on the context, learning processes differ in extent and in style.

Waste policy-making will be better understood when, besides its development of contents, outputs, and impacts, also its roots are studied. Knowing more about the underlying policy styles and political cultures helps to explain the differences between the several waste policy belief systems involved. This requires a general theoretical framework of short-term and long-term policy changes. A major contribution to political theories of policy change and learning is made by Paul Sabatier, who developed a general framework, applicable to a wide variety of policy domains and political systems. This is the Advocacy Coalition Framework (Sabatier, 1987; Sabatier and Jenkins-Smith, 1993), which focuses on both policy learning as well as the effects of system-wide events on the resources and constraints of subsystem actors.

According to the Advocacy Coalition Framework (ACF), policy change over time is a function of three sets of processes:

(1)   The interaction of competing *advocacy coalitions* within a policy subsystem. An advocacy coalition is an analytical construct. It consists of actors from a variety of positions (elected and agency officials, interest group leaders, researchers, etc.) who share a particular belief system, and who show a nontrivial degree of parallel action over time. Coalition actors seek to translate their beliefs into public policies throughout the intergovernmental system. The

concept of an advocacy coalition assumes that it is shared beliefs that provide the principal 'glue' of politics.

(2)   *Changes external to the subsystem* in socio-economic conditions, public opinion, system-wide governing coalitions, and decisions from other policy subsystems.

(3)   The effects of *relatively stable system parameters*: the basic attributes of the problem area, the basic distribution of natural resources, fundamental socio-cultural values and social structure, and the basic constitutional structure.

The ACF proposes that belief systems of advocacy coalitions are structured into three categories, arranged in order of decreasing resistance to change:

(1)   A Deep Core of fundamental normative and ontological axioms that define an actor's underlying personal philosophy;

(2)   A Near Policy Core of basic strategies and policy positions for achieving deep core beliefs in the policy area or subsystem in question;

(3)   A set of Secondary Aspects comprising a multitude of instrumental decisions and information searches necessary to implement the policy core in the specific policy area.

Policy-oriented learning

The framework defines policy-oriented learning as relatively enduring alterations of thought or behavioural intentions that result from experience and are concerned with the attainment (or revision) of public policy. Policy-oriented learning involves perceptions concerning external dynamics, and increased knowledge of problem parameters and the factors affecting them. The framework assumes that such learning is instrumental, that is, that members of various coalitions seek to better understand the world in order to further their policy objectives.

Policy-oriented learning is a form of information and argumentation management. The ACF distinguishes two types of policy-oriented learning: *within* a coalition's belief system, and *across* the belief systems of different coalitions. The first type of learning means that members of an advocacy coalition are seeking to improve their understanding of variable states and causal relationships consistent with their policy core ('puzzle-solving'). The second type of learning refers to a productive analytical debate between members of different advocacy coalitions. One or more coalitions are led to alter policy core aspects of their belief system (or at least very important secondary aspects) as a result of an observed dialogue rather than a change in external conditions. The basic argument, however, of the ACF is that, while policy-oriented learning is an important aspect of policy change and can often alter secondary aspects of a coalition's belief system, changes in the policy core aspects of a governmental programme are usually the results of outside the subsystem, altering the distribution of political resources among coalitions within the subsystem.

The ACF is but one model in the tradition of policy learning (cf. Bennett and Howlett, 1992). Nevertheless, it is different from several other theories on policy learning who all emphasize *levels* of learning. These general categories are: instrumental learning and conceptual learning. *Instrumental learning* refers to an improvement of policy instruments without questioning the underlying policy objectives. It is a reaction to ineffective decisions. *Conceptual learning* refers to a revision of policy concepts, i.e. fundamental policy positions. It is a reflection on problem definitions, policy goals and strategies. The general levels of learning can be combined with the forms of learning according to the ACF. These four types of learning are related in the sense that instrumental and/or conceptual learning may occur within one coalition belief system or across – two or more – coalition belief systems (see table 8.1).

Table 8.1   Types of Policy Learning

	Learning within a belief system	Learning across belief systems
Instrumental learning	active change of secondary aspects of coalition A	interactive change of secondary aspects of one or more coalitions
Conceptual learning	active change of policy core beliefs of coalition A	interactive change of policy core beliefs of one or more coalitions

It should be noted that 'instrumental learning' is, in fact, the same as policy-oriented learning according to the ACF. Both can cause changes at the level of secondary aspects of a policy actor's belief structure. However, whereas 'conceptual learning' points to changes at the policy core level, the equivalent factor according to the ACF would be 'perturbations in non-cognitive factors external to the subsystem'.

Analysing processes of policy change and learning according to the advocacy coalition approach enables one to structure both institutional and constructivist aspects of the policy process. This is especially appropriate to a policy field as dynamical as waste management.

Advocacy coalitions in Dutch and Bavarian waste incineration subsystems

Waste management is a comprehensive policy domain. Specific empirical data has been gathered concerning Dutch and Bavarian waste policy developments in the subsystems of municipal and hazardous waste incineration (Eberg, 1997). Waste incineration subsystems can be mapped out along cognitive lines by advocacy coalitions and the corresponding belief structures which (most) 'member' actors have in common. Policy subsystems and advocacy coalitions are continuously changing. Coalitions may change in terms of size and relative strength, and coalition age might sometimes be confusing for not all coalition actors 'step in' at the same time. It is assumed that co-ordination is mainly informal. Members of the same coalition are rather striving for the same policy programme (elements) instead of following a joint and formally developed strategy, although the latter might well be the case when several actors are closely co-operating within their institutional field.

The Dutch waste incineration subsystem consists of three advocacy coalitions regarding the incineration of municipal waste, and three coalitions regarding the incineration of hazardous waste. In Bavaria, two advocacy coalitions were found to be involved in municipal waste incineration, and just one in hazardous waste incineration. There is some overlap with respect to the policy actors that are members of these coalitions. For example, the Dutch Rijnmond Waste Processing (AVR) incinerates municipal as well as hazardous waste, and some environmental organisations actively oppose both types of waste processing. The following review is confined to the most directly involved policy actors.

Advocacy coalitions involved in Dutch municipal waste incineration are:

(1)   The Thermal Recycling Coalition, which considers waste-to-energy processes as 'green electricity': incinerators, their interest organisation the Dutch Waste Processing Association, and like-minded actors from the waste processing (technology) sector.

(2)   The Incineration Prevention Coalition, which considers incineration as a hazard to public health and the environment: environmental protection organisations (the Netherlands Society for Nature and Environment; Dutch Greenpeace; the Foundation Waste and Environment; and the Dutch Friends of the Earth), and 'green' political parties at different administrative levels.

(3)   The Incineration Supervision Coalition, which considers incineration as one of different processing possibilities that have to be weighed against socio-economic developments: governmental agencies (the Ministry of Housing, Physical Planning and Environmental Management, VROM; provinces, municipalities, the Dutch Waste Management Council, and the National Institute of Public Health and Environmental Management.

The three advocacy coalitions involved in hazardous waste incineration are:

(1)   The Incineration Procedural Coalition, which thinks that hazardous waste incineration is both a necessary and efficient way of internal end-processing that should be part of agreed T&D procedures: AVR-Chemicals, its shareholder companies, the municipality of Rotterdam, the provinces, and the Ministry of VROM.

(2)   The Incineration Prevention Coalition, opposing hazardous waste incineration for the same reasons as municipal incineration: the environmental protection organisations mentioned earlier.

(3)   The Processing Development Coalition, which endeavours to raise the quality of hazardous waste processing by means of self-responsibility and self-regulation: the Dutch Association of Chemical Waste Processors (NVCA) and its members from the hazardous waste processing sector.

Bavarian advocacy coalitions with respect to municipal waste incineration are:

(1)   The Incineration Prominence Coalition, which beliefs incineration to constitute an important part of waste management: central government agencies (the Bavarian Ministry of Land Development and Environment,

StMLU; the Bavarian Bureau of Environmental Protection, LfU), waste incinerators and their interest association, the waste industry, and large energy firms.

(2)   The Incineration Prevention Coalition, which fiercely opposes waste incineration, considering this as part of a dissipating economic-technocratic structure: citizens' groups (led by *Das Bessere Müllkonzept*, BMK), environmentalist organisations (e.g. *Bund Naturschutz Bayern, Robin Wood*), and political parties (the Greens; the *Ökologisch-Demokratische Partei*).

The one advocacy coalition concerning hazardous waste incineration in Bavaria is:

(1)   The Processing Procedural Coalition, which strives for integrated hazardous waste management, using state-of-the-art technology. This is standard procedure since the very beginning of hazardous waste management in Bavaria. The coalition consists of government (StMLU, LfU), hazardous waste generators, and the two organisations for the management of hazardous waste: ZVSMM in the district of Central Franconia and GSB for the rest of Bavaria. Opposing or alternative coalitions are absent, mainly because of the early establishment and well-functioning of the existing hazardous waste T&D structure.

Learning processes in Dutch and Bavarian waste incineration subsystems

Instrumental learning within a belief system

In all four waste incineration subsystems, there has been an almost continuous improvement of policy instruments, either on the basis of trial-and-error, experiences in other situations, or innovations that reinforced the resources to support the policy objectives. In the Netherlands, instrumental learning within belief systems was found in the case of municipal waste incineration where the Incineration Supervision Coalition and the Thermal Recycling Coalition not only strengthened but also broadened their belief structures by the expertise of the Waste Management Council and Waste Processing Association respectively. The same holds for the Dutch Association of Chemical Waste Processors in the Processing Development Coalition concerning hazardous waste incineration. The Incineration Procedural Coalition in this case attributed its regulatory and technological progress to 'learning by doing' and 'learning by experience'.

In Bavaria, learning within belief systems was more common which can be explained by the dominance of the Incineration Prominence Coalition and the solitude of the Processing Procedural Coalition. Both coalitions reinforced their belief systems by extension of knowledge and influence. The former convinced executive waste authorities of the importance of a municipal waste incineration infrastructure. The latter endeavoured to apply the best technical means and performance in order to keep its leading position.

Instrumental learning across belief systems

Policy-oriented learning across belief systems occurred with several issues. In general, both municipal waste incineration cases showed that policy beliefs of the Incineration Prevention Coalitions were incorporated into the belief structures of other subsystem advocacy coalitions. In the Netherlands, this applied to ideas about risk management and the use of alternative processing methods. In Bavaria, a clear example emerged from the confrontation of the two advocacy coalitions during a 'national' plebiscite over the 1991 Waste Act. The Incineration Prominence Coalition included accommodated beliefs from the Bavarian Incineration Prevention Coalition on the role of municipalities, the funding of new MVAs, and controlling emissions and immission. The Dutch case, in addition, revealed a mutual adoption of beliefs between the Thermal Recycling Coalition and the Incineration Supervision Coalition. The first adopted the belief that economic and environmental interests should be balanced, while the second adopted the belief that waste incineration is also a useful means of energy recovery.

As far as hazardous waste management is concerned, this type of learning could only occur in the Dutch multi-coalition subsystem. It pointed to a similar role of the Incineration Prevention Coalition compared to municipal waste incineration. Furthermore, there has been an adoption of instrumental beliefs by the Incineration Procedural Coalition from the Processing Development Coalition, i.e. that the share of end-processing should decrease in favour of more 'upstream' processing, and that the role of permits should decrease in favour of environmental management systems.

Conceptual learning within a belief system

Revision of policy concepts as a result of reflection on problem definitions, policy objectives and strategies is quite an incidental learning process, but has nonetheless taken place in all four subsystems. In the Netherlands, the Incineration Supervision Coalition expanded its policy goal of protecting public health and the environment to environmental management, which introduced an integrated approach to waste problems. Furthermore, both the Incineration Supervision Coalition and the Thermal Recycling Coalition adjusted their disposal strategies towards the concept of 'thinking from fractions', which means collection and treatment of separate waste streams. Regarding hazardous waste management, the Processing Development Coalition incorporated environmental care into the goals for its activities.

In Bavaria, an early conceptual change was marked by the transformation from disposal to prevention and recycling in the waste policy programme of the Incineration Prominence Coalition. This was part of the Bavarian land development plan for economic and ecological modernisation. In accordance with this, the Processing Procedural Coalition (hazardous waste) adopted a public-private monopoly model of integrated hazardous waste management, including risk management by responsibility, in the early 1970s. At the end of the 1980s, this coalition incorporated the concept of public participation in their risk management strategy.

Conceptual learning across belief systems

This type of learning, finally, was rare. One example can be found in the Netherlands where the Incineration Prevention Coalition expanded their policy strategies with the belief of deliberation and dialogue from the Incineration Supervision Coalition. Similar processes of conceptual learning probably also happened the other way around. These are indicated as conceptual learning within belief systems. Nevertheless, these changes have, most likely, been influenced by the Incineration Prevention Coalition. In Bavaria, where this type of policy learning could only occur in the municipal waste management subsystem, it was not found. The most plausible reason for this is the large difference in coalition strength.

The impact of national policy styles

As it appeared from the Dutch and Bavarian cases on municipal and hazardous waste incineration, policy learning should be recognised as one of different forces and mechanisms that contribute to (waste) policy changes. However, we should also acknowledge that these processes are embedded in a national political structure which to a great deal determines the preconditions for policy change and learning.

General waste policy developments show that Bavaria, as compared to the Netherlands, made an early start and kept its lead until today. Roughly stated, waste policy in Bavaria was already quite mature at the beginning of the 1980s, whereas at that time Dutch waste policy was getting afoot. Besides the difference in tempo of waste policy development, there is also a difference between the two countries in the mode of that development. Bavarian waste policy has been confidently structured and thoroughly elaborated from the beginning, while waste policy in the Netherlands has been seeking its way through to find balance. Regarding the whole period of waste policy development, both major differences may characterise this development in Bavaria as smooth and steadfast, and in the Netherlands as fragmented and restless.

The early and steady development of the Bavarian waste management sector resulted from specific policy initiatives that were taken under specific conditions. This enabled cultural preservation and economic progress to go hand in hand fruitfully. Furthermore, the political climate was stable, and the ruling CSU was dominant and influential at every societal level, which facilitated decision-making. In the Netherlands, both the conditions for waste policy to develop as well as the forming of advocacy coalitions were different. Government was less anticipatory, government and business acted less concertedly, and policy positions were distributed over more belief systems of advocacy coalitions.

The 'why' of waste policy change and learning in the Netherlands and Bavaria can be explained by the long-term developments in the political and cultural climate of the individual policy systems, which result in specific institutional structures and policy styles. Especially since the work of Richardson (1982, also Richardson and Watts, 1985), we speak of policy styles as the central characteristics of the policy process in particular countries. Richardson (1982: 13) defines policy style as 'the interaction between (a) the government's approach to problem-solving and (b) the relationship between government and other actors in the policy process'. This leads to a categorisation of societies into four basic policy styles: anticipatory/active problem-solving vs. reactive problem-solving in combination with either a consensus relationship or an imposition relationship. According to this, the Dutch policy style would be typified as reactive-consensual, and the Bavarian style as active-impositional. However, this does not leave much room for gradation. The concept of policy style can also be defined in a broader manner as a characteristic way of policy-making and policy implementation which is supported by the sum of institutions underlying the policy process. Subsequently, this can be specified into four categories of policy style aspects:

(1)   historical-cultural aspects, like state formation and the development of socio-cultural 'pillars';
(2)   juridical-administrative aspects, like the development of a constitutional system and bureaucratic structure;
(3)   socio-economic aspects, like modernisation and the development of production sectors; and
(4)   political-organisational aspects, like democratisation and the development of decision-making structures.

All these aspects contribute to the evolution of a specific political-administrative tradition. A combination of these aspects will provide a unique portrait of the national (or, in a case like Bavaria, state) policy.

The national policy style is an important explaining factor for the waste policy of a country. As Richardson and Watts (1985: 2) remark: '[..] countries tend to regulate, say, pollution, in much the same way (style) as they regulate other policy sectors'. In addition, the specific sector policy of waste and environmental issues is also influenced by two more factors. First, the national image of nature, which is expressed by -historically shaped- beliefs about the value of nature and the connections between man and nature (cf. Eder, 1993; Dobson and Lucardie, 1993). Secondly, policy style and image of nature are indissolubly linked to the physical-geographical aspects of a country, like its location and ecological structure, constituting basic constraints and possibilities.

The Netherlands vs. Bavaria

Together, the national policy style aspects, the national image of nature, and the physical-geographical aspects of a country, encompass the 'relatively stable parameters' and 'external (system) events' of the Advocacy Coalition Framework, and more. It requires thick description to go into all these aspects in detail for the Netherlands and Bavaria. Therefore, the following gives a synoptic (and for that reason also somewhat stereotypical) impression.

The Netherlands is a flat, densely populated, and intensively cultivated country. Its sea and rivers formed the basis for a transit-economy with heavy industry. Dutch culture is imbued with commerce and Calvinism, as well as with a tradition of pragmatic tolerance. In this century, this tradition was expressed by pacification, pillarisation, and 'a policy of the lesser evil' (*gedoogbeleid*). Furthermore, the officialdom has no clear identity, policy-making suffers from fragmented institutionalisation, and decision-making is directed to negotiation and consensus. The Dutch image of nature is connected to the eternal struggle against the water. Real nature is gone, and the environment is considered part of the economy. Commitment to the environmental issue is rather extrinsic: the Dutch devotion to fight today's waste problems is derived from the Calvinist moralisation of the domestic, and the rites of cleanliness.

Bavaria is an inland state that has been decentrally cultivated in conjunction with the mountainous and wooded mid-European structure. It has experienced a tempestuous post-war transformation from an agricultural land to a modern, high-tech service economy. The Bavarian Model of tradition and progress is rooted in a culture of 'national' identity, federalism, constitutionalism, centralism, formalism, and *Vorsorge* (precaution). The public administration system is characterised by a 'Weberian' bureaucracy, based on rational-legal authority. The Bavarian image of nature has been nourished by Romanticism and the ensuing '*Wald-im-Kopf*' mentality (or involvement with the weal and woe with the wood). The environment is considered part of the culture. This induced a rather intrinsic commitment to the environmental issue: environmental protection as cultural conservationism.

The policy styles of the Netherlands and Bavaria have their impact on both policy implementation and policy learning. The Netherlands can be labelled as a country of 'tolerance and tortuosity'. Laborious pursuit of consensus is superior to all other political rules of the game. Hence, its environmental policy shows signs of 'window-dressing'. Achievements do not meet the ambitious goals, and while environmental policy has become considerably professional and procedural, there is a gulf between the policy intentions on paper and the policy impacts in practice. Waste policy has been fragmented and bothered by an implementation deficit.

Bavaria can be labelled as a country of 'prudence and precaution'. It inclines to follow a preventive and calculative course in order to avoid risks, both regarding the environment and the economy. In result, the government continuously played a pro-active and participative role concerning environmental policy, and employed *Vorsorge* as a leading principle. Waste policy has been planned and implemented in an integral way.

Learning styles in the Netherlands and Bavaria

The Dutch and Bavarian policy styles are also reflected in the characteristic waste policy learning styles of each of these countries. In the Netherlands, there are no harsh conflicts between the advocacy coalitions. On the one hand, disagreements are genuine and every advocacy coalition will try to do its best pursuing its case. But on the other hand, policy positions in the end appear to be flexible and matters get settled. The multi-coalition subsystem with coalition powers more or less equally distributed, leads to learning processes with the emphasis on communication, deliberation, and co-operation. This can be qualified as consensus-oriented learning, and as 'learning by interacting' (cf. Lundvall, 1988). In addition, the considerative attitude of the advocacy coalitions also implied a certain degree of reservedness, waiting, and safe play. This resulted in an adoptive learning style.

In Bavaria, a quite different learning 'climate' prevailed. The developments in the subsystem of municipal waste management can be characterised as formal, persuasive, and full of conflict. The common feature was the picture of earnest and committed advocacy coalitions. However, waste management in Bavaria has been dominated by the Incineration Prominence Coalition and the Processing Procedural Coalition, which implied mainly coalition-internal policy learning. In this process, emphasis was put on quality, responsibility, and dutifulness. This resembles what Van Gunsteren (1985) has called 'learning by analysis and instruction': experts carry out analyses, after which a rationally presented solution will be instructed by the authorities to the rest of the community. Furthermore, the coalitions followed a vocation of professionalisation and progress, which can be described as an innovative learning style.

The waste policy learning strategies of the Netherlands and Bavaria can also be described by Wildavsky's (1988) ideal-type concepts of, respectively, resilience and anticipation. The Dutch strategy of resilience refers to trial-and-error or learning by experience. Changes are dealt with after they have become manifest; a concept like sustainability is gradually discovered. The Bavarian strategy of anticipation refers to trial-without-error or learning by foresight. Changes are averted, unless there is sufficient evidence that they will have no or negligible impact; sustainability is chosen *a priori*. Aspects of the Dutch and Bavarian learning styles are summarised in table 8.2.

Table 8.2   Learning Styles in the Netherlands and Bavaria

The Netherlands	Bavaria
'Learning by interacting' (consensual)	'Learning by analysis and instruction' (hierarchical)
Adaptive learning style (following)	Innovative learning style (pioneering)
'Resilience' (trial-and-error)	'Anticipation' (trial-without-error)

Learning between countries: adopting waste management directives

The case studies on waste management and waste incineration in the Netherlands and Bavaria reveal two important lessons to improve the implementation and internationalisation of environmental policy. First, a set of general directives for modern waste management. Second, possibilities to learn from the relatively successful policy concept of *Vorsorge*, which is being practised mostly in German environmental policy. This concept of precautionary politics has its roots in Bavaria and will be discussed in the next section.

Starting with the general directives that can be adopted, implementation of national waste policy will be furthered when the following recommendations are applied:

(1)   The present scale of waste processing needs national planning and steering. The principal goal remains to establish a system of integrated waste management, which basically means implementing a priority order for taking waste policy measures, in which prevention has the highest priority and, subsequently ranking down, product recycling, material recycling, useful application, waste-to-energy, and secured landfill should only be applied when necessary. This principle is germane to both municipal and hazardous waste (although the heterogeneity of hazardous waste thwarts the priority order for some waste streams). In practice, this goal is very difficult to achieve. As many people in the waste sector acknowledge, waste is like water: it flows to the lowest level, that is, to the lowest *cost* level. This calls upon government co-ordination to constrain market forces and steer waste streams. Regarding the international dimension, exports should be limited to special waste stream processing or volume exchange agreements, and illegal export should be strictly controlled and severely punished.

(2)   A further challenge is to arrange the municipal waste processing infrastructure according to the ladder principle of waste T&D priority ranking, and to link this to an appropriate scale of waste prevention, treatment, and disposal. Prevention should be pursued on a small scale, at the producers of waste (households, businesses); waste separation and recycling on a municipal scale; composting or anaerobic digestion on a scale of co-operating municipalities; incineration on a regional scale; and landfill on a national scale. Each treatment method is perfectly suitable for its scale. Processing capacity for hazardous waste can best be arranged on a national scale and concentrated at one site.

(3)   It will eventually be safest to practise precaution, e.g. not to fight risks but to anticipate them; to act in advance in order to prevent what is possibly unacceptable. Because this is not yet incorporated in the behaviour of institutions everywhere, it remains, therefore, essential to employ all regulatory and technological instruments to prevent possible future damages to public health or the environment from waste treatment. This was necessary in the case of dioxins, and will be compulsory in the case of diffuse pollution by slags and ashes (as the other residues from waste incineration).

(4)   To force and facilitate environmental technology has been proven to yield favourable results. Modern incineration technology is increasingly capable of efficiently combining economic and environmental demands. More attention, however, should be given to biological-mechanical techniques to process municipal waste, and recycling techniques to process hazardous waste.

Adopting these elements of modern waste management would be to learn from a virtual country. The suggested policy improvements are derived from the comparative study of Dutch and Bavarian waste policies. It is an idealised image. Not unattainable though, but there are no countries yet that work this way. Not even the Netherlands and Germany, although they do come close. The point is, however, that this body of politics can be set as an example. Subsequently, motives are created for learning between countries; between the Netherlands and Bavaria, and between these and other countries.

Learning between countries: adapting *Vorsorge* politics

A more specific occasion for policy oriented learning between countries would be a form of lesson-drawing (Rose, 1993). Rose developed a typology of 'alternative ways of drawing a lesson' (ibid: 30):

(1)   Copying   Enacting more or less intact a programme already in effect in another jurisdiction.

(2)   Adaptation   Adjusting for contextual differences a programme already in effect in another jurisdiction.

(3)   Making a hybrid   Combining elements of programmes from two different places.

(4)   Synthesis   Combining familiar elements from programmes in a number of different places to create a new programme.

(5)   Inspiration   Using programmes elsewhere as an intellectual stimulus to develop a novel programme.

The discussion on national policy styles and cultural constraints proved that the alternatives of 'copying' and 'making a hybrid' are not really possible. The most effective alternative would be 'adaptation', followed by 'synthesis' as a good runner up alternative, and finally 'inspiration' as a supplementary alternative. Adaptation does justice to the specific institutional context of the countries involved.

Adaptation occurs when a programme in effect elsewhere is the starting point for the design of a new programme allowing for differences in institutions, culture, and historical specifics. [..] Adaptation involves two governments in a one-to-one relationship of pacesetter and follower. Japan's late nineteenth-century adaptation of programmes from the United States and European countries is a textbook example of this relationship (ibid: 31).

Because of its relatively more successful implementation of environmental policy, it should be inviting to draw lessons from Bavaria, and use (parts of) their policy programme as a guide to what can be done. The characteristic of Bavarian environmental policy is *Vorsorge*, or politics of precaution. This means taking preventive measures independent of full scientific certainty to justify these measures, or: uncertainty is no excuse for doing nothing. *Vorsorge* is an integrative concept, combining the acceptance of challenges and innovations, anticipation of new regulatory structures, and aversion of new risks and their effects. This principle can be applied in general, but is pre-eminently suitable for environmental policy where feedback is problematic, uncertainties are manifest, and risks are high.

The precaution principle is part of German environmental policy. This is not a coincidence, but a result of the German administrative culture and policy style. According to Weale (1992), the precaution principle is supported by a technocratic and legalistic administrative structure. This structure is marked by carefulness, and an important influence of experts and courts on the policy process. Consequently, opportunities rise for 'best technical means' and common interests. Environmental policy benefits from this. So, it is not that Germany is this intrinsically environmentally sound country. There was, however, a fertile political-cultural soil for the ideology of ecological modernisation.

Bavaria takes this ideology even one step further by the vigorous conservation and protection of its own culture. And 'culture' in Bavaria encompasses intellectual, material, as well as natural values. In Bavaria, ecological modernisation found even richer soil, because of the rapid economic and technological progress, the natural heritage, and the political conditions for long-term planning. Moreover, the roots of *Vorsorge* politics lie in the early nineteenth-century Bavarian 'public service pragmatism', which demanded expertise and dutifulness from its officials, and was adopted in large parts of Germany. In the waste management system of Bavaria, government identified itself as a risk manager and played an active role. It implemented a detailed regulatory structure, and pays much attention to monitoring, control, public information and technology development. Adjustments and changes in relation with environmental policy are perceived as economic chances, not as costs.

It is clear that the politics of *Vorsorge* can not be integrally adopted by just any other country. *Vorsorge* is a structural element of the Bavarian and German policy style and, therefore, quite difficult to transfer. It is, however, perceivable that countries learn by adaptation, and that certain parts or elaborations of this policy concept will be applied on an international scale. Examples can be found in the fields of interdisciplinary research, sustainable technology development, and interactive policy-making. In the Bavarian waste management system this is elaborated as follows:

(1)   Interdisciplinary research; the Bavarian Institute for Waste Research (BIfA) is an independent, interdisciplinary institute for applied research on waste management and waste technology, and provides a link between university and company research activities regarding waste issues. When the Japanese Waste Research Foundation discovered this unique model of integrated waste management research, they adopted it.

(2)   Sustainable technology development; The two organisations for the management of hazardous wastes in Bavaria (GSB and ZVSMM) and the Bavarian R&D Centre for Hazardous Waste Management (FES) patented several technological devices (e.g. air pollution control and measurement), and market their know-how of integrated processing on a world-wide scale. Bavarian government supported various waste processing technologies, including pyrolysis which formed the basis of a new technique for the processing of municipal waste developed by Siemens.

(3)   Interactive policy-making; The Municipal Waste Management Office in Munich (AfAW) deploys professional and voluntary municipal waste consultants to inform citizens about prevention, recycling, and the organisation of waste management. In Germany, this has become a widespread phenomenon. The model of voluntary waste consultancy is of Bavarian origin, where people can follow a training in this type of work at the Munich Folk High School (or public education centre). Municipal waste consultants also fulfil a role as intermediaries between citizens groups and local government.

Prospect of a European environmental policy

Since the end of the 1980s, precautionary politics have been noticed by several countries. For example, in the Netherlands, the internalisation of environmental responsibility of target groups (*verinnerlijking*) has been advocated for years; and, from the fourth edition of 1986, the Environmental Action Programmes of the European Union propose a preventive policy approach. Yet, these are still only translations into policy objectives. As a strategy in practice, the precautionary principle is mainly applied by Germany (and outside Europe by California). Adaptation as a way of lesson-drawing between countries could promote the diffusion of practical anticipatory environmental policy.

Learning by adaptation is both desirable and necessary. It is desirable in order to harmonise and enhance environmental policy in Europe. And it is necessary in order to keep up with economic development in the process of europeanisation. Besides developments in the field of European environmental regulations, the change towards European unity is predominantly economic by nature. Waste management is a fine example of this. The scale of waste processing has become ever more larger. Due to environmental standards and new technological possibilities, there has been an increase of the treatment and disposal of separate waste streams. This can only be done remuneratively when markets are being expanded. For many markets, as in the case of the processing of batteries, this means Europe.

An economic europeanisation of waste management, however, causes all kinds of negative effects for the environment. Especially open frontiers and a free market will result in less supervision possibilities for the control of waste streams, and will affect the structure of self-provision of countries with high quality processing capacity. The unique Bavarian system of hazardous waste management seems hard to maintain. For this reason, there should also be an ecological europeanisation of waste management. This requires a uniform regulatory structure for waste processing, and a consistent policy approach. For instance, it has to be prevented that definitions of 'waste processing', 'useful application of wastes', and 'recycling' are interpreted very differently among countries. Until now, inconsistency in national waste policies has caused recyclable waste streams to end in waste incinerators, and waste for municipal or hazardous waste incinerators to go to (poorly regulated) cement industries.

An ecological europeanisation of waste policy will benefit from a further integration of waste policy on a European level. This can be supported by a convergence of national policy styles, a difficult process though. Or, as Van Waarden (1995: 364) puts it: 'Political integration in the EU-suprastate is more likely to produce a convergence of regulations than a convergence of regulatory styles'. Nevertheless, the increase of international relations and transnational interactions will cause national policy styles to slowly become alike. In the long run, also an internationalisation of environmental policy will grow. Policy learning between countries, either one-sided or on a mutual basis, is a good start. It might, in addition to efforts like the European Environmental Agency (1994), also be another contribution to a possible future European Environmental Union.

9 Mobilisation and Institutionalisation in Decision-making Processes around Large Scale Infrastructure

PAUL PESTMAN[1]

Introduction

This chapter gives an overview of a research project concerning the long term effects of mobilisation processes in the field of transport and infrastructure. The project will be carried out between 1996 and 2000. First, the empirical background of the project will be highlighted. Following that, the research questions are formulated. Maarten Hajer's argumentative approach is discussed in the third section. Subsequently, a framework based on Hajer's work and designed to study processes of mobilisation and institutionalisation will be introduced. In the final section, a format for the analysis of policy issues is presented.

The Dutch debate on infrastructure, planning and the environment

In recent years there has been an intense debate in the Netherlands concerning a number of large infrastructural projects. These projects include a High Speed Train connection to Belgium and France and a new rail freight connection to Germany, known as the *Betuweroute*. In both projects economic argumentations as well as environmental argumentations were used to mobilise actors in favour or against the realisation of the projects. One line of argumentation used by those in favour of construction is that railroad traffic produces less CO_2, as compared to air traffic and lorry traffic, which would help to fight the greenhouse effect. Another argument is that inland shipping is seriously ignored and should be stimulated in order to make new railroad for freight superfluous. A third line of argument states

197

that the premise on which the Dutch economy is based, the role of the distribution-sector, is false. Distribution would not add much value to goods, it should be priced for its contribution to environmental degradation and it is in the long term unwise to build the economy on such a sector.

At the same time, plans for railway construction caused a lot of commotion in local communities, especially in those areas which are located at the junction of several transport axes. The discussion was therefore not only between economy and ecology but between different spatial scales as well. The environmental movement for example found itself stuck between supporting local groups, who were fighting for the protection of their landscape and local environment on the one hand, and the reduction of CO_2 on the other.

Furthermore, a lot of the opposition of local governments was not directed against the plans itself but against the way the plans were presented by the state. As a result of the national government's desire to accelerate normal procedures, which serve to secure public participation, legal protection and consultation, new legal arrangements were made. These regulations, based on 'national interests', are intended to rule out 'NIMBY-objections (Not In My Backyard). It is questionable whether these regulations will be effective, since local governments can operate strategically within the legal framework (Aarts, 1995). At the end of an intense debate, it was decided to construct both railways. Especially in the case of the *Betuweroute*, the decision left a large number of local governments and citizens frustrated at the end of the process.

It seems however that the tide is turning. Recently, the Ministry of Transport has taken a somewhat different path of policy-making. The principal decision about the rail freight connection to Germany was a typical example of top-down policy-making, which resulted in a mass mobilisation of local government, environmental movement and citizens. In the successive decision-making processes local governments and NGO's seem to have more room for manoeuvre; public actors are involved in new forms of public participation (Pestman 1998).

The High Speed Railway is being constructed as well. However, in order to protect a rural area between the four largest cities in Holland, commonly referred to as the Green Heart, a tunnel at a length of 10 km will be constructed. Some see this as a form of governmental learning since large tunnels were not at the order of the day at the time parliament discussed the construction of the *Betuweroute*. Others argue that the tunnel only has a symbolic value because of its limited length and see the tunnel mainly as a means of unemployment relief works or as support for the construction industry. In any case, we seem to see some kind of interaction between the mobilisation process and the policies on infrastructure. This interaction process is the key issue in this research project.

Research questions

Processes of mobilisation are always directed to a specific policy proposal or measure. This relationship is, however not the prime object of study here. This type of question on infrastructure has been the object of study before (Huberts, 1988). Instead, this project focuses on the unintended consequences that processes of mobilisation have on future policy practices. The research questions of the project are:

(1) How can we understand the sudden rise in political and financial support for large scale infrastructure in the Netherlands from the beginning of the nineties?

(2) How do processes of mobilisation take place around large scale infrastructure?

(3) What consequences do these processes have on the policy practices at different times and places and on the organisation and the policy paradigm of the policy field?

The argumentative approach

This project takes the argumentative approach as formulated by Hajer as a starting point (Hajer, 1995). Hajer's approach is developed for the analysis of changes in (ways of thinking in) public policy and its institutional consequences. More specific, Hajer studies the emergence and development of ecological modernisation as the new dominant way of conceptualising environmental problems in environmental policy-making processes. The approach focuses on the constitutive role of discourse in policy processes (Hajer, 1995:58). In this approach, changing discourses are related to processes of institutionalisation of practices as well as to actors. From a social constructivist perspective the book argues that the debate on new environmental problems is about their interpretation. In Hajer's argumentative approach policy-making is seen as a struggle between various *discourse coalitions*. Discourse coalitions are defined as an ensemble of a set of *story lines*, the *actors* who utter these story lines and the *practices* in which this discursive activity is rooted. The three elements of the definition of discourse-coalition are clarified below. Discourse is defined as a specific ensemble of ideas, concepts and categorisations that are produced, reproduced and transformed in a specific set of practices and through which meaning is given to physical and social realities (1995:44). Hajer argues that

> discourse is not a medium through which individuals can manipulate the world as conventional social science suggests. It is itself part of reality, and constitutes the discoursing subject. Reference to institutional backgrounds or vested interests is an unsatisfactory circular explanation because institutions are only powerful in so far as they are constituted as authorities vis-à-vis other actors through discourse (1995:51).

What the implications of activities of actors in certain circumstances are depends on contextual and temporary conditions in *practices*. These practices are a key element for the analysis of discourse coalitions.

Story lines form the cement that keep coalitions together (1995:65). They are a kind of metaphors and a generative sort of narrative that allows actors to give meaning to specific problems and in this way reduce discursive complexity (1995:56). Story lines broaden the scope of where participating actors can be located. The example of a story line Hajer gives is *acid rain*. The concept of story lines does not suggest unity in problem definitions. It is possible that, although actors share a specific set of story lines, they can have their own interests and their own interpretations of the meaning of these story lines different from each other. Interests are intersubjectively constituted through discourse (1995:59). Hajer uses the concept of discourse institutionalisation to explain the way in which discourses become anchored in policy practices. In this way he shows how ideas are transformed into institutional bodies. Hajer's main theoretical thesis is 'that one can observe how institutional practices in the environmental domain work according to identifiable policy-discourses that through their story lines provide the signpost for action within these institutional practices' (1995: 264).

Some problems

Hajer's framework is a powerful tool, suitable for application in several fields. However, there are two points on which the analysis can be improved.

Conceptual ambiguity Hajer uses a literary style of description. This can be well explained by his Oxbridge background. Hajer is not always precise in the use of his terminology. Sometimes he refers to acid rain *as* a story line, as an emblematic concept. However, most of the time he distinguishes several story lines *on* acid rain dealing with why an issue is a problem (effects), whether the problem is small or large, who is to blame for it or which strategies can be followed. Clarification on this point would improve the theory. The same holds for the reconstruction of discourses. Hajer does not explain his methodology. A systematic approach could strengthen the empirical analysis. In this research project such an attempt will be made.[2]

The relation between power and discourse   On the relationship between discourses and institutions, Hajer states that

> ...the reference to institutional background or vested interests is an unsatisfactory circular explanation because institutions are only powerful in so far as they are constituted as authorities *vis-à-vis* other actors through discourse. Similarly, interests cannot be taken as given a priori but are constituted through discourse (1995:51).

This position will be adopted in this research as well. Furthermore, Hajer argues that, 'rules, distinctions, or legitimate modes of expression, only have meaning to the extent that they are taken up. It implies that the rules and conventions that constitute the social order have to be constantly reproduced and reconfirmed in actual speech situations, whether in documents or debates'. This is also a point to keep in mind. However, Hajer continues be stating that: 'Consequently, the power structures of society can and should be studied directly through discourse' (1995:55). This is not a logical conclusion. I argue that it is not wise to position discursive interaction as the only starting point for policy research. I have two reasons for arguing this way. First, rules and resources are very visible elements that play a role in processes of decision-making. They point so clearly at power and power structures that is simply a waste not to use them. This has nothing to do with the fact that rules and resources obtain their significance through a powerful discourse.

Secondly, Hajer assumes a direct relationship between discourses and practices. This assumption is problematic, since it ignores the fact that policy practices are the result of many different forms government interventions in different periods of time. Kaufman for instance shows which problems arise when actors try to terminate existing policies (1976). Furthermore, we know from institutional theory that habits like formalised standard operational procedures are very persistent (March & Olsen, 1989). From Beck we learned about zombie-institutions (1994). Beck describes institutions that are no longer backed up by a discourse, but are simply there because no-one questions them; they are taken for granted. In line with this I pose that it is unlikely that this body of institutional forms can be reduced to one or more policy discourses. Some practices can logically be attributed to several different discourses. Of other practices we will not be able to trace their discursive roots. This does not mean that there is not a relationship between discourses and institutions. However, the relation can be shown most clearly when new discourses emerge, since we can observe possible changes in policy practices.

A discursive-institutional framework for analysis

The two problems raised in the previous section are not difficult to overcome. I propose a fourfold adaptation of the argumentative approach:

(1)   a systematic analysis of rules and resources;
(2)   a separate analysis of discourses and story lines;
(3)   introduction of mobilisation as an encompassing concept to study the dynamics of both;
(4)   an analysis of the institutional consequences of these two forms of mobilisation.

Rules and resources: the political room for manoeuvre

The political room for manoeuvre of an actor is here defined as the set of possible options as given by the configuration of actors, rules and resources around a policy issue. For the analysis of political rules, neo-institutional analysis can be applied (March and Olsen, 1989; North, 1990; Steinmo,

Thelen et al., 1992). In contrast to the neo-institutional analysis resources of actors are studies here as well. In political science the analysis of resources has become suspect since the debate on power lead to the conclusion that one can not conclude from availability of resources that an actor is powerful. Usually one refers to the position of the United States during the Vietnam war to make this point (Arts, 1998). I would argue that this example does not mean we must analyse power without the analysis of resources. Instead we should pose the question which resources are relevant in specific situations. Resources become meaningful and important within a specific context. Judicial knowledge only has significance within the appropriate judicial system. Resources should be included in power analysis, but should be studied in relative terms, in context, and in their dynamics.

In large infrastructural projects, technical expertise is an important resource. Other relevant resources are money, real estate, other forms of expertise, public support. Studied in this way resources and rules determine the room for manoeuvre of political actors.

Discourses and story lines in a discursive space

One way to deal with the concepts of discourse and story lines in a more systematic way is by elaborating a third concept, 'discursive space'. The *discursive space* of a policy issue is here defined as the body of accepted conceptualisations, categorisations and problem definitions through which an existing configuration of rules, actors-relations and resources is legitimised. In other words, the political room for manoeuvre cannot be seen apart from the discursive space of the policy issue. The legitimation gives the configuration a certain stability and trust. Within this discursive space several policy discourses can be discerned.

Actors organise around story lines. In the previous section I argued that the concept of a story line is not very clear. Hajer speaks of 'acid rain' as a story line, but discerns several story lines on acid rain as well. This confusion can be overcome by framing acid rain itself as a story line and by defining the diversity within the opinions on acid rain (problem definition, advocated solutions etc.) as the discursive space around the story line 'acid rain'.

The relations between rules, resources and discourses as I see them are not very different from the way Hajer does. Hajer also focuses on a process of institutional change as a result of discursive interaction. What differs is the starting point of the analysis. Hajer uses *story lines* to analyse the discursive space of a theme and the policy practices derived from that. In my research, rules and resources which constitute these practices are systematically investigated separately. Only after this analysis is the question posed whether there is a relationship with certain story lines and discourses through which they are legitimised. In other words, the starting point is different. If no such relationship can be found it does not mean that rules and resources are not important. On the contrary, it becomes justified to assume that they have played an independent role in the decision-making process, regardless from their discursive background.

Dynamics: performative and classical mobilisation

Until now the discussion was mainly focused on the static elements of a decision-making process. Hajer's analysis is dynamic, since it involves discursive interaction and discourse institutionalisation and structuration. If we acknowledge that discourses are not the only starting point for policy analysis, this must have analytical consequences for the dynamic aspects of the framework as well. I think that changes of both discourses and rules and resources can be best conceptualised by means of the concept of *mobilisation*. In this section this will be illustrated.

In sociology mobilisation is used in different modes. Etzioni, for instance, mobilises resources (1968). Others use the term in reference to the mobilisation of people (Klandermans, 1997) or rules (Giddens, 1984). The concept mobilisation is currently often associated with the Resource Mobilisation Approach (RMA) developed by McCarthy and Zald (1982). Despite different approaches, all these studies share one characteristic. They all presuppose a hierarchical relationship between the 'sender' and the 'receiver' of the 'mobilising message'. This conceptualisation may have been valid in a specific period in time, it does not seem to be very adequate to analyse contemporary complex decision-making processes in the Netherlands (Teisman, 1995). Mobilisation is a much more interactive process. In this process several actors try to mobilise each other in order to organise power. Mobilisation is not only something protest groups do, but is a general phenomenon of actors in the policy arena. Mobilisation is a matter of how actors try to qualify themselves in order to transform their preferences into legitimate policies. This process of qualification can be seen as a sudden enlargement of the actors' political room for manoeuvre. This may happen through the enlargement of control over resources, through the formations of coalitions or by using established policy rules. These forms of mobilisation will be classified from now on as *classical mobilisation*. The adjective 'classical' refers to the literature were the concept is derived from. (Etzioni, Klandermans, Zald etc.). It is a general phenomenon in processes of decision-making, and it needs to be studied.

A second form of mobilisation is introduced here. It connects with the notion of story lines as developed by Hajer. This second form deals with the successful introduction of new concepts through which the discursive space of a policy area changes. As a result new coalitions become possible, other resources (e.g. new forms of knowledge) become relevant and new rules are seen as legitimate. This form surpasses the classical form, since a transformation takes place of the discursive space in which classical mobilisation normally takes place. This form of mobilisation will be labelled 'performative'. Performation is a process of change in the social dimension as a result of the introduction of new concepts (Kunneman, 1996). The result of it is a new configuration of actors, rules and resources on the basis of which new patterns of interaction are possible. The approaches mentioned earlier do not distinguish both forms of mobilisation. This does not mean that other authors did not tell us anything about the functioning of good stories. In the RMA this idea is absent, however it is not in the work of Etzioni. The two forms are distinguished here to identify performative mobilisation as a fundamentally different order of mobilisation. In classical mobilisation actors use rules and resources as well, of course. However, these rules play the same role and a specific type of knowledge remains as valuable as it is during the process. The difference is shown in Table 9.1.

Table 9.1   Classical and Performative Mobilisation

Mobilisation	Starting point	Produces changes in
Classical mobilisation	Resources, rules and actors	Political room for manoeuvre of an actor
Performative mobilisation	New concepts	Discursive space of policy issue

The relevance of performative mobilisation becomes clear if we focus on processes of policy change. New policy proposals have a larger chance to be accepted if:

(1)   there is a good fit between the concept at hand and the existing forms of policy and the organisation of it;

(2)   there is conformity of interests, that is when actors perceive the policy proposals as consistent with there own interests at that moment; and

(3)   the material conditions to realise the policy proposal are fulfilled.

Classical mobilisation takes place within the framework of these three conditions. Actors will mobilise on the basis of existing conceptions necessary to further their own goals. They will look for coalition partners based on previous experience and existing rules. Performative mobilisation questions the fundamental relations of the policy field. The introduction of a new performative policy concept raises question like: which actors can form a coalition? Where are the dividing lines between the policy fields? Which new forms of knowledge do we need? And do we need a different form of organisation of the policy field to accomplish our new task?

With this distinction both the process of discursive interaction can be studied as well as the classical form of the gathering of rules and resources. The concepts are therefore suitable to overcome the problem we discovered in Hajer's work, without ignoring the core of his argument.

Institutionalisation

The consequences of these two forms of mobilisation in the long run can be analysed by using the concept of *institutionalisation*. Institutionalisation is here defined as the structuration of the political room for manoeuvre or the discursive space of the policy issue. One can expect that the institutional consequences of performative mobilisation will be larger than those of classical mobilisation. When dealing with infrastructure policies one can distinguish three levels of institutionalisation. First, there is the level of *strategic policy development*. The main question here is whether the place and the function of infrastructure for other policy fields changes as a result of mobilisation and how this becomes visible in the configuration of actors, rules and resources. Changes on this level have a per definition performative character. The second level is the organisation of the policy field. Here we can find changes in views on how the central policy actor should govern, but also changes in the policy context, for example a change in the relationship between local governments and the central government. At this level processes with a classical as well as a performative character play a role.

The third level is that of the practices of design and landscaping of infrastructure. The main question here is whether the practice of the design of infrastructure change as a result of processes of mobilisation and how this becomes visible. Changes at this level seem to be the result of both classical as well as performative mobilisation. To illustrate, some examples of forms of mobilisation and institutionalisation are given below:

Table 9.2   Some Examples of Possible Forms of Institutionalisation of Performative and Classical Mobilisation

Level of institutionali-sation	Nature	Classical mobilisation	Performative mobilisation
Strategic policy development	policy content	nil	a re-orientation of the transport and traffic policies in such a way that the adjoining policy fields become repositioned towards one another
Organisation of the policy field	organisational	a limited revision of formal participation procedures	the implementation of a new practice of decision-making for large infrastructural projects.
Practices of design and landscaping	organisational	the introduction of new methods for the calculation of noise pollution	the implementation of a procedure for the design and planning of new infrastructure (including, political, financial and design aspects).

A format for the analysis of policy issues

In this study political decision-making is considered as a battle between groups of actors about the definition of certain aspects of a policy issue. This battle is not per se a battle between stable coalitions with fixed interests, since these coalitions and interests can be part of this battle of definition as well. The outcome of the battle depends on the political room for manoeuvre (rules, resources in context) and the discursive space through which these are positioned. The extent of this room for manoeuvre can be influenced by processes of mobilisation. Two forms were discerned. First, we acknowledged classical mobilisation where actors, rules and resources are mobilised, but in which case the meaning and position of those elements are not questioned. Secondly, we can speak of performative mobilisation if, as a result of the introduction of new conceptualisations, the meaning of existing actor-relations, rules and resources change.

The outcome of the decision-making process is a temporary definition of the most important aspects of the policy problem. For infrastructural works this means that the organisation and design of the project are a resemblance of the dominant vision on several aspects of the policy field infrastructure. The outcome is at the same time a temporary stabilisation of the configuration of actors, rules and resources. These institutional consequences can be studied at three levels: the level of strategic policy development, the level of the organisation of the policy field and the level of the practices of design and landscaping of infrastructure.

In order to reconstruct decision-making it is necessary to select the crucial policy issues of a decision-making process. For each of these issues six related questions need to be answered. These questions deal with stability and change of the policy process as well as with the discursive and institutional dimensions of the process (see table 9.3).

The approach outlined here offers the possibility to analyse the strategic, institutional and discursive aspects of power and its long term consequences. In table 9.2 some examples were already given of institutional consequences in the field of infrastructure. The relation with the environment seems evident. A repositioning of land use planning, nature conservation, economics and environmental policy with respect to one another has major implications for environmental policy-making, the introduction of new forms of public participation has this as well. (For an overview of the effects of participation on decision-making processes see

Coenen, Huitema and O'Toole, 1998). Addressing the effects of mobilisation on long term policy change also identifies the possibility of what can be called *next round effects*. As an example of a next round effect one can think of a specific technical solution that is advocated in a certain decision-making process, is not choosen at that time, but is applied in the next project (Pestman, 1998).

Table 9.3   Format for the Analysis of Policy Issues

	Static	Dynamic	Discursive	Institutional
1. What are the relevant actors or coalitions?	X			X
2. What is the existing configuration of rules and resources?	X			X
3. What are the dominant story lines?	X		X	
4. What is the discursive space of the policy issue?	X		X	
5. Which forms of classical and performative mobilisation take place?		X	X	X
6. Which forms of institutionalisation take place?		X	X	X

Notes

1   This chapter is based on a research note presented at the IRNES-seminar in Firenze, Italy, 28th June 1996. The paper was revised on the basis of research activities in 1997 and 1998.

2   Of course Hajer's writing style has a charm of its own. Nonetheless I would argue that more could be gained from the theoretical insights he offers by a more systematic approach.

Bibliography

Aarts, J. H. W. M., Huigen, J. and D.H. van der Rijdt (1995), 'Snelheid van uitvoering onder Tracewet, op weg naar pervertering van de verhouding tussen rijksoverheid en medeoverheden?', *Bestuurswetenschappen*, vol. 4, pp. 278-92.

Aguilar, S. (1997), 'Subsidiarity, Shared Responsibility and Environmental Policy in Spain', in Collier, U., Golub, J. and Kreher, A. (eds), op.cit.

Albrow, D. (1996), *The Global Age. State and Society Beyond Modernity*, Polity Press, Cambridge.

Alexander, J.C. (1995), *Fin de Siècle Social Theory. Relativism, Reduction, and the Problem of Reason*, Verso, London.

Almond, G. (1990), *A Discipline Divided: Schools and Sects in Political Science*, Sage, Beverly Hills, CA.

Argyris, C. (1976), 'Single-loop and double-loop models in research on decision-making', *Administrative Science Quarterly*, vol. 21, pp. 363-75.

Armstrong, K. and Bulmer S. (1998), *The Governance of the Single European Market*, Manchester University Press, Manchester.

Arts, B. (1998), *The Political Influence of NGOs. Case Studies on the Climate and Biodiversity Conventions*, Van Arkel/International Books, Utrecht.

Axelrod, R. (1994), 'Subsidiarity and Environmental Policy in the European Community', *Journal of International Environmental Affairs* vol. 6 (2), pp. 115-32.

Azzi, G. (ed.) (1985), *The Implementation Of Community Law By Member States*, European Institute of Public Administration, Maastricht.

Bahro, R. (1982), *Elementen voor een nieuwe politiek*, Van Gennip, Amsterdam.

Baker, S. (1996), 'The evolution of EU environmental policy: from growth to sustainable development' in Baker, S., Kousis, M., Richardson, D. and Young, S. (eds), *The Politics of Sustainable Development*, Routledge, London.

Baker, S., Kousis, M., Richardson, D. and Young, S. (1997) 'Introduction: The Theory and Practice of Sustainable Development in EU perspective', in: Baker, S., Kousis, M., Richardson, D. and Young, S. (eds.) *The Politics of Sustainable Development: Theory, Policy and Practice within the European Union*. Routledge, London, pp. 1-40.

Barav, A. (1975), 'Failure of Member States to Fulfil Their Obligations Under Community Law', *Common Market Law Review*, 369-83.

Bartelmus, P. (1994), *Environment, Growth and Development*, Routledge, London.

Bauman, Z. (1992), *Intimations of Postmodernity*, Routledge, London.

Bauman, Z. (1993), *Postmodern Ethics*, Blackwell, Oxford.

Becher, T. (1989), *Academic Tribes and Territories*, Open University Press, Milton Keynes.

Beck, U. (1992), *Risk Society. Towards a new modernity*, Sage Publications, London.

Beck, U. (1994), 'The Reinvention of Politics: Towards a Theory of Reflexive modernization' in: Beck, U., Giddens, A. and Lash, S. (eds.), *Reflexive Modernization, Politics, Tradition and Aesthetics in the Modern Social Order*. Polity Press, Oxford, pp. 1-55.

Beck, U. (1996a), 'Risk Society and the Provident State', in S. Lash, B. Szerszynski and B. Wynne (eds), *Risk, Environment and Modernity. Towards a New Ecology*, Sage, London, pp. 27-43.

Beck, U. (1996b), 'World Risk Society as Cosmopolitan Society? Ecological Questions in a Framework of Manufactured Uncertainties', *Theory, Culture and Society*, vol. 13, no. 4, pp. 1-32.

Beck, U. (1998), 'Politics of Risk Society', in J. Franklin (ed.), *The Politics of Risk Society*, Polity Press, Cambridge, pp. 9-22.

Beck, U., Giddens, A. and Lash, S. (1994) *Reflexive Modernization. Politics, Tradition and Aesthetics in the Modern Social Order*, Polity Press, Oxford.

Bennett, C.J. and Howlett, M. (1992). 'The lessons of learning: Reconciling theories of policy learning and policy change', *Policy Sciences*, vol. 25, pp. 275-94.

Bennulf, M. and Holmberg, S. (1990) 'The Green Breakthrough in Sweden', *Scandinavian Political Studies* vol. 13 (2), pp. 165-84.

Bercusson, B. (1994), 'Social Policy at the Cross roads: European Labour Law after Maastricht.', in Dehousse, R. (ed.) (1994), *Europe After Maastricht: An Ever Closer Union ?*, Beck-Law Books in Europe, München.

Berger, P. and T. Luckmann (1966), *The Social Construction of Reality. A Treatise in the Sociology of Knowledge*, Penquin Books, Harmondsworth.

Birnie, P. (1992), 'International Environmental Law: Its Adequacy for Present and Future Needs', in A. Hurrell and B. Kingsbury (eds), *The International Politics of the Environment*, Clarendon Press, Oxford, pp. 51-84.

Blumer, H. (1951) 'Elementary Collective Behavior', in: McClung Lee, A. (ed.), *New Outline of the Principles of Sociology*. 2nd revised edition (first: 1939). New York: Random House, New York, pp. 166-222.

Blyth, M. (1997) 'Any More Bright Ideas?: The Ideational Turn of Comparative Political Economy' *Comparative Politics* vol. 29:2, pp.229-50.

Boehmer-Christiansen, S. (1995), 'Reflections on Scientific Advice and EC Transboundary Pollution Policy', *Science and Public Policy*, vol. 22 (3), pp. 195-203.

Brand, K.-W., Eder, K. and Poferl, A. (1997) *Ökologische Kommunikation in Deutschland*, Westdeutscher Verlag, Opladen.

BSPB, NFU and UKASTA (1998), 'Guidelines for Growing Newly Developed Herbicide Tolerant Crops', *British Society of Plant Breeders*, Ely, Cambridge.

Burley, A. Mattli, W. (1993), 'Europe Before the Court: A Political Theory of Integration', *International Organisation*, vol. 47, no. 1, pp. 41-76.

Butt-Philip, A. (1994). 'Old Policies and New Competences.', in Duff, A., J.Pinder, R.Pryce (eds.) (1994), *Maastricht and Beyond: Building the European Union*, Routledge, London.

Caporaso, J. (1997), 'Across the Great Divide', EUI Working Paper RSC 97-58, EUI, Florence.

Caporaso, J. and Keeler, J. (1995), 'The EU and Regional Integration Theory', in Rhodes, C. and Mazey, S. (eds), *The State of the EU*, Lynne Rienner, Boulder, CO.

Carraro, C., Galeotti, M. and Gallo, M. (1995), 'Environmental Taxation and Unemployment: Some Evidence on the Double-Dividend Hypothesis in Europe', Nota di Lavora 34.95, Fondazione Eni Enrico Mattei, Milano.

Castells, M. (1996), *The Information Age. Economy, Society and Culture. Volume I: The Network Society*, Blackwell, Malden USA/Oxford UK.

Castells, M. (1997), *The Information Age. Economy, Society and Culture. Volume II: Power and Identity*, Blackwell, Malden USA/Oxford UK.

CEC (Commission of the European Communities) (1993), 'Interinstitutional Agreement between the European Parliament, the Council and the Commission on procedures for implementing the principle of subsidiarity.' Reproduced in full in CEC (1993) 'Interinstitutional declaration on democracy, transparency and subsidiarity', in Bulletin on the European Community, Issue 10, pp 119-20.

CEC (1994), 'Report to The European Council on The Application of the Subsidiarity Principle'. COM (94) 533 final.

CEC (1995), 'Better Law-Making; Commission report to the European Council on the Application of the Subsidiarity and proportionality principles, on simplification and on consolidation.' CSE (95) 580.

CEC (1998), 'Commission Proposal on the Revision of Directive 90/220', COM(1998) 85 final, 98/0072 (COD).

Ciuffreda, G. (1996), 'Ecologia, un passo indietro', *Il Manifesto*, 2/3/96, p.15.

Coenen, F., Huitema, D. and O'Toole, L.J. Jr. (eds.) (1998). *Participation and the quality of environmental decision-making*, Kluwer Academic Publishers, Dordrecht.

Collier, U. (1994), *Energy and Environment in the European Union: the Challenge of Integration*, Avebury, Aldershot.

Collier, U. (1997a) 'Liberalisation in the energy sector: environmental threat or opportunity?' in Collier, U. (ed) *Deregulation in the European Union: Environmental Perspectives*, Routledge, London.

Collier, U. (1997b), 'Developing responses to the climate change issue: the role of subsidiarity and shared responsibility', in Collier, U. Golub, J. and Kreher, A. op.cit.

Collier, U. and Golub, J. (1996), 'Environmental policy and politics' in Rhodes, M., Heywood, P., and Wright, V. (eds), *Developments in West European Politics*, Macmillan, London.

Collier, U. and Löfstedt, R. (1997), *Cases in Climate Change Policy: Political Reality in the European Union*, Earthscan, London.

Collier, U. Golub, J. and Kreher, A. (1997) (eds), *Subsidiarity and Shared Responsibility: New Challenges for EU Environmental Policy*, Nomos Verlag, Baden-Baden.

Committee of the Regions (1996) *Regional and Local Authorities: Protagonists in the Political Union of Europe*, Draft Report of the Commission on Institutional Affairs, CdR 282/96.

Common, M. (1995), *Sustainability and Policy*, Cambridge University Press, Cambridge.

Cotgrove, S. (1982), *Catastrophe or Cornucopia: The Environment, Politics and the Future*, John Wiley & Sons, Chichester.

Crepaz, M. M. L. (1995) 'Explaining National Variations of Air Pollution Levels: Political Institutions and Their Impact on Environmental Policy-Making', *Environmental Politics* vol. 4:3, pp. 391-414.

Daintith, T. (ed.) (1995), *Implementing EC Law in the UK: Structures for Indirect Rule*, Wiley Chancery Law, Chichester.

Dalton, R. J. (1991), 'Responsiveness of Parties and Party Systems to the New Politics', pp. 39-56 in: Klingemann, H.-D., Stöss, R. and Weßels, B. (eds.) *Politische Klasse und politische Institutionen. Probleme und Perrspektiven der Elitenforschung*, Westdeutscher Verlag, Opladen.

Dalton, R. J. (1994), *The Green Rainbow. Environmental Groups in Western Europe*, Yale University Press, New Haven.

Dalton, R. J. and Kuechler, M. (eds.) (1990), *Challenging the Political Order*, Polity Press, Oxford.

Dashwood, A. White, R. (1989), 'Enforcement Actions Under Articles 169 and 170 EEC', *European Law Review*, vol. 14, pp. 388-414.

Dearlove, J. and Saunders, P. (1991), *Introduction to British Politics* (2nd edition), Polity, Cambridge.

Dehousse, R. (1994) 'Community Competences:Are there limits to Growth', in Dehousse, R (ed.) *Europe After Maastricht-An Ever Closer Union ?*, Law Books Europe, München, pp. 103-25.

Della Porta, D. and Rucht, D. (1995) 'Left-Libertarian Movements in Context: A Comparison of Italy and West-Germany, 1965-1990', in: Jenkins, J. C. and Klandermans, B. (eds.), *The Politics of Social Protest. Comparative*

Perspectives on States and Social Movements, UCL Press, London, pp. 229-72.

Diani, M. and Lodi, G. (1988), 'Three in One: Currents in the Milan Ecology Movement', in: Klandermans, B., Kriesi, H. and Tarrow, S. (eds.), *From Structure to Action: Comparing Movement Participation Across Cultures*, JAI, Greenwich (Conn.), pp.103-24.

Djerft, M. (1996), *Göna Nyheter: Miljöjournalistiken i Televisions Nyhetssändningar 1961-1994*, Institutionen för journalistik och masskommunikation, Göteborg.

Dobson, A. and Lucardie, P. (eds) (1993), *The Politics of Nature. Explorations in Green Political Theory*, Routledge, London.

Docksey, C. and K. Williams, (1994), 'The Commission and the Execution of Community Policy', in Edwards, G. and D. Spence (eds), *The European Commission*, Cartermill Publishing, London.

Dogan, R. (1997), 'Comitology: Little Procedures with Big Implications', *West European Politics*, vol. 20, no. 3, pp. 31-60.

Douglas, M. and Wildavsky, A. (1982), *Risk and Culture: An Essay on the Selection of Technological and Environmental Dangers*, University of California Press, Berkeley.

Downs, A. (1972) 'Up and down with Ecology – the "Issue-Attention Cycle"', *Public Interest* vol. 28, pp. 38-50.

DRI (1994), *Potential Benefits of Integration of Environmental and Economic Policies*, Graham and Trotman, London.

Dryzek, J.S. (1997), *The Politics of the Earth. Environmental Discourses*, Oxford University Press, Oxford.

Duff, A. (1994) 'The Main reforms.' in Duff, A., J.Pinder, R.Pryce (eds) (1994), *Maastricht and Beyond: Building the European Union*, Routledge, London.

Easton, D. (1965), *A Framework For Political Analysis*, Prentice Hall, Englewood Cliffs, NJ.

Easton, D. (1979) *A System Analysis of Political Life*. (first 1965), The University of Chicago Press, Chicago.

Eberg, J. (1997), *Waste Policy and Learning. Policy dynamics of waste management and waste incineration in the Netherlands and Bavaria*, Eburon, Delft.

Eberg, J., Van Est, R. and Van de Graaf, H. (eds) (1996), *Leren met beleid. Beleidsverandering en beleidsgericht leren bij NIMBY-, milieu- en technologiebeleid*, Het Spinhuis, Amsterdam.

EC (1988), *Single European Act*, Office for Official Publications, Luxemburg.

EEC (1990), 'Council Directive 90/220 on the Deliberate Release to the Environment of Genetically Modified Organisms', *Official Journal of the European Communities*, L 117, 8 May, pp. 15-27.

EC (1996), 'Commission Decision 96/158/EC of 6 February 1996 Concerning the Placing on the Market of a Product Consisting of a GMO, hybrid herbicide-tolerant swede-rape seeds (B.napus Metzq MS1Bn x RF1Bn)', *Official Journal of the European Communities*, L 37, 15 February, pp. 30-31. (PGS dossier C/GB/94/M1/1).

EC (1997), 'Commission Decision 97/98/EC of 23 January 1997 Concerning the Placing on the Market of Genetically Modified Maize', *Official Journal of the European Communities*, L 31, 1 February, pp. 69-70. (Ciba-Geigy dossier C/F/94/11-3).

EC (1998), 'Commission Decision Concerning the Placing on the Market of a Genetically Modified Maize (Zea mays line 810), Pursuant to Council Directive 90/220/EEC', *Official Journal of the European Communities*, 5 May, L 131, pp. 32-33. (Monsanto dossier C/F/95/12-02).

Edelman, M. (1971), *Politics as Symbolic Action*,. Markham, Chicago.

Eder, K. (1993a), *The New Politics of Class. Social Movements and Cultural Dynamics in Advanced Societies*, Sage Publications, London.

Eder, K. (1993b), 'Die Natur: Ein neues Identitätssymbol der Moderne? Zur Bedeutung kultureller Traditionen für den gesellschaftlichen Umgang mit der Natur', paper, Europäisches Hochschulinstitut, San Domenico di Fiesole (Italy).

Eder, K. (1995), *Framing and Communicating Environmental Issues. Final Report to the Commission of the European Communities*,. European University Institute, Florence and Humboldt Universität zu Berlin, Berlin.

Eder, K. (1996), 'The Institutionalization of Environmentalism: Ecological Discourse and the Second Transformation of the Public Sphere', in: Lash, S., Szerszynski, B. and Wynne, B. (eds.), *Risk, Environment and Modernity: Towards a New Ecology*, Sage, London,. pp. 203-23.

EEB (1996), *Memorandum to the Irish Presidency and EU Member States*, EEB, Brussels.

Elworthy, S. et al (eds) (1995), *Perspectives on the Environment 2: Interdisciplinary Research on Politics, Planning, Society and the Environment*, Aldershot, Avebury.

Etzioni, A. (1968), *The Active-Society, A Theory of Societal and Political Processes*, Free Press, New York.

EU (1992), *Treaty on European Union*, OJ C224, Vol 15, 31.8.1992.

European Commission (1992a), *Towards Sustainability*, COM (92) 23 final.

European Commission (1992b), *A Community Strategy to Limit Carbon Dioxide Emissions and to Improve Energy Efficieny*, COM (92), 246 final.

European Commission (1993), *Growth, Competitiveness and Employment: the Challenges and Ways Forward into the 21st Century*, COM (93) 700 final.

European Commission (1994a), *Directions for the EU on Environmental Indicators and Green Accounting*, COM (94) 670.

European Commission (1994b), *Assessment of the Expected CO2 Emissions from the Community in the Year 2000*, SEC 94 (122).

European Commission (1995a), *Report of the Group of Independent Experts on Legislative and Administrative Simplification*, COM (95) 288 final/2.

European Commission (1995b), *Review of the Fifth Environmental Action Programme*, COM (95) 624.

European Commission (1995c), *White Paper – An Energy Policy for the European Union*, COM (95) 682.

European Commission (1996a), *Implementing Community Environmental Law*, COM (96) xx.

European Environment Agency (1995), *Environment in the European Union*, European Environment Agency, Copenhagen.

European Environmental Bureau (EEB) (1996), *Memorandum to the Irish Presidency and EU Member States*, July 1996:EEB/BEE, Brussels.

Evans, A. (1979), 'The Enforcement Procedure of Article 169 EEC', *European Law Review*, vol. 4, pp. 442-56.

Eyermann, R. and Jamison, A. (1991), *Social Movements: A Cognitive Approach*, Polity Press, Oxford.

Fischer, F. (1993a) 'Reconstructing Policy Analysis: A Postpositivist Perspective', *Policy Sciences*, vol. 25, pp. 333-9.

Fischer, F. (1993b) 'Citizen Participation and the Democratisation of Policy Expertise: From Theoretical Inquiry to Practical Cases', *Policy Sciences*, vol. 26, pp. 165-87.

Flam, H. (1994) (in collaboration with Jamison, Andrew) 'The Swedish Confrontation over Nuclear Energy: A Case of a Timid Anti-Nuclear Opposition', in: Flam, H. (ed.), *States and Anti-Nuclear Movements*, Edinburgh University Press, Edinburgh, pp. 163-200.

Flynn, B. (1996), 'Does Subsidiarity Make a Difference to the EU Environmental Institutions?' Paper presented at the IRNES Workshop 'Institutional Change in Environmental Policy', University of Essex, 28.11.96. (Revised version is Chapter 5 in this book.)

Frankland, G.E. and Schoonmaker, D. (1992), *Between Protest and Power: The German Green Party in Germany*, Westview Press, Boulder, CO.

Franklin, J. (eds) (1998), *The Politics of Risk Society*, Polity Press, Cambridge.

Friends of the Earth (1995), *Towards a Sustainable Europe*, Friends of the Earth Europe, Brussels.

From, J. and P. Stava (1993), 'Implementation of Community Law: The Last Stronghold of National Control?' in Andersen, S. and K. Eliassen (eds), *Making Policy in Europe*, Sage, London.

Frouws, J. and J. van Tatenhove (1993), 'Agriculture, Environment and the State. The development of agro-environmental policy-making in the Netherlands', *Sociologia Ruralis* Vol XXXIII, pp. 220-39.

Funtowicz, S. and Ravetz, J. (1992), 'Three Types of Risk Assessment and the Emergence of Post-normal Science', in S.Krimsky and D.Golding (eds), *Social Theories of Risk*, Praeger, New York, pp.251-74.

Gamson, W. A. (1988) Political Discourse and Collective Action, in: Klandermans, B., Kriesi, H. and Tarrow, S. (eds.), *From Structure to Action: Comparing Movement Participation Across Cultures*, JAI, Greenwich, Connecticut, pp. 219-44.

Gamson, W. A. and Modigliani, A. (1989) 'Media Discourse and Public Opinion on Nuclear Power: A Constructionist Approach', *American Journal of Sociology* vol. 95, pp. 1-37.

Garrett, G. (1995), 'The Politics of Legal Integration in the European Union' *International Organisation*, vol. 49, pp. 171-81.

George, S. (1996), 'The European Union: Approaches From International Relations', in Kassim, H. and Menon, A. (eds), *The European Union and National Industrial Policy*, Routledge, London.

Giddens, A. (1984), *The Constitution of Society. Outline of the Theory of Structuration*, Polity Press, Cambridge.

Giddens, A. (1985), *The Nation-State and Violence*, Polity Press, Cambridge.

Giddens, A. (1990), *The Consequences of Modernity*, Polity Press, Cambridge.

Giddens, A. (1994), 'Living in a Post-Tradition Society', in U. Beck, A. Giddens and S. Lash (eds), *Reflexive Modernization. Politics, tradition and aesthetics in the modern social order*, Polity Press, Cambridge, pp. 56-109.

Giddens, A. (1998), 'Risk Society: the Context of British Politics', in J. Franklin (ed.), *The Politics of Risk Society*, Polity Press, Oxford, pp. 23-34.

Gill, B. (1993), 'Technology assessment in Germany's biotechnology debate', *Science as Culture*, vol. 4, pp. 69-84.

Gill, B. (1996), 'Germany: Splicing Genes, Splitting Society', *Science and Public Policy*, vol. 23, pp. 175-9.

Gitlin, T. (1980), *The Whole World is Watching: Mass Media in the Making and Unmaking of the New Left*, University of California Press, Berkeley.

Goddard, A. and Patel, K. (1998), 'British Jury's out on Food Genetics', *The Times Higher Education Supplement*, 10 July 1998.

Golub, J. (1996a). 'British Sovereignty and the Development of EC Environmental Policy', *Environmental Politics*, Vol.5., pp.700-28.

Golub, J. (1996b). 'Sovereignty and Subsidiarity in EU environmental policy', *Political Studies*, vol. XLIV, p. 686.

Golub, J. (1996c), 'State Power and Institutional Influence in European Integration: Lessons from the Packaging Waste Directive', *Journal of Common Market Studies*, vol. 34, pp. 313-39.

Golub, J. (1997) 'Recasting EU environmental policy: subsidiarity and national sovereignty', in Collier, U., Golub, J. and Kreher, A. (eds), op.cit.

Goodin, R.E. (1992), *Green Political Theory*, Polity Press, Cambridge.

Gordon, I. Lewis, J. Young, K. (1977), 'Perspectives on Policy Analysis', *Public Administration Bulletin*, vol. 25, pp. 26-35.

Gormley, L. (1986), 'The Application of Community Law in the United Kingdon, 1976-1985', *Common Market Law Review*, vol. 23, pp. 287-323.

Gourevitch, P. (1978), 'The Second Image Revisited: The International Sources of Domestic Politics', *International Organisation*, vol. 32, pp. 881-912.

Gourlay, K.A. (1992), *World of waste. Dilemmas of industrial development*, Zed Books, London.

Grant, C. (1994), *Delors: Inside the House that Jacques Built*, Nicholas Brealey, London.

Haas, E. (1964), 'International Integration: the European and the Universal Process', in Hekius, D. et al, (eds), *International Stability*, John Wiley, New York.

Haas, E. (1968), *The Uniting of Europe*, Stanford University Press, Stanford, CA.

Habermas, J. (1968), *Techniek und Wissenschaft als Ideologie*, Suhrkamp Verlag, Frankfurt am Main.

Habermas, J. (1981), *Theorie des kommunikativen Handelns*, 2 Vol., Campus Verlag, Frankfurt am Main.

Habermas, J. (1989), *The Structural Transformation of the Public Sphere*, MIT Press, Boston. Original: *Strukturwandel der Öffentlichkeit. Untersuchungen zu einer Kategorie der bürgerlichen Gesellschaft*, 2nd edition, 1991 (first published 1962), Suhrkamp, Frankfurt am Main.

Haigh, N. (1984), *EEC Environmental Policy and Britain*, ENDS, London.

Haigh, N. (1986), 'Devolved Responsibility and Centralisation: Effects of EEC Environmental Policy', *Public Administration*, vol. 64, pp. 197-207.

Haigh, N. (1992), Manual of Environmental Policy: the EC and Britain, Longman, London.

Haigh, N. Bennett, G. and Kromarek, M. (1986), *Waste and Water in Four Countries: A Study of the Implementation of the EEC Directives in France, Germany, the Netherlands and the UK*, IEEP, London.

Haigh, N. and Lanigan, C. (1995), 'Impact of the European Union on UK Environmental Policy-making', in Gray, T. (ed), *UK Environmental Policy in the 1990s*, Basingstoke, Macmillan.

Hajer, M.A. (1995), *The Politics of Environmental Discourse: Ecological Modernization and the Policy Process*, Clarendon Press, Oxford.

Halfmann, J. (1989) Social Change and Political Mobilization in West Germany, in Katzenstein, P.J. (ed.) *Industry and Politics in West Germany*, Cornell University Press, Ithaca, N.Y., pp. 51-86.

Hall, P.A. (1993), 'Policy Paradigms, Social Learning and the State', *Comparative Politics*, vol. 25, pp. 275-96.

Hall, P.A. (1989) 'Conclusions: Politics of Keynesian Ideas' in P.A. Hall (ed.), *The Political Power of Economic Ideas: Keynesianism Across Nations*, Princeton University Press, Princeton, pp.361-91.

Hall, P.A. and R. Taylor (1996), 'Political Science and Three New Institutionalisms', *Political Studies* vol. 44, pp. 936-57.

Hanf, K. (1982), 'Regulatory Structures: Enforcement as Implementation', *European Journal of Political Research*, vol. 10, pp. 159-72.

Hawkins, K.O. (1984), *Environment and Enforcement: Regulation and the Social Definition of Pollution*,. Clarendon Press, Oxford.

Hayes-Renshaw, F. Wallace, H. (1997), *The Council of Ministers*, Macmillan, Basingstoke.

Heclo, H. (1974), *Social policy in Britain and Sweden*, Yale University Press, New Haven, CT.

Held, D. (1989), *Political Theory and the Modern State. Essays on State, Power and Democracy*, Polity Press, Cambridge.

Held, D. (1995), *Democracy and the Global Order. From the Modern State to Cosmopolitan Governance*, Polity Press, Cambridge.

Hennessy, P. (1990), *Whitehall*, Fontana Press, London.

Hey, C. (1994), *Umweltpolitik in Europa: Fehler, Risiken, Chancen*, Beck'sche Verlagsbuchhandlung, München.

Hildebrand, P.M. (1993), 'The European Community's environmental policy, 1957 to 1992: from incidental measures to an international regime?', *Environmental Politics* vol. 4, pp.13-43.

Hildebrandt, E. and Schmidt, E. (1994) *Umweltschutz und Arbeitsbeziehungen in Europa. Eine vergleichende Zehn-Länder-Studie*, Edition Sigma, Berlin.

Hill, Julie (1998), 'Open Letter from Julie Hill to John Battle, Environment Minister at the DTI', *The Observer*, 12 July 1998.

Hisschemöller, M. and Hoppe, R. (1996), 'Coping with intractable controversies: The case for problem structuring in policy design and analysis', *Knowledge and Policy*, vol. 8, pp. 40-60.

Hix, S. (1994), 'Approaches to the Study of the EC', *West European Politics*, vol. 17, pp. 1-31.

Hix, S. (1996), 'CP, IR and the EU! A Rejoinder to Hurrell and Menon', *West European Politics*, vol. 19, pp. 802-4.

Hix, S. (1998), 'The Study of the EU II: The 'New Governance' Agenda and Its Rival', *Journal of European Public Policy*, vol. 5, pp. 38-65.

Hoffman, S. (1966), 'Obstinate or Obsolete? The Fate of the Nation State and the Case of Europe', *Daedalus*, vol. 95, pp. 862-915.

Hofrichter, J. and Reif, K. (1990), 'Evolution of Environmental Attitudes in the European Community', *Scandinavian Political Studies*, vol. 13.

Holder, J. et al (eds) (1993), *Perspectives on the Environment: Interdisciplinary Research in Action*, Avebury, Aldershot.

Hoogenboom, B. (1998), Mexico and the NAFTA Environmental Debate. The Transnational Politics of Economic Integration, Van Arkel/International Books, Utrecht.

House of Commons (1989), *Environment Committee-Seventh Report. The Proposed European Environment Agency,* 13 November 1989, HMSO, London.

Huber, J. (1985), 'Ecologische modernisering', in E. van den Abbeele (red.), *Ontmanteling van de groei. Leesboek over een andere economie,* Markant, Nijmegen, pp. 161-8.

Huberts, L. W. (1988), *De Politieke Invloed van Protest en Pressie: Besluitvormingsprocessen over Rijkswegen,* DSWO Press, Leiden.

Hunt, Jane (1994), 'The Social Construction of Precaution', in T. O'Riordan and J. Cameron (eds), *Interpreting the Precautionary Principle,* Earthscan, London, pp. 117-25.

Hurrell, A., and Menon, A. (1996), 'Politics Like No Other: Comparative Politics, International Relations and the Study of the EU', *West European Politics,* vol. 19, pp. 386-402.

Inglehart, R. (1989), *Culture Shift in Advanced Industrial Society,* Princeton University Press, Princeton.

Jachtenfuchs, M., Hey, C. and Ströbel, M. (1993) 'Umweltpolitik in der Europäischen Gemeinschaft', in Von Prittwitz, V. (ed.), *Umweltpolitik als Modernisierungsprozess,* Leske + Budrich, Opladen, pp.137-62.

Jackson, T. (1992), *Efficiency without Tears,* Friends of the Earth, London.

Jacobs, F, Corbett, R and Shackleton, M.(1992), *The European Parliament,* London, Longman.

Jacobs, M. (1991), *The Green Economy,* Pluto Press, London.

Jahn, D. (1992), 'Nuclear Power, Energy Policy and New Politics in Sweden and Germany', *Environmental Politics,* vol. 1, pp. 383-417.

Jahn, D. (1993a), *New Politics in Trade Unions,* Dartmouth, Aldershot.

Jahn, D. (1993b), 'The Rise and Decline of New Politics and the Greens in Sweden and Germany: Resource Dependence and New Social Cleavages', *European Journal of Political Research,* vol. 24, pp. 177-94.

Jahn, D. (1996), 'The Colors of the Green Rainbow: Ideology, Strategy and Action of Members of Environmental Organizations in Norway', Discussion paper of the LOS-Center (Norwegian Research Center in Organization and Management) of the University of Bergen.

Jahn, D. (1998a), 'Environmental Performance and Policy Regimes: Explaining Variation in 18 OECD-Countries', *Policy Sciences,* vol. 31, pp. 107-31.

Jahn, D. (1998b), 'Interest Intermediation in Transition: Towards a Cognitive Network Approach', manuscript, The Nottingham Trent University.

Jahn, D. (1999a), 'The Social Paradigms of Environmental Performance: The Scandinavian Countries in an International Perspective', in: Joas, M. and Hermanson, A.-S. (eds.), *The Nordic Environments: Comparing Political, Administrative and Policy Aspects,* Ashgate, Aldershot.

Jahn, D. (1999b), *Zur Institutionalisierung ökologischer Weltbilder in modernen Gesellschaften. Eine Analyse kognitiver Netzwerke der Kernenergiedebatte in Schweden und Deutschland*, Nomos, Baden-Baden.

Jamison, A. (1996), 'The Shaping of the Global Environmental Agenda: The Role of Non-Governmental Organisations', in Lash, S., Szerszynski, B. and Wynne, B. (eds), *Risk, Environment and Modernity: Towards a New Ecology*, London: Sage, London, pp. 224-45.

Jamison, A., Eyerman, R., Cramer, J. and Læssöe, J. (1990), *The Making of the New Environmental Consciousness. A Comparative Study of the Environmental Movements in Sweden, Denmark and the Netherlands*, Edinburgh University Press, Edinburgh.

Jänicke, M. (1993), 'Über Ökologische und Politische Modernisierungen', *Zeitschrift für Umweltpolitik & Umweltrecht ZfU*, vol. 2, pp. 159-75.

Jänicke, M. (1995), 'The Political System's Capacity for Environmental Policy' FFU-report 95-6, Freie Universität Berlin, Berlin.

Joerges, Christian. (1994), 'European Economic Law, the Nation-state and the Maastricht Treaty.' in Dehousse, R. (ed.) (1994), *Europe After Maastricht: An Ever Closer Union ?*, Beck, München.

Johnson, S. (1979), *The Pollution Control Policy of the European Communities*, Graham and Trotman, London.

Johnson, S. P. and Corcelle, G. (1995) *The Environmental Policy of the European Communities*, Kluwer Law International, London.

Jordan, A.J. (1993), 'Integrated Pollution Control and The Evolving Style and Structure of UK Environmental Regulation In The UK', *Environmental Politics*, vol. 2, pp. 405-27.

Jordan, A.J. (1995), Implementation Failure or Policy-making? How Do We Theorise the Implementation of EU Environmental Legislation? CSERGE Working Paper GEC 95-18, CSERGE, London and Norwich, UK.

Jordan, A.J. (1997), 'Post-decisional' Politics in the EC: the Implementation of EC Environmental Policy in the UK,. Ph.D. Dissertation, University of East Anglia, Norwich.

Jordan, A.J. (1998a), 'Step Change or Stasis? EU Environmental Policy After the Amsterdam Summit', *Environmental Politics*, vol. 7, pp. 227-35.

Jordan, A.J. (1998b), 'The Impact of UK Environmental Administration' in Lowe, P. and Ward, S. (eds), *British Environmental Policy and Europe*, Routledge, London.

Jordan, A.J. (1999a), 'The Construction of a Multi-Level Environmental Governance System: EU Environmental Policy at 25', *Environment and Planning C*, vol. 17 (in press).

Jordan, A.J. (1999b), 'Implementation: A Policy Problem Without a Political Solution?', *Environment and Planning C*, vol. 17 (in press).

Jordan, A.J and J. Greenaway, (1999c), 'Shifting Agendas, Changing Regulatory Structures and the 'New' Politics of Pollution', *Public Administration* (in press).

Judge, D (1995), *A Green Dimension for the EU*, Frank Cass, London.

Kassim, H., and Menon, A. (eds), (1996), *The European Union and National Industrial Policy*, Routledge, London.

Katz, R.S. and Mair, P. (1995), 'Changing Models of Party Organization and Party Democracy. The Emergence of the Cartel Party', *Party Politics* vol. 1, pp. 5-28.

Katzenstein, P.J. (1985), *Small States in World Markets: Industrial Policy in Europe*, Cornell University Press, Ithaca.

Kaufman, H. (1976), *Are Government organisations immortal?*, Brookings Institution, Washington.

Keohane, R.O. and J.S. Nye (eds) (1989), *Power and Interdependence. World Politics in Transition*, Scott, Foresman & Company, Glenview.

Kepplinger, H. M. (1988), 'Die Kernenergie in der Presse. Eine Analyse zum Einfluß subjektiver Faktoren auf die Konstruktion von Realität', *Kölner Zeitschrift für Soziologie und Sozialpsychologie*, vol. 40, pp. 659-83.

Kepplinger, M. (1989), *Künstliche Horizonte*, Campus, Frankfurt am Main.

Kingdon, J.W. (1984), *Agendas, Alternatives, and Public Policies*, Little, Brown and Co, Boston, Toronto.

Kitschelt, H. (1986), 'Political Opportunity Structures and Political Protest: Anti-Nuclear Movements in Four Democracies', *British Journal of Political Science*, vol. 16, pp. 57-85.

Kitschelt, H. (1988), 'Left-Libertarian Parties: Explaining Innovation in Competitive Party Systems', *World Politics*, vol. 40, pp. 194-234.

Klandermans, B. (1997), *The social psychology of protest*, Blackwell, Cambridge.

Klandermans, B. (1992), *The Social Construction of Protest and Multiorganizational Fields*, in: Morris, A.D. and McClurg Mueller, C. (eds), *Frontier in Social Movement Theory*, Yale University Press, New Haven, pp. 77-103.

Knill, C. (ed) (1997), *The Impact of National Administrative Traditions on the Implementation of EU Environmental Policy*, EUI, Florence.

Koopman, T. (1994) 'The Quest for Subsidiarity', in Curtin, D and T. Heukels (eds), *Institutional Dynamics of European Integration: Essays in Honour of Henry G. Schermers*, Volume II, Martinus Nijhoff, Dordrecht, p. 55.

Koopmans, R. and Duyvendak, J.W. (1995), 'The Political Construction of the Nuclear Energy Issue and Its Impact on the Mobilization of Anti-Nuclear Movements in Western Europe', *Social Problems*, vol. 42, pp. 235-51.

Krämer, L. (1995), *EC Treaty and Environmental Law*, 2nd edition, Sweet & Maxwell, London.

Kriesi, H. (1993), *Political Mobilization and Social Change. The Dutch Case in Comparative Perspective*, Avebury, Aldershot.

Kriesi, H. (1995), 'The Political Opportunity Structure of New Social Movements: Its Impact on Mobilization', in Jenkins, J. C. and Klandermans, B. (eds), *The Politics of Social Protest. Comparative Perspectives on States and Social Movements*, UCL Press, London, pp. 167-98.

Kriesi, H., Koopmans, R., Duyvendak, J.W. and Giugni, M. G. (1995), *New Social Movements in Western Europe: A Comparative Analysis*, UCL Press, London.

Kumar, K. (1995), *From Post-industrial to post-modern society. New Theories of the Contemporary World*, Blackwell, Oxford.

Kunneman, H. (1996). *Van theemutscultuur naar walkman-ego: contouren van postmoderne individualiteit*, Amsterdam.

Lafferty, W. M. (1996), 'The politics of sustainable development: global norms for national implementation', *Environmental Politics* vol. 5, pp. 185-208.

Lash, S. and Urry, J. (1987), *The End of Organized Capitalism*, Polity Press, Oxford.

Laumann, E.O. and Knoke, D. (1987), *The Organizational State. Social Choice in National Policy Domains*, University of Wisconsin Press, Madison.

Lenschow, A. (1995), Institutional and Policy Change in the EC: Variations in Environmental Policy Integration, Unpublished PhD thesis, New York University, New York.

Leroy, P. and J. van Tatenhove (forthcoming), 'New Policy Arrangements in Environmental Politics: the Relevance of Political and Ecological Modernisation', in F. Buttel, A.P.J. Mol and G. Spaargaren (eds) (1998), Sage, London.

Levidow, L. (1994), 'Biotechnology Regulation as Symbolic Normalization', *Technology Analysis and Strategic Management*, vol. 6, pp. 273-88.

Levidow, L. (1998), 'Democratizing Technology -- or Technologizing Democracy? Regulating Agricultural Biotechnology in Europe', *Technology in Society*, vol. 20, pp. 211-26.

Levidow, L. and Carr, S. (1996), Special Issue on Biotechnology Risk Regulation in Europe, *Science and Public Policy*, vol. 23, pp. 133-200.

Levidow, L. and Carr, S. (in press), 'Market-stage Precautions: Managing Regulatory Disharmonies for Transgenic Crops in Europe', *Proceedings of the 5th International Symposium on The Biosafety Results of Field Tests of Genetically Modified Plants and Microorganisms*, September 1998, BBA, Braunschweig.

Levidow, L., Carr, S., von Schomberg, R. and Wield, D. (1996), 'Regulating Agricultural Biotechnology in Europe: Harmonisation Difficulties, Opportunities, Dilemmas', *Science and Public Policy*, vol. 23, pp. 135-57.

Levidow, L., Carr, S., von Schomberg, R. and Wield, D. (1997), 'European Biotechnology Regulation: Framing the Risk Assessment of a Herbicide-tolerant Crop', *Science, Technology and Human Values*, vol. 22, pp. 472-505.

Liberatore, A. (1991), 'Problems of transnational policymaking: environmental policy in the EC', *European Journal of Political Research*, vol. 19, pp.281-305.

Liefferink, J.D. (1995), *Environmental policy on the way to Brussels. The issue of acidification between the Netherlands and the European Community*, Pudoc, Wageningen.

Liefferink, J.D. and A. Mol (1996), 'Voluntary Agreements as a form of Deregulation? The Dutch experience', Paper prepared for the Working Group on Environmental Studies, European University Florence, 9-11 May 1996.

Liefferink, J.D. and Mol, A. (1997), 'Voluntary agreements as a form of deregulation?', in Collier, U. (1997), *Deregulation in the European Union: Environmental Perspectives*, Routledge, London.

Liefferink, J.D., Lowe, P. and Mol, A. (1993), 'The environment and the EC: the analysis of political integration', in Liefferink, J.D., Lowe, P. and Mol, A. (eds), *European Integration and Environmental Policy*, Belhaven, London.

Liftin, K.T. (1994), *Ozone Discourses: Science and Politics in Global Environmental Cooperation*, Columbia University Press, New York.

Lindberg, L. (1977), 'Energy Policy and the Politics of Economic Development', *Comparative Political Studies*, vol. 10, pp. 355-82.

Lindberg, L., and Scheingold, S. (1970), *Europe's Would-Be Polity*, Prentice Hall, Englewood Cliffs, NJ.

Lindblom, C.E. (1968), *The policy-making process*, Prentice Hall, Englewood Cliffs, NJ.

Lipset, S.M. and Rokkan, S. (1967), 'Cleavage Structures, Party Systems, and Voter Alignment: An Introduction', in Lipset, S.M. and Rokkan, S. (eds), *Party Systems and Voter Alignment: Cross-National Perspectives*, Free Press, New York, pp. 1-61.

Lundqvist, L. J. (1980), *The Hare and the Tortoise: Clean Air Politics in the United States and Sweden*, University of Michigan Press, Ann Arbor.

Lundvall, B.A. (1988), 'Innovation as an interactive process: From user-producer interaction to the national system of innovation', in G. Dosi et.al., *Technical change and economic theory*, Printer Publishers, London.

Lyotard, J.F. (1984), *The Postmodern Condition: A Report on Knowledge*, Manchester University Press, Manchester.

Majone, G. (1992), 'Regulatory Federalism in the European Community', *Environment and Planning C*, vol. 10, pp. 299-316.

Mannheim, K. (1952), Competition as a Cultural Phenomenon, in Kecskemety, P. (ed.), *Essays on the Sociology of Knowledge*, Routledge & Kegan Paul, London, pp. 191-229. First published in German (1929) as 'Die Bedeutung der Konkurrenz im Gebiet des Geistigen', *Verhandlungen des Sechsten Deutschen Soziologentages vom 17. bis 19. September 1928 in Zürich*, Mohr Paul Siebeck, Thüringen.

March, J.G. and Olsen, J.P. (1989), *Rediscovering institutions: the organizational basis of politics*, The Free Press, New York.

Marcuse, H. (1964), *One Dimensional man. The Ideology of industrial society*, Sphere Books, London.

Markovits, A.S. (1986) *The Politics of the West German Trade Unions. Strategies of Class and Interest Representation in Growth and Crisis*, Cambridge University Press, Cambridge.

Markovits, A.S. and Gorski, P. (1993), *The German Left: Red, Green and Beyond*, Polity Press, Cambridge.

Marks, G. (1992), 'Structural Policy in the EC', in Sbragia, A. (ed), *Euro-Politics: Institutions and Policy-making in the 'New' EC*, The Brooking Institute, Washington DC.

Marks, G. (1993), 'Structural Policy and Multi-level Governance in the EC', in Cafruny, A. and Rosenthal, G. (eds), *The State of the European Community*, Longman, London.

Mazey, S. and Richardson, J.J. (eds) (1993), *Lobbying in the EC*, Oxford University Press, Oxford.

McCarthy, J.D. and Zald, M.N. (1982), 'Resource mobilization and Social Movements: A partial theory', *American Journal of Sociology*.

Melucci, A. (1989), *Nomads of the Present: Social Movements and Individual Need in Comparative Society*, Hutchinson Radius, London.

Mendrinou, M. (1996), 'Non-compliance and the European Commission's Role in Integration', *Journal of European Public Policy*, vol. 3, pp. 1-22.

Milbrath, L. W. (1993), 'The World is Relearning Its Story about How the World Works', in Kamieniecki, S. (ed.), *Environmental Politics in the International Arena. Movements, Parties, Organizations, and Policy*, State University of New York Press (SUNY), Albany, pp. 21-39.

Milbrath, L.W. (1984), *Environmentalists: Vanguard for a New Society*, State University of New York Press (SUNY), Albany.

Mol, A.P.J. (1995), *The Refinement of Production. Ecological Modernization Theory and the Chemical Industry*, Van Arkel, Utrecht.

Moravcsik, A. (1993), 'Preferences and Power in the EC: A Liberal Intergovernmentalist Approach', *Journal of Common Market Studies*, vol. 31, pp. 473-524.

Müller-Rommel, F. (1993), *Grüne Parteien in Westeuropa. Entwicklungsphasen und Erfolgsbedingungen*, Westdeutscher Verlag, Opladen.

North, D. C. (1990), *Institutions, institutional change and econonomic performance*, Cambridge University Press, Cambridge.

O'Riordan, T. and Cameron, J. (eds) (1994), *Interpreting the Precautionary Principle*, Earthscan, London.

O'Riordan, T. and Jäger, J. (eds) (1997), *Politics of Climate Change: A European Perspective*, Routledge, London.

OECD (1993), *International Economic Instruments and Climate Change*, OECD, Paris.

Offe, C. (1981), 'The Attribution of Public Status to Interest Groups', in Berger, S. D. (ed.), *Organizing Interests in West Europe*, Cambridge University Press, Cambridge, pp. 123-58.

Offe, C. (1985), *Disorganized Capitalism: Contemporary Transformations of Work and Politics*, Polity Press, Cambridge.

Offe, C. (1986), 'Nieuwe sociale bewegingen als meta-politieke uitdaging', in I. Weijers et.al., *Tegenspraken, dilemma's en impasses van de verzorgingsstaat*, Deel 2, SOMSO, Amsterdam.

Osborn, D. (1992), 'The Impact of EC Environmental Policies on UK Public Administration', *Environmental Policies and Practice*, vol. 2, pp. 199-209.

Paehlke, R.C. (1989), *Environmentalism and the Future of Progressive Politics*, Yale University Press, New Haven.

Paehlke, R.C. and Torgerson, D. (eds) (1990), *Managing Leviathan: Environmental Politics and the Administrative State*, Broadview, Peterborough, Ontario.

Parsons, W. (1995), *Public Policy*, Edward Elgar, Aldershot.

Pearce, D. (1993), *Blueprint 3: Measuring Sustainable Development*, Earthscan, London.

Pelkmans, J. (1987), 'The New Approach to Technical Harmonization and Standardization', *Journal of Common Market Studies*, vol. 25, pp. 249-69.

Pestman, P and J. van Tatenhove (1998), 'Reflexieve beleidsvoering voor milieu, ruimtelijke ordening en infrastructuur', *Beleidswetenschap*, vol. 3, pp. 254-72.

Pestman, P.K., (1998), 'Dutch infrastructure policies, public participation and the environment in the nineties: the politics of interfering logics', in F.H.J.M. Coenen, D. Huitema and L.J. O'Toole (eds), *Participation and the quality of environmental decision-making*, Kluwer Academic Publishers, Dordrecht.

Peters, G. (1994), 'Agenda-Setting in the EC', *Journal of European Public Policy*, vol. 1, pp. 9-26.

Peterson, J. (1995), 'Decision-making in the European Union', *European Journal of Public Policy*, vol. 2, pp. 69-94.

Pinder, John. (1994), 'Building the Union: Policy, Reform, Constitution', in Duff, A., J.Pinder, R.Pryce (eds), *Maastricht and Beyond: Building the European Union*, Routledge, London.

Pretty, Jules N. (1995), 'Participatory Learning for Sustainable Agriculture', *World Development*, vol. 23, pp. 1247-63.

Pridham, G. (1996), 'Developing environmental policies in Southern Europe: problems of enactment and enforcement of European legislation', *Southern European Society and Politics*, pp. 47-73.

Puchala, D. (1975), 'Domestic Politics and Regional Harmonisation in the European Communities', *World Politics*, vol. 27, pp. 496-520.

Purdue, Derrick (1995), 'Whose Knowledge Counts? "Experts", "Counter-experts" and the "Lay" Public', *The Ecologist*, vol. 25, pp. 170-2.

Renn, Ortwin (1995), 'Styles of Using Scientific Expertise: a Comparative Framework', *Science and Public Policy*, vol. 22, pp. 147-56.

Rhodes, C. and Mazey, S. (1995), 'Introduction: Integration in Theoretical Perspective', in Rhodes, C. and Mazey, S. (eds), *The State of the EU*, Lynne Rienner, Boulder, CO.

Rhodes, R.A.W. (1994), 'The Hollowing Out of the State', *The Political Quarterly*, vol. 65, pp. 138-51.

Richardson, G., Ogus, P. and Burrows, P. (1983), *Policing Pollution*, Oxford University Press, Oxford.

Richardson, J. (1996), 'Actor Based Models of National and EU Policy-making' in Kassim, H. and Menon, A. (eds), *The EU and National Industrial Policies*, Routledge, London.

Richardson, J. (ed) (1982), *Policy styles in Western Europe*, George Allen & Unwin, London.

Richardson, J. and Watts, N.S.J. (1985), 'National policy styles and the environment. Britain and West Germany compared', IIUG discussion paper 8516, WZB, Berlin.

Risse-Kappen, T. (1996), 'Exploring the Nature of the Beast: International Relations Theory and Comparative Policy Analysis Meet the EU', *Journal of Common Market Studies*, vol. 34, pp. 53-80.

Rittel, H.W.J., and Webber, M.M. (1973), 'Dilemmas in a general theory of planning', *Policy Sciences*, vol. 4, pp. 155-69.

Robertson, R. (1992), *Globalization*, Sage, London.

Robertson, R. (1995), 'Glocalization: Time-Space and Homogeneity-Heterogeneity', in M. Featherstone, S. Lash and R. Robertson (eds), *Global Modernities*, Sage, London, pp. 25-44.

Rometsch, D. Wessels, W. (eds) (1996), *The EU and the Member States*, Manchester University Press, Manchester.

Rose, R. (1993), *Lesson-drawing in public policy. A guide to learning across time and space*, Chatham House Publishers Inc., Chatham, NJ.

Roy, A. (1998), *Report on France, for 'Safety Regulation of Transgenic Crops: Completing the Internal Market?'*, funded by the European Commission,

DG XII/E5, Open University Centre for Technology Strategy, Milton Keynes.

Rucht, D. (1989), 'Environmental Movement Organizations in West Germany and France: Structure and Interorganizational Relations', in Klandermans, B. (ed.), *Organizing for Change: Social Movement Organizations in Europe and the United States*, International Social Movement Research, vol. 2, JAI, Greenwich (Connecticut), pp. 61-94.

Rucht, D. (1995), 'Parties, Associations and Movements as Systems of Political Mediation', in Thesing, J. and Hofmeister, W. (eds.), *Political Parties and Democracy*, Konrad-Adenauer-Stiftung, Sankt Augustin, pp. 103-25.

Sabatier, P.A. (1986), 'Top-Down and Bottom Up Approaches to Implementation Research: A Critical Analysis and Suggested Synthesis', *Journal of Public Policy*, vol. 6, pp. 21-48.

Sabatier, P.A. (1987), 'Knowledge, policy-oriented learning, and policy change', *Knowledge: Creation, Diffusion, Utilization*, vol. 8, pp. 649-92.

Sabatier, P.A., and Jenkins-Smith, H.-C. (eds) (1993), *Policy change and learning: An advocacy coalition approach*, Westview Press, Boulder, CO.

Sachs, I. (1977), 'Het menselijk leefmilieu', in J. Tinbergen (ed.), *Naar een Rechtvaardige Internationale Orde. Een rapport van de Club van Rome*, Elsevier, Amsterdam, pp. 309-21.

Sandholtz, W. and A. Stone Sweet, (eds) (1998), *Supranational Governance: The Institutionalisation of the European Union*, (in press).

Sbragia, A. (1993), 'The EC: A Balancing Act?', *Publius: Journal of Federalism*, vol. 23, pp. 23-38.

Sbragia, A. (ed), (1992), *Euro-Politics: Institutions and Policy-making in the 'New' EC*, The Brooking Institute, Washington D.C.

Schmitt, H. (1987), *Neue Politik in alten Parteien. Zum Verhältnis von Gesellschaft und Parteien in der Bundesrepublik*, Westdeutscher Verlag, Opladen.

Schnaiberg, A. (1980), *The Environment from Surplus to Scarcity*, Oxford University Press, Oxford.

Schön, D.A., and Rein, M. (1994), *Frame reflection. Toward the resolution of intractable policy controversies*, Basic Books, New York.

Schumacher, E.F. (1974), *Small is Beautiful. A Study of Economics as if People Mattered*, Abacus, London.

Siedentopf, H. and Ziller, J. (eds) (1988), *Making European Policies Work: The Implementation of Community Legislation in the Member States*, Sage, London.

Siegmann, H. (1985), *The Conflict between Labor and Environmentalism in the Federal Republic of Germany and the United States*, Gower, Aldershot.

Skjaerseth, J.B. (1994), 'The climate policy of the EC: too hot to handle?', *Journal of Common Market Studies*, vol. 32, pp. 25-45.

Skocpol, T. (1985), 'Bringing the State Back In: Strategies of Analysis in Current Research' in P. B. Evans, D. Rueschemeyer and T. Skocpol (eds), *Bringing the State Back In*, Cambridge University Press, Cambridge, pp. 3-37.

Smith, R. M. (1995) "Ideas, Institutions and Strategic Choice", *Polity*, vol. 28, pp. 135-40.

Snyder, Francis (1994), 'EMU-Metaphor for European Union? Institutions, Rules and Types of Regulation', in Dehousse, R. (ed.), *Europe After Maastricht: An Ever Closer Union?*, Beck-Law Books in Europe, München.

Somsen, H. (ed.) (1996), *Protecting the European Environment*, Blackstone Press, London.

Spaargaren, G. (1997), *The Ecological Modernization of Production and Consumption. Essays in Environmental Sociology*, Pudoc, Wageningen.

Spaargaren, G. and A. Mol (1992), 'Sociology, Environment, and Modernity: Ecological Modernization as a Theory of Social Change', *Society and Natural Resources*, vol. 5, pp. 323-44.

Spybey, T. (1996), *Globalization and World Society*, Polity Press, Oxford.

Steinmo, S., K. Thelen, et al., (eds.) (1992), *Structuring politics: historical institutionalism in comparative analysis*, Cambridge studies in comparative politics, Cambridge University Press, Cambridge.

Sweet, J., Shepperson, R., Thomas, J.E. and Simpson, E. (1997), 'The Impact of Releases of Genetically Modified Herbicide-tolerant Oilseed Rape', in *Proceeding of the British Crop Protection Conference: Weeds*, British Crop Protection Council, Farnham, Surrey, pp. 291-301.

Szerszynski, B., S. Lash and B. Wynne (1996), 'Introduction: Ecology, Realism and the Social Sciences', in S. Lash, B. Szerszynski and B. Wynne (eds), *Risk, Environment and Modernity. Towards a New Ecology*, Sage, London.

Sztompka, P. (1993), *The Sociology of Social Change*, Blackwell, Oxford.

Tarrow, S. (1995), 'The Europeanisation of Conflict: Reflections From a Social Movement Perspective', *West European Politics*, vol. 18, pp. 223-51.

Taylor, P. (1983), *The Limits of European Integration*, Croom Helm, London.

Teisman, G. R. (1992), *Complexe besluitvorming: een pluricentrisch perspectief op besluitvorming over ruimtelijke investeringen*, VUGA, 'sGravenhage.

Thelen, K. and S. Steinmo (1992), 'Historical Institutionalism in Comparative Politics' in S. Steinmo, K. Thelen and F. Longstreth (eds.), *Structuring Politics: Historical Institutionalism in Comparative Analysis*, Cambridge University Press, Cambridge, pp. 1-32.

Toft, J. (1996), 'Denmark: Seeking a Broad-Based Consensus on Gene Technology', *Science and Public Policy*, vol. 23, pp. 171-4.

Toth, A. (1992), 'The principle of Subsidiarity in the Maastricht Treaty.', *Common Market Law Review*, vol. 29, pp. 1079-105.

Touraine, A. (1977), *The Self-Production of Society*, University of Chicago Press, Chicago.

Touraine, A., Wieviorka, M. and Dubet, F. (1987), *The Workers' Movement*, Cambridge University Press, Cambridge.

UK delegation (1996), 'Proposal at the 1996 Intergovernmental Conference, On the Application of the Principle of Subsidiarity, submitted by the UK delegation' reproduced in *The European Review*, vol. 3, Centre for European Studies at the University of Essex, pp. 40-2.

Ullrich, O. (1979), *Weltniveau*, Rotbuch Verlag, Berlin.

UNICE (1995), *Releasing Europe's Potential through Targeted Regulatory Reform*, UNICE, Brussels.

United Nations (1992), *Agenda 21: The United Nations Program of Action from Rio*, United Nations Publication, New York.

United Nations (1992), *The Global Partnership for Environment and Development: a Guide to Agenda 21*, UNCED, Geneva.

Van Ermen, Raymond & EEB/BEE, (1996), *Review of the Vth Action Programme*, EEB, Brussels.

Van Gunsteren, H.R. (1985), 'Het leervermogen van de overheid', in M.A.P. Bovens and W.J. Witteveen (eds), *Het Schip van Staat. Beschouwingen over Recht, Staat en Sturing*, Tjeenk Willink, Zwolle, pp. 53-74.

Van Horn, C. (1979), *Implementation in the Federal System*, Lexington Books, Lexington, MA.

Van Tatenhove, J. (1993), *Milieubeleid onder dak?*, Pudoc, Wageningen.

Van Tatenhove, J. and J.D. Liefferink (1992), 'Environmental Policy in the Netherlands and in the European Community, a conceptual approach', in F. von Benda-Beckmann and M. van der Velde (eds), *Law as a resource in agrarian struggles*, WSS, no. 33, Pudoc, Wageningen, pp. 267-93.

Van Tatenhove, J. and B. Arts (1998), 'Political Modernization: The Dynamics of Environmental Policy Arrangements', paper presented at the XIV World Congress of Sociology, RC 24, July 26- August 1, Montréal, Canada.

Van Tatenhove, B. Arts and P. Leroy (forthcoming), *Changing Environmental Policy Arrangements: From Political Modernisation to Policy-making*.

Vogel, D. (1986), *National Styles of Regulation: Environmental Policy in Great Britain and the United States*, Cornell University Press, Ithaca, NY.

Voisey, H., Beuermann, C., Sverdrup, L. and O'Riordan, T. (1996), 'The political significance of local agenda 21: the early stages of some European experience', *Local Environment*, vol. 1, pp. 33-50.

von Schomberg, R. (1996), 'Netherlands: Deliberating Biotechnology Regulation', *Science and Public Policy*, vol. 23, pp. 158-63.

Waarden, F. van (1995), 'Persistence of national policy styles: A study of their institutional foundations', in B. Unger and F. van Waarden (eds), *Convergence or diversity? Internationalisation and economic policy response*, Avebury, Aldershot, pp. 333-72.

Wagner, P. (1994), *A Sociology of Modernity. Liberty and Discipline*, Routledge, London.

Wallace, H. (1971), 'The Impact of the European Communities on National Policy-making', *Government and Opposition*, vol. 6, pp. 520-38.

Wallace, H. (1977), 'National Bulls In the Community China Shop', in Wallace, H. Webb, C. and Wallace, W. (eds), *Policy-making in the European Communities*, John Wiley, Chichester.

Wallace, H. and Wallace, W. (eds) (1996), *Policy-making In The EU*, Oxford University Press, Oxford.

Wallace, W. (1982), 'Europe as a Confederation: the Community and the Nation State', *Journal of Common Market Studies*, vol. 21, pp. 57-68.

Wapner, P. (1995), 'Politics Beyond the State. Environmental Activism and World Civic Politics', *World Politics*, vol. 47, pp. 311-40.

Ward, N. (1998), 'Britain, Europe and Water Quality Policy', in Lowe, P. Ward, S. (eds), *British Environmental Politics*, Routledge, London.

WCED/World Commission on Environment and Development (1987), *Our Common Future*, Oxford University Press, Oxford.

Weale, A. (1992), *The New Politics of Pollution*, Manchester University Press, Manchester.

Weale, A. (1993) 'Ecological Modernisation and the Integration of European Environmental Policy' in J.D.Liefferink, P.D.Lowe and A.P.J. Mol (eds), *European Integration and Environmental Policy*, Belhaven Press, London.

Weale, Albert (1994) 'Environmental Protection, the Four Freedoms and Competition Among Rules' in M. Faure, J. Vervaele and A. Weale (eds), *Environmental Standards in the European Union in an Interdisciplinary Framework*, Maklu, Antwerpen.

Weale, Albert (1995) 'The Kaleidoscopic Competititon of European Environmental Regulation', *European Business Journal*, vol. 7, pp. 19-25.

Weale, A. (1996), 'Environmental Rules and Rule-Making in the European Union', *Journal of European Public Policy*, vol. 3, pp. 594-611.

Weale, A. and Williams, A. (1993), 'Between economy and ecology? The Single Market and the integration of environmental policy', *Environmental Politics*, vol. 1, pp. 45-64.

Weaver, R. Kent and Bert A. Rockman (1993) 'Assessing the Effects of the Institutions' in R. Kent Weaver and Bert A. Rockman (eds), *Do Institutions Matter?: Government Capabilities in the United States and Abroad*, Brooking Institution, Washington DC.

Wildavsky, A. (1988), *Searching for Safety*, Social Philosophy and Policy Centre/Transaction Publishers, New Brunswick/Oxford.

Williamson, P.J. (1989), *Corporatism in Perspective. An Introductory Guide to Corporatist Theory*, Sage, London.

Wils, W.P. (1994), 'Subsidiarity and EC environmental policy: taking people's concerns seriously', *Journal of Environmental Law*, Vol. 6, pp. 85-91.

Wissenburg, M. (1997), 'Epistemology, Policy and Diversity', *Episteme*, vol.1, pp. 123-44.

Wit, Th. W.A. de (1995), 'De ontluistering van de politiek. Over "Eén-partij staat Nederland" en postmoderne democratie', *Socialisme en Democratie*, vol. 4, pp. 155-65.

WWF (1998), *The Living Planet Index*, WWF, Gland.

Wynne, B. (1992), 'Uncertainty and Environmental Learning: Reconceiving Science in the Preventive Paradigm', *Global Environmental Change*, pp. 111-7.

Young, O. (ed.) (1997), *Global Governance: Drawing Insights from the Environmental Experience*, MIT Press, Cambridge, Mass.

Index